C0-AWY-650

INTERGROUP EDUCATION

Methods and Materials

JEAN DRESDEN GRAMBS

INTERGROUP EDUCATION

Methods and Materials

sponsored by
The Anti-Defamation League of B'nai B'rith

Prentice-Hall, Inc., Englewood Cliffs, New Jersey

Library of Congress Catalog Card No.: 68-24186

Current printing (last digit):
10 9 8 7 6 5 4 3 2 1

Printed in the United States of America

Prentice-Hall International, Inc., *London*
Prentice-Hall of Australia, Pty. Ltd., *Sydney*
Prentice-Hall of Canada, Ltd., *Toronto*
Prentice-Hall of India Private Ltd., *New Delhi*
Prentice-Hall of Japan, Inc., *Tokyo*

PREFACE

The material in this book comes from many sources. The experiences in methods have been gained through a number of teacher's institutes, workshops, college classes, and public school classrooms. Teachers' reports of successes and failures have been a rich resource, as has been the published literature.

Particular impetus to put this all in writing came from three main sources. One was the conference on "Negro-Self Concept" held at the Lincoln Filene Center, September, 1964, when the author presented a paper identifying sources of self-concepts, with particular relevance to educational remedies. The conference was jointly sponsored by the U.S. Office of Education and the President's Commission on Juvenile Delinquency. Another grant from the U.S. Office of Education to the Lincoln Filene Center, 1965-1966, enabled the writer to draw together educational research which would underlie efforts to develop materials and methods which would reach students in elementary grades with information about race and cultural diversity. With two field teams trying out some of the suggestions, we learned a great deal about what more needed to be done, and got some ideas about what could be done.

Finally, under a grant from the U.S. Office of Education to the State Department of Massachusetts, the author was privileged to present two television programs on WBGH-TV, incorporating some of the most promising methods and materials in the intergroup area. The reception given these two presentations was enthusiastic. These, together with the other programs in the series "Education and Race Relations," became the basis for a National Defense Education Act institute grant to Tufts University, for the teachers of the disadvantaged. As a result, the author was asked to put in more extended form the visual material from the TV presentations. In the process of doing this, naturally, the scope of the materials and methods to be covered grew vastly, as did the bibliography. This final statement based on the TV series appears as a chapter in another book, which includes material from other Tufts conferences and programs.[1]

With encouragement from Oscar Cohen, Director of Education for the Anti-Defamation League of B'nai B'rith, these various pieces were pulled together into this book, which includes much of what was in the original TV program, plus additional material from the previous papers written for the Lincoln Filene Center Projects, as well as ideas and data garnered from subsequent activities and experiences.

The purpose of this work is to be as helpful and specific as possible for the classroom teacher. The list of materials will inevitably be out of date within a short time. However, it is hoped that teachers will find the sources listed, and the suggestions for ways of using them, of maximum practicality. Some background from the research has also been provided to show to what extent education in intergroup understanding is possible.

Special acknowledgment for encouragement, both financial and personal, goes to the members of the staff of the Lincoln Filene Center. Dr. Franklin Patterson, formerly Director of the Center, now President of Hampshire College, Amherst, Massachusetts, was the source of the original concept, and has been of continued encouragement in the development of this book. Dr. John Gibson, Center Director, has provided support for the program through many writings and rewritings of project proposals and innumerable trips to Washington to gain support for the several projects. Dr. Tom Curtin, of the State Board of Education of Massachusetts, was the inspiration for the TV series and pioneered in providing statewide interest in the significant field of race relations. Other staff members of the Lincoln Filene Center, Dr. William Kvarceus, Astrid Anderson, Harvey Pressman, and Wyman Holmes, have been continually helpful. Miss Anderson in particular worked closely with the author during the field trials in the winter and spring of 1966.

A special note of appreciation is due students in the author's classes and in the Human Relations Institute at Bowie State College, Bowie, Maryland, 1967, who read earlier versions of this book and gave freely of their criticisms, reactions, and comments, as well as pointing out errors of grammar and typing. But errors of judgment, or of inclusion or exclusion of sources, are those of the author alone.

JEAN DRESDEN GRAMBS

[1] William C. Kvarceus, John S. Gibson, and Thomas J. Curtin, eds., *Poverty, Education and Race Relations* (Boston: Allyn & Bacon, Inc., 1967).

CONTENTS

Part I

WHO NEEDS INTERGROUP EDUCATION?

INTRODUCTION

If a person can learn to hate and distrust others, he can learn to like and trust others. This is the basic assumption of intergroup education.

Education assumes change. The person who has learned something acts in a different fashion from the person who has not learned this same thing: the first person has been "educated"; the second person has not. Intergroup education similarly assumes that, as a result of selected materials and methods, individuals will be changed, that their attitudes and behaviors toward persons of other groups, and toward members of whatever group they themselves belong to, will be changed. The change will result in *more* acceptance of persons who differ and *more* acceptance of one's own difference from others.

Intergroup understanding and acceptance do not occur just because we want them to. Children do not "just naturally" like other children. They learn a great deal about other people in the process of growing up, and much of this learning does not necessarily lead to liking and trust. The deliberate education of the child about himself and others is one of the obligations of the educator. Such learning cannot be left to chance.

In education we talk about the "teachable moment." When my little boy puts his finger on the hot stove and yowls, I have a teachable moment. I say promptly, "Peter, hot stoves burn. Don't put your finger on hot stoves." Peter learns to show great respect for stoves, and he finds out if they are or are not hot before he explores them further.

In intergroup education we can wait for the teachable moment or we can, to use the analogy above, create our own "hot stoves."

There are literally thousands of teachable moments in any classroom or group of children. Gillham (K14)* points out the many incidents that occur when a group of children are together. A teacher, by intervening at such moments, can aid children in understanding and acceptance. Stendler and Martin (K35) describe ways of exploiting ordinary classroom situations for their carry-over into intergroup relations. One report of an eighth-grade class (Taba and Elkins, H32) provides a perceptive and illuminating diary of how a teacher can observe and utilize the many moments in which human relations insights can become educational resources.

Unfortunately, many teachers are not aware of the "teachable moments" when they do occur. Sensitive teachers note the times when a child seems left out, or when cliques form and tension rises, or when some individual appears to be the scapegoat of a group. Socio-economic and religious cleavages, which we know occur in classrooms at every grade level and in every part of the country, are often unseen, or dismissed as irrelevant, by the teacher. Teachers may notice when the fat boy is teased, but be unaware of the silent treatment accorded the Puerto Rican student in the same classroom.

Knowing about such situations is one thing; doing something about them is still another thing.

Many points at which lack of intergroup understanding makes for conflict, tension, and unhappiness are outside the immediate awareness of the teacher. She may not have been in the hallway when someone was pushed, nor on the playground when an offensive term was used. One third-grade boy always seemed to be the last to leave the classroom and, unlike his classmates, did not run madly for the nearest playground exit. Instead he ambled as slowly

* The bibliography has been divided into a number of categories, indicated by letter. The items in each category have been numbered sequentially. Thus a reference cited as Taba (H32), means that this item will be found in category H and is number 32 in that category.

as possible toward home. When questioned by the teacher he admitted that he was angry at the children from a neighboring parochial school. The two groups passed each other on the same street, morning and evening. There were frequent clashes, name-calling by both groups, and books, papers, and crayon boxes being snatched and thrown. Why did the children from these two schools clash? What could be done about it? Was it up to the teacher to do anything? As often happens, she chose to ignore it, feeling it was up to the child to cope with the situation as best he could.

A tenth-grader astounded his family by announcing that he was going to learn karate. The reason he gave was his need to be able to defend himself against the extortion demands of a gang of lower-class youngsters who had identified him with a group from a wealthier part of town and were demanding a "pay-off" each day. The school knew nothing about this.

Such events, and many like them, occur constantly and in most schools, whether school personnel acknowledge this or not. We cannot wait until such moments occur to embark on deliberate education for better human relationships.

Intergroup feelings and attitudes are learned very early. If we wait for the teachable moment to conduct our lesson in intergroup relations, we may wait forever. Thus we create our own teachable moments, or light our own "hot stoves." What kinds of devices, situations, materials, and methods are most useful in intergroup education? The answer to this question is our major concern in this book.

WHO NEEDS INTERGROUP EDUCATION?

Human relations education or intergroup education—and the two terms can be used interchangeably—is not a special need of any special group. As will be pointed out later, some minority groups—notably Negroes, Puerto Ricans, and Mexican-Americans—may benefit as they begin to perceive their own group membership in more positive terms. Research has shown that the culturally disadvantaged child can gain a great deal of personal ego-strength by being aided in an examination of his own place and history in American life and culture (Kvarceus *et al.*, K20). But equally "disadvantaged" is the child who lives isolated in the affluent cocoon of suburbia, who knows nothing except what he may hear or read about the problems that face minority-group children and children of poverty (Miel and Kiester, K27).

The educator who says with pride and security, "But we don't have any problems here; see, our children all come from the same type of nice middle-class home," is denying in fact a very major problem. The children who come to such a school are not being educated in life as it occurs in the larger world. They are, in Jules Henry's terms, "learning how to be stupid" (A22). They are learning that what is taught in school bears no relationship to the outside world. If they dare contradict the teacher and suggest that "Dick and Jane" are not the sum total of human experience, or that the happy picture of the plantation slave is a distortion of the facts, they are apt to be reprimanded, ignored, or both.

Every effort of educators to "group" children in order to reduce educational differences has resulted in decreasing the range of some kinds of differences while ignoring others. No group of children, even those with identical IQ's, will come from identical homes; they will vary in their religious beliefs, in the emotional climate of their families, in their experiences with birth, death, illness, and other emotional traumas, and they will have had each in his own way a special education regarding "our groups" and "those others." Surface homogeneity masks undercover heterogeneity. All children are different; the differences are important and must become part of our curriculum.

Every school has a problem of education for human understanding. One does not have to have Negroes in the school to realize that all children need to gain insight into what the sources of the contemporary situation of the Negro are, and why the role of the Negro is a critical problem in American life.

The localities most insulated from the mainstreams of American life, the ghetto and the rich suburb, have much in common; children in both areas are deprived of a larger view of life.

In the rich suburb the problem is more acute in one very significant sense: out of these suburbs come leaders of the future—the politicians, the bankers, the corporation officers, the military leaders, the opinion-makers. If they have been badly served by their earlier education, then they will serve their nation badly when they are called upon to make decisions regarding the future of all persons, not just others like themselves.

A recent study of suburbia has evoked considerable discussion and controversy (Miel and Kiester, K27). The results of the study reveal a lack of interest and awareness on the part of parents and educators as to the intergroup needs of suburban children. It is very easy to dismiss the "problem" when the community is seemingly heterogeneous. The too typical attitude of the community—shared by teachers—to ignore a problem if it is not of immediate apparent concern is distressing. In the case of the suburban community studied by Miel and Diester, when there was temporary integration of the schools the teachers chose to ignore or gloss over interracial incidents, illustrating once again the tendency to evade that which is unpleasant or difficult to deal with.

The suburban school is not as isolated as commentators suggest. In most such communities there are pockets of poverty, or ethnic islands whose workers provide the service personnel for the more affluent middle-class white community. The children reflect their parents' values, and also they see but do not see, hear but do not hear, the prejudices and stereotyped remarks and behaviors of the adults around them. Poor people are poor because they choose to be; some people are better off as servants; we don't want "those others" in our neighborhood because they will do something that will make us have to move—such are the reactions of typical suburban youngsters, who naturally reflect what they hear the adults around them say.

Educational intervention is perhaps more difficult yet more critical with the children of the isolated suburban community than with the child of the inner-city ghetto. The child of the ghetto at least knows that life as he sees it is not good, and perhaps could be better; the child of suburbia is isolated in his smugness. How can the realities of poverty and discrimination be brought to the suburban child so that his smugness is not reinforced? Trips to the slums may only make him more convinced that the poor deserve what they get and they ought to stay where they are. Contact may not breed friendship, but may breed distrust and suspicion. What are the alternatives for the teacher in suburbia? The suggestions for practical classroom approaches, in later sections of this book, are designed for schools of all kinds. Use of role-playing; open-ended scripts, stories and films; use of flat pictures; reading of novels and authentic history—these techniques can bring alive the problems of all people everywhere.

So, the development of empathy, insight, and understanding is essential for both the suburban child and the ghetto child. The responsibility rests perhaps more heavily on the teacher in suburbia, but also the pressures against such education may be greater than elsewhere. Who wants to rock the boat? Why bring up that which is unpleasant? Students must be made ready to get into college, not dabble in social problems! How familiar are the arguments—and how disastrous. Suburban schools, just because they tend to enroll the elite—economically and intellectually—should make special efforts to see that it is a *responsible* elite able to assist in the solving of social problems within the context of a concerned and informed democratic environment. Any school system that does not have a consistent, coherent, and continuous program for intergroup understanding, including interracial, interethnic, interreligious, and intereconomic class groups, is failing in its responsibility to our country.

There is ample evidence that prejudice against others is widespread throughout the United States and does not depend on whether or not a child has any actual contact with a given group (Allport, B1). The mass media have been as effective as any other device in spreading the general notion of stereotypes about ethnic and racial groups in the United States (Berelson and Stimer, A5, pp. 495-525). When will children learn that there were great *Negro* cowboys, too? (Durham and Jones, L42; Leckie, C35).

In one "enrichment" program in an Eastern community for primary-grade children, a *real* Indian Chief and his *real* Indian teenage daughter were brought from the far West. How many had ever seen a "real" Indian? When their appearance was announced to one group of five-year-olds, one child burst into frantic tears. He was scared; Indians shoot people, don't they? He'd seen it all, week after week, on TV. Only now is one beginning to see movies that provide a respected role for Negroes as Negroes, and as part of the general social and cultural scene. Advertisements now show Negroes as well as whites in group pictures. When will an Indian be perceived, too, as "one of us"?

EDUCATORS, TOO, MUST SEE

Cultural blindness is all around us. In a recent report of a social studies project, for instance, one runs across the following passage: "All classes listened to many Christmas stories and poems and told many stories. The story of the first Christmas was used in all classes and the story of Hanukah was used in classes where there were Jewish children." [1] How was it decided that only Jewish children needed this extra dose of religious understanding? In this same project, in the fifth grade a study is to be made of persons from foreign countries who came to the United States, yet no mention is made of Negroes—only "other" immigrant groups—although "In early days, many people settled in the north to avoid competing with the slave labor of the south." Listed under "activities" to develop a better understanding of race, the following is suggested:

> See a movie, "The Pussycat That Ran Away."
> Children of *our race* live in other countries.
> This is an adventure of children in Norway. [Italics added]

What definition of "race" is used here?

A rather different approach to intergroup education is the human relations program of the Wilmington Schools. The project, reported by Crosby (H5), emphasizes the broader interpretation of intergroup education. One can agree with the premise of this project, that adequate human relationships underlie adequate intergroup understanding; but one searches in vain throughout the report for specific discussions with children about race and the meanings of race, although the project was one aspect of the school's efforts to facilitate the desegregation process in the schools of the city. Did race and problems of race fail to come to the attention of children? Does the report merely omit them, or did the project *not* explicitly deal with the real problems of school desegregation in that city?

Without our even knowing it, we may be expressing attitudes toward groups as stereotypes. A junior high school teacher who used a pair of bookends that depicted Mexican peasants reclining under a cactus, with a serape draped over their shoulders and a hat over their faces, was providing an education in intergroup relations

[1] Clyde Martin, *An Elementary Social Studies Program* (Austin: University of Texas Press, 1963).

daily to all her students—the wrong education. In a first-grade classroom there was a very clever frieze (commercially published) to introduce numbers to children. Illustrated by little "Indian" girls with black pigtails and a feather, it read: "One (1) little Indian; two (2) little Indians . . . [etc.]." In a class composed mostly of Negro girls, a teacher giving a lesson in arithmetic was also stroking the straight shining hair of a Puerto Rican girl sitting in the front row. As the observer stated, "Each stroke must have been like a knife in the heart of each Negro girl, with her natty, or frizzy, black hair."

Recent outcries against all-white textbooks have resulted in the appearance of new texts which "color them brown" in order to indicate that the books are "integrated." It is interesting to note that the brown color produces merely "tan Nordics," rather than realistic pictures of Negro-Americans. Some texts are utilizing actual photographs of children of different racial and ethnic backgrounds. But they still show mainly the happy, smiling—though now integrated—world that text critics have long decried (Klineberg, P19).

Textbooks are changing, however. The Urban Social Studies Series of one publisher (Holt, L167), the Skyline Series (L155), and more recently, *Citizens All* (McClellan *et al.,* L113) are all attempts to bring reality into the inner-city classroom. The photographs used by the Holt series, and the realistic action in the Skyline Series and in *Citizens All,* provide a setting where it is natural for classrooms to be integrated, for children to have friends across race lines, and for things both good and bad to happen. Inevitably, the good wins out. But for the first time, as in *Citizens All,* there is a Negro teacher and a Negro principal, Puerto Ricans are shown in white-collar government jobs, the problems of urban renewal are explored, and a Negro woman judge is presented. Such efforts to break the stereotype are admirable. It will be interesting to see how far such books penetrate within the urban ghetto and beyond, to suburbia.

The appearance of such books, benign as they are, is long overdue. Interest in providing integrated text material is not recent (Taba *et al.,* H31). The biased discussion of population groups and the history of various ethnic and racial groups have been presented in the literature of education for many decades (Grambs, H16). Only recently, with Negroes sitting in large numbers on the book selection committees of major metropolitan school districts (which incidentally enroll most of the children in the United States), have book publishers and educators responded to the critics of the lily-white text and of the disappearance of the Negro from American history books after the Civil War.

A question of immediate practical interest to educators is whether it does in fact make a difference whether or not texts have integrated pictures. The classic study by Trager and Yarrow (K42) demonstrated over twenty years ago that it did, in fact, make a difference to the kindergarten and first-grade children what intergroup "loading" their instructional materials convey. Research in this area is practically nonexistent. Many teachers attest, however, to the startled response of Negro students when for the first time they come across a textbook with Negro children pictured.

But the mere use of integrated material may not turn out to be the panacea the teacher expects. As Walton pointed out:

> Other stories . . . are those with a Negro hero or with some Negro characters where no mention is made of color and the plot of the story does not deal with race. However, in some of these the reader is supposed to get the idea that race does not matter. The problem is that it does. Many of these stories are good as stories, and beautifully illustrated, but since race is not mentioned *per se* both teachers and children get the idea that you aren't supposed to talk about it. The child will, however, talk about it—but not with the teacher. I have known Negro children in nursery schools who have disliked *Two Is a Team* [Beim and Beim, L7], and I believe that it is partly due to things white children have said to them about the story. I have heard white children say of the scooter race, "I hope the white boys win!" They also giggle and point and say, "That boy's colored," or to a Negro child, "That's you." This may be, and often is, at least for the first time, said without malice. However, some Negro children have felt it so painful to be black that any calling it to their attention is felt as an attack.[2]

This report by Walton underlines our previous comment about capturing the "teachable moment." If children respond to a very good piece of children's literature in such a way, then the teacher should recognize what is taking place and make immediate plans for further class discussion. "Why did you want the white boy to win?" she may ask. She would let the children express their feelings,

[2] Jeanne Walton, "The American Negro in Children's Literature," Eliot-Pearson School *News,* Tufts University, February, 1964.

and explore with them what it may mean to others to be identified racially. "Susan has red hair and Jane has brown hair; do you think Susan should win a race because she has red hair?" Analogies like this could help children see beneath their words. Further, the teacher would bring in more stories, such as *Fun for Chris* (Randall, L140). One teacher found that reading *All About Us* (Evans, L47) a chapter at a time, followed by class discussion, proved very valuable for her fifth-grade class.

The teacher described her technique:

> . . . it was pointed out how people's appearances changed. We discussed carotene and melanin as being the determinants of skin color and also mutations that occur in cells. When we started to discuss "Negro" in class, the teacher was aware of the glances that were sent to the two Negro boys. The glances seemed a little sly and hidden and appeared to question how the boys were taking this sort of frankness and matter of factness in talking about race. For their part the Negro boys looked only at the teacher with a blank, indifferent air that appeared to say, "Why should all this talk about Negroes affect me?" To lessen any amount of embarrassment, we also talked about people of other lands and their origins. The Mongolians, Eskimos, and American Indians are always interesting to children of this age.

One young woman, enrolled in the Neighborhood Youth Corps program, commented on her educational experience by saying, with feeling: "I am sick and tired of George Washington Carver and his damn peanuts." As a Negro, she was asking for a more accurate as well as a less patronizing approach to the Negro in American life and history.

It is of interest to note that some bibliographies of children's books make a virtue out of the fact that, although the main character or one of the characters is a Negro, no mention is made of race in the book (Wolfe, T31; Huus, T14). A really astonishing bibliography is one provided for the Office of Economic Opportunity by the American Library Association (T30). One assumes these books were selected because they would further the programs of the OEO in dealing with children from disadvantaged areas. A book entitled *The Happy Garbage Man* presents a "jovial introduction to the sanitation department." The list has two supplements: one for Spanish-speaking children of Cuban background and one for Spanish-speaking children of Puerto Rican background.

Furthermore, the book *Your Face Is a Picture,*[3] which presents in an extremely sensitive and effective way, via photographs, that all children all around the world share similar feelings and situations, is placed in the list for the Cuban children! Many books listed are identified by their having Negro characters, but no special listing for Negro youngsters is provided.

Other bibliographies designed to encourage better intergroup understanding do point out the human relations problems which are the focal points of the books (Crosby, T9; Kircher, T17; Keating, T16a). Of particular value in this respect is the bibliography provided by Kircher of other lists that suggest ways in which books may be used to aid young people in dealing with their problems as growing persons.

In examining many textbooks, one is struck by the fact that, although they are now appearing with integrated pictures (in some editions, not in others), the teachers' guides and the student material rarely if ever refer to the fact that there are indeed persons of different races in the pictured material.

The book *Citizens All,* with its strong emphasis on the ways in which members of minority groups are naturally represented in positions of prestige and importance, does not refer to race or ethnic differences in the teachers' edition. No mention is made of Negro or the word "race." In the bibliography, references include some books with Negro heroes or heroines, but the identification of these individuals as Negro is minimal. Is the word Negro not to be used? The teachers' guide for this book is primarily devoted to development of language concepts, such as words that show action, words that describe, etc. The very obvious factors of ethnic and racial differences, made vividly clear by the pictures and by the names of the children, is in no place referred to for the teacher to use as an instructional addition.

The series *Call Them Heroes* (O4), written by educators in the New York City Schools, makes it quite clear that individuals were selected *because* of their differences. These were people who rose to competent personal achievement despite handicaps of poverty, race, religion, or other kinds of handicaps. This series is meant for the reluctant reader in the secondary schools; the volume *Citizens*

[3] Eth Clifford and David Clifford, *Your Face Is a Picture* (Indianapolis: The E. C. Seale Co., 1963).

All is for students reading at the third- or fourth-grade level. Evidently, at the lower reading level they should not be exposed to the realities of race and ethnic origin specifically.

Nontext material for children does not do much better. For instance, in discussing the year's crop of books on anthropology for young people, the reviewer Turnbull reported:

> The very disappointing volumes of part of a series published by Lyons and Carnahan, *Indian Legends of Eastern America* and *Indian Legends of the Great West*. Both cite Johanna R. M. Lyback as author, but give no indication as to how she came by the legends or the translations. Both volumes also carry exactly the same extraordinarily condescending introduction by G. Walso Browne, full of such paternalistic nonsense as: "The Indian, like a child, had a mind remarkably acute in one direction, but undeveloped in others. He could grasp but one truth, and that without any abstract reasoning."
>
> The tales are not arranged in a way that convinces us of the abstract reasoning power of those responsible for the books' contents . . . [and] as science they are worthless.
>
> Another book that does not make the grade is *The Art of the North American Indian,* by Shirley Glubok (Harper & Row). It is lavishly presented with excellent photographs, type, and other publishing minutiae, but the text is not worth the space it takes. . . . And where the text is more generous with information, it is frequently generalized to the point of being misinformation, or is couched in unfortunate terms. . . . As for the pictures themselves, they are presented merely as a museological gallimaufry.
>
> There are, however, two good books about North American Indians. Needless to say, one is by Robert Hofsinde. His *Indians at Home* (Morrow) follows his usual, straightforward, simple format. The type is bold and the author's line drawings show something important. In making the home his central theme, Hofsinde again limits himself to a subject he can handle with ease and clarity in a short book. . . .
>
> Also good, but written at greater length, is *Home of the Red Man,* by Robert Silverberg (New York Graphic Society). Early in the book the author writes: "If anything, white men, with their pinkish skins, deserve the name of 'red men' more than the Indians!" I, therefore, wish another title could have been chosen. The book deserves it, for it is a sensible and sensitive general introduction to a study of North American Indian peoples. . . .
>
> Turning to Africa, we are faced with another problem book. Stories from Africa (Duell, Sloan and Pearce) are "retold by Shirley Goulden"

and gloriously illustrated in color by Maraja. There are only six tales, and although each stands fully on its own, I again wish we could have been told more about how the tales were collected and from where. . . .

Africa: Adventures in Eyewitness History, by Rhoda Hoff (Walck), claims to tell us about African history through the written word of observers from Herodotus on. It does nothing of the sort. Presenting African history is not without problems, but there are much more reliable ways of doing it than by citing miscellaneous individuals whose only common qualification seems to be that they have at one time or another set foot on the African continent. . . . Many of the authors are bigoted, ignorant, or idiotic, and it is difficult to see what one can derive from this book except the jaundiced vision and understanding of most of those quoted. . . .[4]

The similar review undertaken by *Natural History* for the 1965 publishing year is interesting because, as the author, Metraux, notes:

As the prospect for the future broadens and deepens for the younger generation—who live with the exploration of space and move in a world that has become one network of communicating peoples—it is significant that so much writing intended for today's youth attempts to open a broader view to the past. The majority of the books that take young Americans to unfamiliar places are concerned, not with men living in the contemporary world, but with earlier civilizations.[5]

Though the criticism of texts' treatment of various ethnic groups is not new, and has been amply documented, one continuing curiosity remains. In discussions of immigrants, the Negro is omitted or hardly mentioned. As an example, Kraus [6] devotes about two paragraphs to the "forced" immigration of the Negro to America. The balance of this book on the story of immigration is devoted to an extensive discussion of the kinds of problems faced by all other immigrant groups—never returning to the Negro and *his* adjustment and *his* situation. The question can be asked, of course, as to whether the Negro is an "immigrant." [7] What happens then to our

[4] C. M. Turnbull, "1964 Survey of Science Books for Young People," *Natural History,* LXXIII (November, 1964), 4.

[5] Rhoda Metraux, "1965 Survey of Science Books for Young People," *Natural History,* LXXIV (November, 1965), 4.

[6] Michael Kraus, *Immigration, the American Mosaic* (Princeton, N.J.: D. Van Nostrand Co., Inc., 1966).

[7] K. E. Tauber and F. Alura, "Is the Negro an Immigrant Group?" *Integrated Education,* I (June, 1963), 25-28.

units on "contributions of immigrant groups to America?" Other works discussing immigration give the Negroes a very minor position, despite the fact that as a "different" element they now constitute the most significant minority in America [8] (Handlin, O12). Where does the American Negro "come from"? No one writing for young people seems to have devoted attention to the fact that today's Negro-American is often a product of the nonlegal offspring of many immigrant strains, so that the Negro not only may inherit a very *distant* (over 200 years) residue of African culture, but also may be sensitive to the problems of later ethnic migrants to the United States. In addition, of course, the *real cultural inheritance* of the American Negro is the extremely harsh personal situation of slavery and generations of subsequent economic bondage and political peonage.

When critics condemn the treatment of minority groups, history books are the first ones to take a beating; after that come literature books and language arts texts. One area that is significantly overlooked is science books. What is taught in biology courses about the evolution of the different groups of mankind? A cursory examination of some of the most widely used textbooks in biology revealed some unacceptable material. In one book, for example, the evolutionary theory of the development of man is portrayed in a graphic chart. Who is at the end of the evolutionary cycle? Of course—a white male! [9] (One wonders how this evolutionary cycle can continue without at least a white female!) Is the white individual more at the "end" of the evolutionary cycle as perceived in current history than the Negro, the Mongoloid, or any of the other varieties of the human species? Another text disclaims any association with the racist theories of the Nazis, and spends almost a page and a half in virtuous condemnation of the nonscientific nature of such ideologies, yet an interesting footnote then appears, which reads:

> Anglo-Saxons, or their descendants, are not a race, anyhow, or any other arbitrarily definable biological population. Neither, incidentally, are Jews,

[8] Franklin Scott, *Emigration and Immigration* (Washington, D.C.: Service Center for the Teaching of History, 1963), No. 51.

[9] J. H. Otto and A. Towle, *Modern Biology* (New York: Holt, Rinehart & Winston, Inc., 1965), p. 548.

although some groups Jewish in religion have tended to become so, as have some other religious groups.[10]

Thus, we have an obligation to examine all the instructional materials that we use in the schools. What messages are they conveying? Are these accurate, authentic, commensurate with current research, designed to help young people gain a true understanding of their own inheritance and that of others who differ? Look at spelling books, arithmetic books, home economics books—any text or supplementary material that enters the school—with the same sensitive eye, and unfortunately one may find painful evidence of omissions or inclusions.

Critical reviews of textbooks, particularly in the social sciences, have been recently published (See Sect. P). Teachers and others on selection committees should be alert to distortions and omissions in books that are presumably written by the most impeccable of authorities. No single text, however well designed, can serve to present a total picture of as diverse a nation as ours. It would be valuable for the teacher to look beyond a single text to other materials for presenting a well-rounded picture of our national history and of the diverse groups who have been part of this history.

It is necessary, as a corollary of the above, that school libraries be well stocked with supplementary material. The facts, however, are not much more reassuring as regards school libraries than school texts. In many instances books that have integrated situations, books such as those listed in the bibliography of this volume, may not be on the "approved" list of public school libraries. Who approves the lists from which schools may purchase supplementary and library books? What books are reviewed by American Library Association reviewers? Are some of the biases and prejudices of educators apparent in reviews by librarians? That is, regarding books that present "problems," that show life as not all rosy and happy, that suggest that growing up is difficult for some children because of poverty or discrimination—to what extent are such books included on "approved" lists or given approving reviews?

Unfortunately, books that focus on problem areas are apt to be the last ones found on school or library shelves. Often librarians

[10] G. G. Simpson, and others, 2nd ed., *Life* (New York: Harcourt, Brace & World, Inc., 1965), p. 687.

themselves do not know of their existence. Sometimes the books are screened out before ever being listed. The freedom of teachers and librarians to have access to such books is most urgently needed, as is the freedom to purchase such books for the use of children and adults (U20).

Generations of miseducation in the role of minority groups is not easily overcome. It takes more than brown-colored pictures or stories in an urban setting to provide depth to our intergroup education efforts.

THE PARTICULAR NEEDS OF MINORITY-GROUP CHILDREN

INCIDENT

by Countee Cullen

Once riding in old Baltimore,
Heart filled, head filled with glee,
I saw a Baltimorean
Keep looking straight at me.
Now I was eight and very small
And he was no whit bigger,
And so I smiled, but he poked out
His tongue and called me "Nigger."
I saw the whole of Baltimore
From May until December,
Of all the things that happened there
That's all that I remember.[11]

Many minority-group children have learned at a very early age just what society thinks about the group to which they belong. Such learning is often painful, disturbing, drastic, and always permanent. The negative identity with which Negro children are saddled must be corrected by counter messages. Part of the process of counteracting the early negative message is to find and use materials in which the child can see some common elements, something in the material that speaks directly *to him.*

We have some clues as to the kinds of materials that may make most sense to the child of a minority group. He will, we are fairly

[11] Countee Cullen, "Incident," from *On These I Stand*. Copyright 1925 by Harper & Brothers; renewed 1953 by Ida M. Cullen. Reprinted by permission of Harper & Row, Publishers, Incorporated.

sure, respond most readily to those materials and situations that have most relevance to himself. He will pay attention to a movie in which, if he is a Negro, he sees Negroes as part of the scene. He will further be moved to develop more positive feelings about himself if this portrayal of Negroes makes it clear that they have a respected social and cultural role (Hoban, R44; Hoban, R45). It was observed that handicapped children tended to write more voluminously about pictures showing handicapped children than about those showing normal children. It would be reasonable to conclude that this would also be true of children of any particular group identification. Boys respond far better to material in which boys play a major role, or in which male or masculine traits are exemplified (Maccoby and Wilson, R55).

The special learning problems of the culturally different child make this assumption even more significant. Deutsch [12] noted that in all-Negro elementary classes that he observed children were most attentive during studies of Negro history.

As Hess and Shipman (G11) point out, the "meaning of deprivation is a deprivation of meaning." Yet those who are cognitively impoverished may not be responsive even to material apparently most relevant to them as perceived by the adult. Or, the relevance of the material may actually be evaded or avoided by the teacher. The concept of race is disclaimed by parents and teachers, so that any child of any race is left in a state of confusion as well as ignorance. He may be highly responsive to differences, his own and that of others, but he has no help in making sense out of it all. Our task, then, as educators is to aid the child in understanding the relationships and differences among people, and also to understand what meaning these concepts have for him.

For the child who is a member of a minority group there is a further educational step to be taken: He needs to learn ways of coping with the prejudiced view others have of the group with which he is identified. How should he respond when someone calls him "kike" or "nigger" or "hunkie" or "Christ-killer" or "whitey" or "chink"?

This is not an easy question to answer. Some suggestions for

[12] Martin Deutsch, *Minority Group and Class Status as Related to Social and Personality Factors in Scholastic Achievement,* Monograph No. 2 (Ithaca, N.Y.: Society for Applied Anthropology, Cornell University, 1960).

answering are given on pages 26-58. There is considerable controversy, unresolved by any research findings, as to what *is* a good answer. In a celebrated exchange of views, Bettelheim and Lewin (B5) take opposite sides of the debate regarding what kind of preparation helps the Jewish child cope best with expected discrimination. Bettelheim feels that the child is best prepared who is loved and helped to feel secure within his group, without necessarily so labeling it. Lewin, on the other hand, feels that it is imperative to provide the child with a sense of his group so that he can gain feelings of pride and security. Later discriminatory acts or attacks are then deflected against his armor of self-respect.

In his brilliant book, *Stigma: Notes on the Management of Spoiled Identity,* Goffman (B16) suggests that minority-group status is only one of the many stigmata which interfere with normal interaction among human beings. As insight is gained into the ways in which all persons respond who bear a visible stigma—the blind, deaf, crippled, colored—and who bear an invisible stigma—a prison record, a history of mental illness, alcoholism—then there may be developed more appropriate ways of educating "normals" and "deviants." The purpose to be served would be that of reducing the individual's distortions of the world and of himself, and thus enlarging the chance each person may have of leading a satisfying personal life.

Cultures establish different valuations for differences. In one Indian tribe, for instance, a person who was epileptic was considered to be endowed with unique powers because his seizures were seen to be communications with the gods. In the United States, valuations are made on the basis of the individual's degree of conformity with a kind of "standard" American—white, preferably of Anglo-Saxon background, Protestant, middle class. Although most people deviate from this norm in one fashion or another, it is still the folk (or TV) norm. When such an obvious difference as skin color is observable, there is a very visible way of making gross distinctions among people. Thus it is that the Negro, because of his visibility, can be identified as being most different from the "standard" American. Other non-Caucasian groups—Chinese, Japanese, Hindus, Malayans, Eurasians—are similarly perceived as being different because the differences are so obvious in appearance. The closer a group member comes to the "standard" version, the less likely is he to encounter the closed door of opportunity, or the harsh tones of prejudice.

The basic educational problem is *identifying those differences that make a difference,* and those that do not. The educational need is to study and understand why some differences are made significant and are socially and individually destructive, and why some differences that *should* be recognized as important are ignored. There is an educational need for developing a creative use of differences. Differences challenge us to see ourselves more clearly, differences are productive of new insights, and differences are what make each person unique, himself, and infinitely valuable.

WHAT ARE THE SOURCES OF RESISTANCE?

It is probable that most who have read this far agree with the premises stated and are already aware of the data regarding distortion of historical facts and the omissions from teaching material which in turn result in bias and ignorance. What are other reasons that we fail to practice what we preach?

Teachers bring to the classroom their own cultural education. A study (Gottleib, K16) of the attitudes of Negro and white teachers toward their teaching task in the schools of an inner-city area—predominantly Negro—showed that the white teachers identified the source of their teaching dissatisfaction as "lack of parental interest" and "student behavior or discipline problems." Negro teachers, on the other hand, frequently reported that they lacked the proper equipment and had overcrowded schools. In describing their students, Negro and white teachers saw them through different-colored eyes. The white teachers selected adjectives to describe their Negro students in markedly different terms than did their Negro colleagues. The Negro teachers felt their students to be ambitious and cooperative; the white teachers perceived them to be lazy and talkative. Teacher perceptions clearly influence the message they will convey to students, overtly or covertly.

Furthermore, the very problem of race and cultural diversity is one heavily loaded emotionally for all teachers.

In a discussion with a group of teachers at a summer NDEA Institute for Teachers of the Disadvantaged it was found that the questions of interracial living and interracial understanding could be discussed by the adults, but not by the adults *with the children* in the camp setting of this particular institute. One anecdote is particularly revealing: a ten-year-old Negro boy in the camp wanted to write a note to a white girl because he liked her. He had never spoken to her, and in fact did not even know her name. But to his ten-year-old mind, it was perfectly reasonable that he might write her a note. He asked his counselor (a Negro teacher) for help. The teacher told him he did not think it was wise for him to write to the girl. When the child asked why, the teacher's response was, "When you get home ask your parents; they will explain to you."

Another Negro teacher reported, with feelings of great pride and warmth, that the two Negro and two white girls in her cabin group were very devoted to one another. Integration was working out just fine. She did not want to "upset" anything by making any comments. When asked if it would be helpful to the girls to recognize that, in fact, they were living harmoniously together in an interracial setting, which was not the case back home, the teacher looked stunned. The others in the group seemed equally startled, and in a few instances upset.

To talk about race and race relations with children was as taboo for these teachers as talking about sex. It would be interesting to speculate on the similarity in origin of the two taboos. Race, then, is an extremely sensitive subject to discuss. Our experiences in talking with Negro parents and educators support the comment by Goodman (K15, p. 113) about parental responses:

> There is a prevalent feeling among our parents that race, like sex, is a rather hazardous topic and one best left alone, at least so far as the children are concerned.

Although most Negro parents may report that they try to explain to their children that differences in color are hereditary accidents which really don't make too much difference (Rowan, A37), at the same time there is considerable evidence that there is extreme concern over color in most Negro homes which induces conflict in children about what color means to them (Brody, B7; Redding, O21; Drake, A39).

Interestingly enough, in our search of the literature of intergroup education, practically nothing of recent publication was found for young children to read on the question of race or skin color (Johnson, L85; Showers, L153; Evans, L47).

Religion is another sensitive area. One does not question anyone else's religion, nor does one explain one's own. This is likely to be difficult, however, as one suburban community found out. Because of various coincidences, it was found that the majority of the children in school were Jewish. The schools closed, of course, on the traditional Christian holidays—Christmas and Easter. They remained open during the Jewish holidays, but the teachers were unhappy because so few children were in school and so much study time was wasted. As one teacher put it, "Christmas just isn't fun any more!" Why? They could not sing the good old Christian Christmas songs, nor have the usual traditional Christmas pageants or programs. In fact, one got the impression that it was not fair for the Jewish children to be Jewish—or at least not so many of them. Yet again, one was struck over and over by the reluctance of the teachers to talk together about the situation. ("We don't want to hurt the feelings of some of our Jewish teachers—of course, we don't have very many," one supervisor remarked.) Nor did the teachers seem to be able to talk with the children about the situation.

These anecdotes could be supplemented by many more. They take the place of more adequate research and study of teachers' feelings, attitudes, and responses in the area of cultural diversity. The reports we have either are dated, mainly those of the *Intergroup Education Project* (Taba *et al.,* H31) of the American Council on Education, which took place during the late 1930's and early 1940's, or are scattered and fragmentary.[13]

We lack insight into the core problem of the teacher as the instructional mediator in the area of cultural diversity. Teachers, like the children they teach, have been reared in a national climate that makes significance out of racial, ethnic, and religious differences. They bring these feelings to class, despite any disclaimer offered to the contrary.[14]

[13] Robert E. Doherty, "Attitudes Toward Labor: When Blue Collar Children Become Teachers," *School Review,* LXXI (Spring, 1963), 87-96. Arthur Jersild, *When Teachers Face Themselves* (New York: Columbia University, Teachers College Press, 1955). Chapter 5, "Sex," pp. 100-105.

[14] Jean D. Grambs, "Are We Training Prejudiced Teachers?" *School and Society,* XI (April 1, 1950), 196-98.

It is somewhat disheartening to note, too, that women by and large appear to be more prejudiced than men.[15] And since most of the teachers in elementary schools are women, where the most effective indoctrination of attitudes takes place, we can readily understand why the problem of intergroup understanding is one that meets deep teacher resistance.

In light of the paucity of materials on teacher attitudes in this critical field, one must note that those most likely to stimulate such research, educational psychologists, have evidently been least interested. At least one study analyzing content trends in educational psychology textbooks[16] indicates that between 1948 and 1963 teachers in training were increasingly more likely to learn about learning theory and increasingly less likely to be instructed in problems of human growth and development and personality and adjustment. Thus teachers not only are taught less about attitudes and feelings of the children they teach, but are less likely to be the objects of study regarding their own attitudes and feelings.

It would be hoped that new ideas in teacher training could be one by-product of efforts to develop innovative materials in this highly charged area of cultural diversity. Through teacher institutes, models might be developed of ways of educating and re-educating adults which could become part of general teacher-education practices.

It might, for instance, be suggested that older students be involved in some of the experimental work with very young children. Such older students (already used now in tutoring programs in some of the poverty programs) have been found to be highly effective instructors and aides to innovations in some difficult areas.[17] Those with genuine teaching potential could be encouraged to continue. College freshmen could be similarly involved, as aides. The rationale here is that by the time the student is "finished" at

[15] Robin M. Williams, *Strangers Next Door* (Englewood Cliffs, N.J.: Prentice-Hall, Inc., 1964).

[16] Derek N. Nunney, "Trends in the Content of Educational Psychology, 1948-53," *Journal of Teacher Education,* XV (December, 1964), 372-77.

[17] Arthur Pearl and Frank Riessman, *New Careers for the Poor* (New York: The Free Press, 1965), and Ronald Lippitt, "Roles and Processes in Curriculum Development and Change," in *Strategy for Curriculum Change,* ed. Robert Leeper (Washington, D.C.: National Education Association, 1965), p. 24.

age 21 or 22 and has been subjected to the anticreative and prejudiced atmosphere of many of his peers in colleges and universities, it is too late or too difficult to make significant attitude change.

It is rather discouraging to contemplate the quarter of a century or more of workshops in human relations and intergroup relations sponsored by the Anti-Defamation League, National Conference of Christians and Jews, and local groups that have enrolled literally thousands of teachers, and yet have to report how little has seeped into classrooms and teaching materials. Such workshops, with good purposes and high motives, may have assuaged a few guilt feelings and reassured already good teachers that what they felt was okay to feel; but certainly they roused no spreading demand for the kind of educational program we are discussing here. It took a tired lady in Montgomery, Alabama, to get Americans to the point of doing something daring, different, and effective. The teachers unfortunately, might still be sitting at the back of the bus—or the front, as the case might be.

A new factor in influencing teacher change has been introduced by government-financed institutes and other training programs. Under the NDEA Institute Act, many special institutes have been authorized for teachers of culturally disadvantaged children. Other Federal funds, under Titles I and III of the Elementary and Secondary Education Act of 1965, and under Title IV of the Civil Rights Act of 1964, have also been used to provide special training programs in intergroup understanding and in meeting problems attendant upon desegregation or upon large numbers of children from the poverty levels of society.

We can contemplate, therefore, a vastly stepped-up interest in this area, and also a much larger impact upon the school population as a whole of the knowledge and skills gained in the past few decades of effort.

What about the school system as a source of resistance to change? We have already noted that teachers may be reluctant to change, and that school materials need vast changes. Now what about our institutional situation itself? Knowing that we seek to make some changes in the ways in which cultural diversity becomes a part of the content and process of education, how can such a change be achieved?

Discussions of the problem of inducing innovation in education are quite recent.[18] There are some optimistic notes sounded in these reviews and others. But some observers, such as Goodman,[19] Friedenberg (M7), Henry (A22), and Grambs (H16), find the schools, as they now are, less than adequate.

Some frantic, even drastic, efforts are being made (well-financed) to encourage and even force innovation in education, and successful innovation has been achieved in such areas as mathematics, science, and foreign language. The Federal government, under Title III of the Elementary and Secondary Education Act of 1965, *specifies* that the money allocated be used to demonstrate new ways of dealing with persistent educational problems.

In the social sciences, despite all efforts, the schools are considerably less open to innovation. Many hypotheses may be advanced to explain this situation. There is certainly a lack of research which in any definitive sense could establish what should be taught in the social sciences, to whom, at what level, and in what sequence. But it goes farther than that, of course: "Our antiquated social studies curriculum in secondary education . . . is a monument to local American mores." [20]

Though schools have made some interesting adaptations in terms of organizational structure and, as mentioned, in some of the special subject areas, social science concepts or concepts that touch on taboo areas of society pose special problems for the innovator.

Our utmost ingenuity will be needed to devise procedures and materials that will have maximum impact on students, at the time and a. the point where most helpful, which teachers in general will use, and which will not interfere with accepted institutional mores.

In many communities the proposal to discuss contemporary race problems, to discuss the sources of prejudice, to spend much time on "human relations" problems of young people, comes under at-

[18] Robert R. Leeper, ed., *Strategy for Curriculum Change* (Washington, D.C.: National Education Association, 1965). Matthew B. Miles, ed., *Innovation in Education* (New York: Columbia University, Teachers College Press), 1964. Henry M. Brickell, *Organizing New York for Educational Change* (Albany, N.Y.: State Department of Education), 1961.

[19] Paul M. Goodman, "The Universal Trap," in *The School Dropout,* ed. Daniel Schreiber (Washington, D.C.: National Education Association), 1964.

[20] Paul F. Lazarsfeld and Sam D. Sieber, *Organization Educational Research: an Exploration* (Englewood Cliffs, N.J.: Prentice-Hall, Inc., 1964), p. 56.

tack. In one community, topics such as these are reported to be sponsored by subversive elements. In other places the claim is that the schools are trying to introduce "mental health" materials, which in turn are labeled as an invasion of the child's psychological privacy.

It is important that those who are interested in a wider discussion of the real human relations problems facing us in America, and with implications for our international role as well, must be prepared to face such critics.[21] It is probable, as we move into ever more complex world situations, that the curriculum of the elementary and secondary school will move further in the direction of understanding what it means to be human and civilized, and spend less time on the disciplines of technology. We now know more about the atom than we do about people; it may soon become apparent that this imbalance is dangerous. It is only as man learns to understand himself and others that he can cope constructively with the incredible tools that his scientific genius has provided him.

The threat of self-understanding is a real one; who wants to know about his own worst self? The Group for the Advancement of Psychiatry,[22] in discussing the psychiatric aspects of desegregation, pointed out the unconscious motivations that lie behind many of the beliefs and actions of those persistently (and even violently) insisting on a segregated society. The whole field of intergroup education inevitably involves one in personal feelings, and these rarely have a rational basis (Coles, K6; Grossack [23]). It is no wonder then, that despite the work of educators and others for many years, we are still wondering about how we can provide intergroup understanding in our schools.

[21] Harvey Schechter, *How to Listen to a John Birch Society Speaker* (New York: Anti-Defamation League of B'nai B'rith), 1966.

[22] Group for the Advancement of Psychiatry, *Psychiatric Aspects of School Desegregation, Report #37* (New York: The Group). (Reprinted in shorter form as *The Emotional Aspects of School Desegregation,* 1960.)

[23] Martin Grossack, ed., *Mental Health and Segregation* (New York: Springer Publishing Company, 1963).

Part II

PROMISING PRACTICES

In the following pages are introduced some promising practices in intergroup education. As has been stated earlier, little if any of what is being said here is new. Most of these approaches have been in the education literature in one form or another, and in the teaching repertoire of good teachers, for years. The need now is to help more teachers use more such methods and materials in many more classrooms.

SOME MAJOR ASSUMPTIONS

1. The first assumption basic to intergroup education is that changes in attitudes toward others can be achieved through educational means. That is, children's feelings and attitudes *can* be affected by deliberate education, and the earlier this occurs, the more effective it will be.

2. All persons are affected by the social valuations of groups: who is good, who is not so good, who rates, and who does not rate. In the culture of the United States today it is almost impossible for a child to grow up without an awareness of group differences and of the social valuations accorded to these differences[24] (Bettelheim and Lewin, B5).

[24] Martin L. Hoffman and Lois W. Hoffman, eds., *Review of Child Development Research* (New York: Russell Sage Foundation, 1964). Volume I, p. 297.

3. Learning to like and trust persons in one situation is not necessarily transferred to other situations with other people. A child who is comfortable with persons whom he has been taught are to be trusted does not necessarily transfer this sense of trust to other persons who differ from him and whose differences have been pointed out to him by his culture. Transfer of feelings of trust and acceptance must be made explicit. This is as true for adults as it is for children.[25]

4. Learning new attitudes and new feelings and gaining understanding of familiar attitudes and feelings about others and oneself occur through *the intellectual exploration of experience.* It is not sufficient to have a child burn his finger on a hot stove; he must see some connection between the hot stove and the burned finger. Similarly, in intergroup education, merely experiencing a congenial interracial situation will not necessarily produce lasting or visible changes in feelings and behaviors in other settings unless the experience has been explored intellectually: discussed, identified, labeled, argued about, researched, and tried again and again, vicariously and in actuality.

As Loban has pointed out, experience is the basis for learning:

> Modern societies have never fully envisioned the educational uses of experience and as a result our schools remain excessively verbal in their emphasis and incomplete in their accomplishments. . . .
>
> Through experience and through language we learn.
>
> Experience needs language to give it form.
>
> Language needs experience to give it content (Loban, G20, pp. 63-73).

METHODS AND MATERIALS, GENERAL COMMENTS

Discussion regarding the differentiation between materials and methods in education is futile. Any given type of material makes a particular method or spectrum of methods necessary or inevitable. In the intergroup area, methods and materials are inextricable.

[25] Grambs, "Are We Training Prejudiced Teachers?" John D. Campbell, Leon J. Yarrow, and Marian Radke Yarrow, "A Study of Adaptation to a New Social Situation," "Acquisition of New Norms: A Study of Racial Desegregation," "Personal and Situational Variables in Adaptation to Change," and "Leadership and Interpersonal Change," *Journal of Social Issues,* XIV, No. 1 (1958), 3-59.

Some methods may depend on specially prepared materials or on materials utilized in a special manner. There are some methods whose only "material" will be the imagination of the teacher and the interactions of children.

Many of the methods and materials we will discuss have been with us for some time. The pioneer research and study in the field of intergroup relations, undertaken under the direction of Hilda Taba in the 1940's, included most of what we would consider relevant methodology in intergroup relations today (Taba *et al.*, H31).

WHAT METHODS OR MATERIALS SHOULD ONE USE?

Just as children and schools vary, so do teachers. A method that one teacher finds congenial may be difficult or impossible for another to use or adapt. Materials that some teachers find valuable may seem inadequate or limited in another situation when viewed by other teachers. We can offer, then, primarily a "cafeteria" of methods and materials for teachers, school systems, and children to explore and try out, to find which seems to accomplish the task best within any particular setting for any particular group of children.

The best guidelines for utilization of instructional methods and materials in intergroup education appear to be the following:

Teachers will tend to use materials that:

—are intellectually sound and stimulating
—are authentic
—support creative use
—are not overdemanding on teacher out-of-class time
—are easy to utilize with groups of 25-30 children in a standard school situation.

Children are most apt to respond to and be engaged by methods and materials that:

—enable them to become participants
—are honest and unsentimental
—report the real world as children already know it.[26]

There is some evidence that "verbal *and* pictorial stimuli may tend to interfere with rather than reinforce each other . . . multi-

[26] Franklin K. Patterson, unpublished remarks at Conference on Education About Diversity, Lincoln Filene Center, Tufts University, Medford, Mass., 1965.

media presentations may not be as effective as single-channel presentations." [27] In seeking the most effective means to reach students, then, the teacher should use many media, but only one at a time.

We know that individuals learn through many sensory channels, but we may overload the channels if we expect them all to be functioning at once. The child can pay attention to a picture, talk about it, wonder about it, write about it, argue about it. He does not need to have background music to help this process along. He does not need a narrator to tell him what it is he is to see in the picture. Children may close their eyes and keep their ears open as they learn to listen: to sounds of different kinds, to voices, to feelings in voices, to stories told, to their own voices. The distraction of a colorful moving picture along with the voices, and maybe some song dubbed in behind, may all come out just a jumble of noise.

As each of us can testify, we screen out those sounds or objects that interfere with the task at hand. This kind of concentration has taken years of growing up to achieve. Some individuals never become very adept at keeping distractors out of range. Other people can become so absorbed in something that they are literally deaf to sounds or blind to objects outside their point of focus. We are so used to our automatic screening of sensory impressions that we take it for granted, yet the hard-of-hearing person, putting on a hearing aid for the first time, suddenly realizes that the mechanical "aid" does not do much screening; all sounds come in at once. Persons can be retrained to screen out unwanted sounds. Some children, whose home and neighborhood may be too full of sounds and sights, may be in special need of help in singling out the *one* sound that is a dripping faucet, the *one* voice that is a friend's, the color that says "stop" and the color that says "go." As a report on the research by Travers points out, we may be adhering to an outworn concept of how messages get transmitted and the conditions under which learning can occur:

> As for the other popular assumption—that appealing to several senses (modalities) simultaneously is more effective than concentrating on one—*the fact is that when the human learner is exposed to information coming to him from different sources he either suppresses all but one "message" or*

[27] Murray G. Phillips, "Learning Materials and Their Implementation," *Review of Educational Research,* XXXVI (June, 1966), 376.

blocks off all but one channel of communication, or he shifts from one to another in pretty much random fashion. Researchers have concluded that when this shifting takes place the total amount of information picked up is no more than would have been got by staying with one source, and in fact it may be less because of the time consumed in making the shifts.

In other words, the human nervous system acts as though it is capable of handling information from only a single source at any one time; trying to crowd it may be more of a hindrance than a help. The common notion that one can pick up useful bits and pieces of information while concentrating on some one source is ill-founded. As Travers says, "The picking up of incidental information peripheral to a common task is symptomatic of a poorly organized learning situation."

An important role of the teacher becomes that of finding simplified representations of the environment which are compatible both with the objectives of learning and with the information-handling mechanism of the learner.[28]

Many children, particularly those from the lowest socio-economic levels, need more than the "typical" amount of oral activity. Such children need more talking time, time when they are aided in finding the words for their world, and enlarging their word-world, than children who have ample talking time at home. All children can utilize extended opportunities to talk about people, feelings, and relationships.

The procedures selected here, and the resource list that follows, are designed to elicit the greatest possible involvement on the part of students. Through these means we would hope to encourage teachers to learn with students about the complex intellectual and emotional dimensions of the students' intergroup relationships, whether from the inner city, from the affluent suburb, or in rural America.

DIAGNOSING THE INTERGROUP SITUATION IN YOUR SCHOOL

Although many teachers are intellectually convinced that there is a need for intergroup educational efforts in their own schools, they do not know where the particular point of tension or conflict or misunderstanding or mythology is most evident. There are several ways of finding out: In one of the best of the series produced under

[28] Robert Travers, "The Transmission of Information to Human Receivers," *AV Communication Review,* XII (Winter, 1964), 373-85.

the direction of Hilda Taba (K38), the small book *Diagnosing Human Relations Needs* suggests many ways in which teachers can get insight into those problems that vex *her* students. Included are sociometrics, diaries, observation guides, interview procedures, etc. In a recent publication, Thomas (K40) expands ways teachers can understand classroom social relations.

Another very useful device is the "Shadow Study." An individual teacher "follows" a child through his school day. A record is kept of what is taking place every five or ten minutes for that child, for the other children, and in the general classroom setting. This kind of view of the school as the student experiences it is particularly useful for the segmented junior or senior high school situation. A report of a nationwide study of what was happening in eighth grades all over the country, using the "Shadow Study" technique, is given in *The Junior High School We Saw* (ASCD, M1). For all those who participated in this study, the experience was memorable.

One teacher found out that her first-grade all-Negro class was extremely color conscious by showing them a series of pictures of Negro youngsters. There was almost total rejection by the class of the pictures of the darkest Negro child. Another teacher found out that her first-grade all-Negro class had already internalized the concept believed to be held by the white group that Negroes are dangerous: She showed them a picture of a Negro woman peering at her flat tire. She asked, "Who would stop to help this woman?" The class rejected the idea that a white man would help: "He thinks she would hurt him. She has a knife in her purse." A white woman? "She is afraid of her; she has a knife in her purse." A Negro man? "Yes, he is one of us." This simple device showed the teacher the apparent expectation on the part of these young children that white people by and large perceived Negroes as dangerous. Such a self-image obviously is going to interfere with positive intergroup relations in the years ahead, and re-education is essential. Other groups of children, of course, might not react this way at all.

When shown the short film, "I Wonder Why? . . ." based on the Burden (L26) book, several members of an all-white third-grade class were clearly able to see why the girl was not liked because she was a Negro. One boy made it very clear. "She stinks," was his succinct report.

Thus these teachers, using informal or formal means, were able to diagnose the status of intergroup insight on the part of their students. At this point, then, the teacher knows better where to start. Some advertisements have recently shown Negro as well as white children engaging in activities. The teacher can use such an advertisement as a kind of "instant social-distance scale" to determine: "Who belongs in our group? Who does not? With whom would you prefer to play? Anyone here you would not want to play with? Why?" The teacher makes no evaluative statements about the children's responses; instead she notes down who reacts, and the quality of the reaction. This will guide her in the selection of material to be used next.

The diagnosis may reveal some ugly attitudes as well as the ugly words they are phrased in. What shall the teacher do when the children use racial epithets? In a diagnostic sense, such epithets certainly tell the teacher what more needs to be done. But one does not give a lecture on safety while a fire is burning; one puts the fire out and then talks about playing with matches.

In response to a child's use of such inflammatory names as "nigger," "kike," "wop," etc., the teacher can do several things. Possible lines of action are listed below, with their probable consequences:

Action	*Consequence*
Teacher: "Jane, we don't call people by such names in this school."	Immediate arousal of interest on the part of other children to learn the forbidden name. Jane is shamed, but angry.
Teacher: "Class, Bob used a word which could make someone unhappy. Bob, would you repeat what you said. Can anyone tell me why this would make someone unhappy?"	Puts Bob on the spot. He may refuse to answer. However, if he does not, the teacher can continue the discussion. The class will probably provide the reasons why the name is undesirable. If the children do not know, tell them.
Teacher: "I heard Ellen say a naughty word. Now I don't want to hear this word from anyone ever again."	Children will immediately turn to Ellen to find out her naughty word, and try it out on other people.

Teacher: "I just heard something that reminded me of an old saying:

"Sticks and stones can break my bones but words can never hurt me."

Children, do you think this is so? Have you ever heard a word or words that hurt?"

Teacher directs children's attention to the *general* way in which a word can be hurtful. She can eventually work back to the word she heard which started the discussion. A list of "hurt words" can be made by each child. A public listing, particularly with small children, may be misused.

Teacher: "See this word I just wrote?" (She writes *Shorty*—or some similar word—on the board.) "When I was your age, people called me this. You know, it hurt my feelings. I was the tallest in my room. Why do you think they called me Shorty?"

Teacher directs children at the use of words to hurt by using a personal experience. She will eventually come back to the "hurt" word used in the class.

Teacher: "Bob, if I ever hear you say that again in this room you will be sent to the principal. You know we have a rule against such things in this school."

Over-reaction: Bob will now know how to get the teacher angry. So will his friends.

Teacher: "I heard what you said, Suzy, but I am going to ignore it this time. I want you to write on a piece of paper why you think I am not happy about what you said."

Is this a guessing game? Will Suzy learn a lesson or just learn to dislike the teacher and feel the "bad" word is a useful way to get attention?

Teacher: "Sometimes people say things without thinking. I heard John say something just now which puzzled me. I wonder, John, if you thought really about what you were saying?"

Puts John on the spot. However, provides an intellectual way out for him; also suggests a possible avenue of class investigation.

The above samples of possible teacher behavior and possible student response suggest some of the things to do—and not to do. It is unwise for the teacher to ignore an obviously inflammatory use of derogatory names. But the way in which she handles the situation can make it worse rather than better.

Name-calling is almost always a sign for needed investigation. In many instances the teacher would be advised to ignore the first incidence of name-calling so that she can think out a line of action which will lead to positive understanding by all the students. Too quick a response, while very natural, may be more damaging than a delayed response well thought out. For this reason, before reacting one should consider very carefully any incidents that seem to have a hostile interracial or intergroup overtone. Racial epithets may be used in situations where the real problem is personal animosity, and the racial aspects are quite beside the point. But it is important for educators to bring to the attention of students that the use of such loaded language has more to it than just a way to get at an enemy. If someone wants to call John a name, that is part of the game, but the name should be unrelated to his racial, ethnic, or religious group. It is the latter "hurt names" that provide the continued ammunition for intergroup warfare. In a country and a world of many groups, we are seeking ways to declare a truce in intergroup hostilities.

WHAT TO USE:

1. The Real Thing

Learning about the achievements of Ralph Bunche *may not,* says Ginzberg (M8, p. 107), "be as helpful a guide to the average Negro youngster as the knowledge that individuals not too different from himself have risen one or two rungs on the ladder." Students, whether members of a minority group or not, not only will be impressed by the admonitions of the dentist to brush their teeth, but may also be impressed if he is Negro, Chinese, Cuban, or of whatever cultural group is least likely to be thought as a dentist.

Using the "real thing"—the live representation of the thing we wish to demonstrate—speaks far louder than the words we say. If teachers claim, for instance, that all kinds of people can get along well, then it would be valuable if the school faculty were a demonstration of that very fact—an integrated faculty. The most telling argument for school integration at all levels, both in classroom and in adult personnel, is that this in itself is the "acting out" of what the child may see in the school text. Yes, the class pictured in the text is integrated; see, so is ours. The book is talking about a world we know.

The use of resource visitors has special merit when such visitors are the parents of students in the classroom. Bill's father, who works in the post office, can talk about his work; Jane's father, who works for the transit company, can talk about his work, and so on. It must be remembered that many children who dwell in slums do so primarily because of housing restrictions. Many have parents who are responsibly employed in significant middle-echelon jobs. *For the slum child whose parents are not so fortunate, it is useful to bring to him over and over again the "live" lesson of achieved opportunity.*

Seeing Negroes and other minority-group members as persons employed in a variety of settings, utilizing a variety of talents, is also a very significant lesson for the white student. Visits to industrial plants, government offices, and military establishments in which integrated work experiences can be observed are valuable experiences. Not only will the student gain from learning about the particular enterprise, but the teacher needs to make it quite obvious that one noticeable point was the fact that many persons of different ethnic and racial backgrounds were employed at all levels of work.

The logistics of a field trip are often enough to make a teacher blanch; many school systems put so many barriers in the way of field trips that teachers are unable to use this extremely effective educational device. It would be worthwhile for teachers and administrators who are interested in deliberate intergroup education to examine policies governing field trips.

Although there has been much talk recently of the value of the "enrichment" experience—seeing a play, going to an opera, visiting a museum or the zoo—there is considerable merit in field trips that take students into the world of work, if only to demonstrate the point made above. Such trips are particularly important for the defeated child of the slums who cannot see himself striving for these kinds of jobs; the only jobs he has heard of—other than living on welfare—are menial, dirty, unskilled, insecure, and exploitative. On the basis of such contact with reality, the stories of success reported in such booklets as *Call Them Heroes* (O4) or noted in each issue of *Ebony* magazine (U8) will sound feasible to the student.

As this book goes to press, the publisher of *Ebony* is collaborating with the United States Department of Labor to produce a pamphlet which will include the pictures and vignettes of these middle-echelon Negro workers who have succeeded in almost every variety of job that one can imagine, a fact useful for both white and Negro youngsters to realize. *I Have a Dream* (Sterne, N162) is another valuable alternative to "live" demonstrations of real achievement.

Communities, however, can also provide real data, though it takes a brave teacher to utilize the community in this fashion. For instance, the Miel study of attitudes in suburbia (K27) causes hackles to rise whenever the findings are presented to a PTA or faculty group in similar situations. One enterprising teacher introduced her class to a genuine experience in social research which could be an exemplary model for others:

> During a current-events session, one of my sixth graders read a review of *The Shortchanged Children of Suburbia* by Alice Miel with Edwin Kiester, Jr., a report on the self-segregation of the affluent suburbs. After a heated class discussion, the children composed a letter to Dr. Miel telling her that they disagreed with the reported findings and would be willing to conduct a local survey.
>
> As the children prepared for the survey, she offered valuable suggestions on format and types of questions. The class formed committees that went through magazines looking for pictures of different groups of people. They also began to make up questions that they felt would help to form a profile of the student body.
>
> To prevent bias in conducting the survey, the class recruited survey teams from other classes to administer the test—an eight-picture projection and a 54-question profile—to 124 sixth grade pupils.
>
> When the results came back, we turned to mathematics and began to tabulate, organize, and analyze the findings. When the children had found averages, they began to check on possible correlations. They wanted to know, for example, how many of the students who said they would not associate with a Negro classmate also said they would not attend a party with a Negro or stated they had never had a Negro friend or neighbor.
>
> When the survey was over, the children discovered—to their surprise and dismay—that their findings agreed with Dr. Miel's.
>
> During the entire process, the pupils were highly motivated. What's more, they saw how their language arts and mathematics skills could serve them.

They learned a lot about themselves and the problem of hidden prejudice.

(Philip A. Shart, sixth grade teacher, Middleville Junior High School, Northport, New York, in *NEA Journal*, Vol. 56, December, 1967, page 76.)

2. *Role-Playing*

Role-playing (or dramatic play) provides a challenging way to try out the ways in which people feel and the ways in which others respond to them. The technique is relatively simple: a dramatic situation or confrontation is identified by the teacher or the class. The persons involved in the situation are described, and the action is outlined or the outcome is suggested. The role-players "try out" the situation. The class may offer comments regarding the reality of the action or the authenticity of the role-taking. The scene may be played again with new actors, or with the first ones trying to follow the instructions of the class. Following one or two enactments, the class discusses the problem raised by the role-play and their response to it. The emphasis is on spontaneity of response: no lines are written, no script is memorized, the "solution" comes from the enactment itself.

Although not a new technique, role-playing is still relatively infrequently used in classrooms. One reason is that it does require a teacher who is sensitive to the feelings of the group and is able to accept any direction the role-playing may take. For instance, in role-playing a situation in which a group of girls is trying to face the fact that their hitherto all-white club may be confronted by the decision about accepting a Negro member (as presented in the open-ended script in Appendix B), one group may decide to let the whole decision rest with the adult advisor. Another group may work the whole thing out and decide that the club's purposes include accepting any person who applies. Still another group may be quite unable to find a way out of the dilemma. No matter how a given group develops a role-play situation, the teacher must deal with any solution offered. Thus a teacher who uses role-playing must be comfortable with ambiguity and uncertainty. One can never be sure how a role-playing situation will be handled from group to group. This, of course, is part of the adventure of using role-playing in teaching; it is a constant challenge to the teacher. Role-playing will be difficult and hazardous for teachers who feel uncomfortable with the unknown.

The teacher must be sure that the class understands that whatever solution a group arrives at is to be accepted as *that* group's efforts—and is worth discussing. The teacher who uses role-playing cannot use such phrases as, "Oh no, that's not the right thing to say," or "Let's see if we can get a *better* solution," or "I don't think that was the right answer to the problem, do you?" Instead, the teacher must be prepared to use phrases like, "How did you feel about your solution to the problem?" and "Is there another way that would be just as good that could be used to solve the problem?" and "Could someone suggest another answer that Mary could have given when faced with the problem?" and "Who would like to try Mary's role and see if another solution is possible?" Thus, no matter how a group may resolve a given situation, the teacher can suggest there are other alternatives, even if the one provided by the role-players is, on the face of it, feasible and reasonable. What the teacher is suggesting is that there are many ways to solve complex human relations problems.

In one situation, using a role-play revolving around an adolescent's demand for more freedom than his family would allow, an experienced teacher, playing the role of the adolescent, stated after the role-play that such a situation was just what had once happened to him in his own life. After experiencing the role-play, he realized that there were other ways he could have handled the situation in his youth; he had not had a chance (which role-play provides) to "see" other alternatives. The only alternative he knew was one of bitter, angry, hostile fighting with his family. Role-playing can provide members of a group with a repertoire of different ways to respond to a troublesome situation.

A class is usually very quick to analyze a role-play enactment, and quick to identify the authenticity and reasonableness of the situation as presented. If an individual is out of character, that is, if he does not act as a real father would, the group will quickly ask for a replay. The teacher would accept such constructive responses, and either coach the original "father" in his role, with the help of the class, or have the person who made the suggestion for the new solution try his hand at being the father.

Sometimes one presents a class with three variations on a theme.

For instance, in a teacher-training example, three members were selected as "teachers" and sent out of the room. Each was given a slip of paper on which was written:

> You have been told by the teacher on yard duty that members of your group have been heard calling racial epithets at other children on the playground, even though your class is racially integrated. The class is just coming in from recess and you want to do something.

Each of the three "teachers" was given the same problem. The first teacher could not do anything with the situation at all; she just froze, after telling the class what she had heard. The instructor accepted her inability to deal with the situation and she took her seat with the class. The second teacher talked with the class to the point where it was agreed they would not call names again. Finally, the third teacher presented an entirely different strategy for dealing with the situation, which ended with the class agreeing to apologize to the victims of their persecution.

The instructor then discussed the three different modes of behavior. Though none might have worked in the real classroom, at least the group of teachers-to-be were able to think about a situation which might very well face them in their teaching, and see how one might find different ways of dealing with the situation. Each member now had new additions to their behavorial repertoire of teaching strategies.

Sometimes a single enactment may include five or six different solutions, with persons switching roles: the father taking the place of the son, the mother changing seats with the daughter, the student becoming the teacher. Sometimes the teacher may enter into the act, becoming a new member of the cast, who was not previously identified. For instance, in one human relations workshop, the group was given the task of discussing their response as white teachers to the new principal, who was Negro. The scene was just after the first teachers' meeting of the year. The group in the role-play was being very "nice." The leader of the session decided someone had to be the devil's advocate, so she entered the scene herself. She was able to say all the prejudiced, unpleasant, and difficult things which needed to come out, and which, she well knew, were on the minds of the participants. In the course of being in the role-play, one of the most bigoted members of the group did her best to persuade the role-play bigoted teacher that she was wrong!

Typically, however, the role of the teacher is to support the role-play. The teacher must decide when to stop an enactment that is not getting anywhere, or that is too "hammy" or too unrealistic. The teacher may interrupt to remind role-players of their role, or to instruct the audience to be as serious as the role-players are. Usually, once a role-play gets underway, the players are so involved in what is going on that they ignore the laughter of an audience. The teacher, by a gesture or a glance, reminds the audience of the essential seriousness of the situation.

The teacher, as noted before, then helps in the follow-up of the role-play. The role-play is essentially designed to induce reflection and discussion. It is not to produce or train great actors nor is the acting itself the primary interest. Role-playing is utilized to provide an immediate, common experience for a group which involves the group at an emotional as well as an intellectual level. The persons who play a role are typically very much affected by the emotional demands the role-playing makes upon them, and this in turn influences their feelings and attitudes and learning.

When exposed to persuasive messages, persons who are required to play a role that entails putting the content of the message in their own words to others will be more influenced than those who are more passively exposed. This tendency toward "saying is believing" has been found to occur even when role-playing is artificially induced, as in experiments dealing with the effects of communications designed to modify . . . *evaluations* of previously disliked tasks, policies or ethnic groups. . . . The tendency to accept personally the content of a message that one is required to verbalize to others has been found to increase as the amount of *improvisation* increases. . . .

The success of improvised role-play might be attributed to several psychological processes. Festinger suggests that the main gain from role-playing comes about from efforts to reduce dissonance between what one is saying and what one actually believes. . . . An alternative explanation is in terms of self-persuasion: When attempting to put the message across to others, the role-player is likely to think up new formulations of the arguments, illustrations, and appeals that are tailormade to be convincing to himself . . . role-playing under acceptable, benevolent sponsorship produces more attitude change than role-playing under seemingly manipulative or exploitative sponsorship. (Smith and Janis, J25.)

Role-play also has a significant effect upon the audience viewing the enactment, not just through subsequent discussion, but while the situation is being developed and throughout the process of selecting actors and the ensuing dramatic development (Grambs, J14).

Role-playing may be introduced by way of incompleted stories, as described by the Shaftels (J20; J21), by Nichols and Williams (J18), and by the Citizenship Education Project (J11) materials. Riessman (F26; J19) considers role-playing a particularly useful device for the culturally deprived child.

The most comprehensive and useful discussion of role-playing is provided in the recent publication of the Shaftels (J22). This guide should be carefully read by any teacher who wishes to use this technique. Additional help is provided by Corsini, Shaw, and Blake (J9), who use instances from business and industry, but whose examples and discussion of technique is readily adaptable to the secondary school situation. This volume has a particularly excellent annotated bibliography. An older guide, that of Klein (J16), also reports ways of using role-playing with adults, with obvious analogies to ways of using the variations of this technique with adolescents.

A rather unusual type of role-playing is described by Rosemary Lippitt (J17), who showed how the use of empty chairs could provide a substitute for "live" actors in a role-playing situation. This device, although not widely used in school settings, could be of great value particularly for the teacher who is not too sure of role-playing technique. The chairs can represent people, and the class can help to describe how someone *sitting in that chair* might feel, what he might do, how he might react. The chairs can be shifted at will and can represent many kinds of situations and persons. With a large group, where role-playing might be quite difficult, the empty-chair technique can be quite successful. The audience is drawn into dramatic imagining of what might be the feelings of the persons sitting in the empty chairs. In one such demonstration with an audience of more than 150 teenage girls, the author was able to elicit remarkably free and spontaneous remarks and questions about the sensitive problems of race (in a Southern state), and to facilitate later small-group discussion of feelings among Negro and white girls.

Another variation of role-playing may be developed through the use of hand puppets. These may be constructed by the children or purchased from Creative Playthings or other children's toy manufacturers. The children, protected by the puppet, may feel more able to express their real feelings and emotions in an area in which there may be tension. Masks, bought or class-made, also can be used for the same purpose. Similarly, doll play with family dolls which are both Negro and white (available from Creative Playthings) can permit children to manipulate the dolls through scenes which they have devised. See Appendix A and Appendix B for examples of materials to start role-playing enactments.

3. *Open-Ended Situations*

The open-ended stories developed by the Shaftels (J22) and others are designed specifically for role-playing. They do not solve a problem, but present a dramatic confrontation in which several possible alternatives are available for resolution. Other open-ended material may be used either for role-playing or for class discussion. With older children, written endings may be requested; these endings may be developed by groups or by individuals. A class may then discuss various endings and evaluate which ones seem to be most feasible. Essential to the use of any open-ended type of material is the recognition that *there is no single right answer.* There may be many answers, depending on the way in which the students choose to define the situation, the aspects of it which make most sense to them, and what they know about their own world. A teacher who uses role-playing or any open-ended device must be fully able to accept many answers, and many of these may be far from what she might consider "right" or "proper." To invoke teacher judgment of what is the right or proper response is to destroy the value of these techniques.

However, the teacher may find the answers students give highly revealing, and therefore useful in a diagnostic sense. She may note that students reject solutions that would be appropriate in terms of the world they live in. This may suggest to her the need for further discussion and wider experiences. Take, for instance, a group of Negro students presented with an open-ended story about a job-seeking youngster who is undecided whether to go into the store with the sign "messenger wanted" because he is afraid he will be refused on account of his color. The class may agree that he should not try for the job. In the teacher's eyes this might not be a "good" answer, though in reality the class is saying that they fear rebuff, have experienced it too often, and therefore will not test the situation. Exploration of the reality of job discrimination should certainly become an important lesson for future classes.

Using role-playing, one youth worker in the Watts area of Los Angeles helped young people develop insight into their intergroup problems.[29] Recent issues of the *NEA Journal* have carried short open-ended stories for student completion. A collection of these is now available (K29). Issues of *Scope* (U24) and *Read* and some of the commercial children's magazines publish open-ended stories. Stories from *Read* are available in one pamphlet (N173). Noteworthy in most instances, however, is the fact that problems of ethnic or religious or social-class differences are absent.

From the Community Relations Service, the open-ended story, "Somebody's Brother," by Anne Kurflink may be obtained (L99). This story focuses on how a parent can answer a child's question, "Mother, why did they call me 'nigger'?" Adolescents and PTA groups might find this short story a challenging way to start a discussion of the impact on children of desegregation and racial name-calling. See the Appendix for examples of open-ended short stories for both younger children and adolescents.

A careful reading of some stories may show the teacher how to cut a story so that the children can then write or act out what would happen next. A good example is the story, "The Shoes."[30] This very brief story, describing vividly the feelings of poverty and its degradation, makes a superb open-ended story if it is cut at the point where the principal, who was thought of as the enemy, approaches the young boy: "I could feel my face getting red as I began to move my feet up under me. But before I could ease them up he. . . ." The story continues. But the teacher stops, and asks, "Well?" The children are then free to create their own ending. Comparing endings will be an interesting adventure for all concerned. In the instance cited, the teacher can then provide the "real" answer given by the story. With this as a model, children can

[29] Washington, D.C. *Star,* Friday, March 4, 1966.

[30] Paul E. Mawhinney, "The Shoes," *NEA Journal* (October, 1966), 12-14.

write their own beginnings of stories. It is surprising how inventive children can be when once started on this kind of creative experience. Teachers, with the help of their students, can devise their own open-ended stories from the real life around them.

Open-ended scripts such as those prepared for the Y-Teen program of the YWCA (Grambs, J13; also see example in Appendix B) can be developed by the teacher by tape recording role-play situations. These are then transcribed, they are modified somewhat, and the endings are removed. The reading of the script sets the stage for the problem, establishes the roles and the characters, and then, by leaving the cast in midstream, forces them to act out their own solutions. Or if the class prefers, the group can discuss the possible alternatives for the problem.

Another useful open-ended device is the film, although few such films are available. It is unfortunate that more open-ended films have not been made, since they provide a dramatic springboard for either role-play or discussion.

The following are some open-ended films suitable for use with adolescents:

Right or Wrong? (Should one tell on one's playmates when apprehended for a window breaking?) (R90)

Teaching: A Question of Method (What is the responsibility of the teacher when a religious issue comes up?) (R106)

All the Way Home (Shall a house be sold to a Negro when the neighborhood is all white?) (R3)

Politics: The High Cost of Conviction (Should a politician vote as he believes, or as his supporters want him to vote?) (R81)

Vandalism: Crime or Prank? (An adult sees a friend's child break a statue; should he report it or forget it?) (R115)

I Wonder Why, based on the Burden (L26) book, can be used with elementary school children from third grade on. The lack of other open-ended films for young children is to be deplored. Talking is the activity to be encouraged, but the typical film provides the problem *and* the solution, and there is little left to talk about.

Another superb device for providing discussion are problem pictures. These are pictures suggesting a situation which is familiar to children or youth, but which leaves the analysis quite open. The *Focus* pictures (Q9) prepared by the National Conference of Christians and Jews are one such set. In the Singer Social Studies Series (Hunnicutt and Grambs) (L81) there are a number of problem pictures which, although they do not specifically center on intergroup problems, do provide an opportunity to discuss typical human relations situations with children. The teacher seeking to make more explicit the intergroup content could ask: "Would your answer to the problem be any different if this child were of another race?" "Why?" And the discussion can roll from there. A series of problem pictures developed by the Shaftels (Q24) will also be very useful for providing intergroup discussion. A set of pictures being developed by Raymond Muessig promises to be very useful.

Another open-ended situation is created by the asking of "open questions," or incomplete sentences. Examples of these are given by Wright (H37):

How I felt when . . .
I felt left out when . . .
Others like (or dislike) me because . . .
Things I don't like about people are . . .
I'd like to move because . . .

It has been stated that the incompleted tasks are likely to be the ones that are remembered longest. There is a human urge to finish something, to know the ending. Thus the open-ended device, whichever one may choose to use, draws the class into involvement because of this need to find a satisfying and satisfactory solution. The fact that there may be many solutions, and that these may be debated, tends to increase the level of involvement as well as the level of remembering.

4. Flat Pictures

We live in a pictorial culture. Illustrations are used everywhere. A book without pictures would not interest a very young child, particularly a beginning reader. Only adults read books without pictures, and even for adults there is a wide (and expensive) market for the lavishly illustrated history or art book.

Currently there is a renewed interest in the value of flat pictures and photographs for intergroup education. A large folio series published by The John Day Company is one example (*Urban Education Studies,* Q29). These folios include series of large photographs around such themes as:

Growing Is . . . .
A Neighborhood Is . . . .
Recreation Is . . . .
A Family Is . . . .

The materials have been arranged in the sequence developed for each folio on the basis of the underlying theory and organization of the editor. However, a teacher may wish to separate the folios, using pictures in another sequence or several from different ones or encouraging children to organize their own sequence. The pictures in this group, and those in other sources (see Section Q) are designed to evoke children's responses with their photographic reality.

Although not designed specifically for classroom use, some recent and not so recent volumes of photographs are to be highly recommended. Beginning with *The Family of Man* (Steichen, Q25a), the teacher would find such books as *The Child* (Bermont and Langston, Q2), *The World is Young* (Miller, Q13), *Willie* (Heyman and Mason, Q10), *Family* (Mead and Heyman, Q12), *Your Face is a Picture*[31] (Clifford), and *The Sense of Wonder* (Carson, Q3) very valuable source material. It would be the height of educational luxury if several copies of each of these books were available so that teachers could cut them up and mount the pictures, thus allowing children to develop their own sequences, to use pictures for classwork or individual work, and to utilize them in innumerable other creative ways. The Children's Museum of Boston has pioneered in developing a picture collection designed for flexible classroom use. The program "Match Boxes" is described in the December 1966-January 1967 issue of *American Education* (Vol. 3, No. 1, p. 9) published by the United States Office of Education.

The City Box, for instance, introduces first and second graders to "cityness." They listen to recordings of city sounds, see films on the city and on

[31] Eth Clifford and David Clifford, *Your Face is a Picture* (Indianapolis: The E. C. Seale Co., 1963).

man's life in the city, study photographs of the city, and manipulate models of buildings included in the Box. These overlapping activities not only give the children an idea of the meaning and the feeling of the city, but, more importantly, give them an opportunity to express their own feelings about the city and city life. They speculate.

To date the Boxes have received an excellent report card from the Boston schools where they have been used. "We think this concept has vast potential," reports one administrator; "it puts the kids in the driver's seat," says another; "makes book-learning old-fashioned," says a third.

And from one of the kids, sitting back after scraping a deerskin from the Algonquin Box: "No wonder the wigwam was so dirty."

There are, in addition, books that focus particularly on intergroup relations and use pictorial material to increase the impact of the problem presented. Such volumes as *The Shame of a Nation* (Stern, F30), *Mississippi from Within* (Tucker, E49), *The Movement* (Hansberry, New York, Simon and Schuster Inc., paperback, [n.d.], *Our Faces, Our Words* (Smith, Q25), and *I Wonder Why . . .* (Burden, L26), are sources of pictorial material of particular value for upper-grade and secondary school students.

The large pictures produced by the Seabury Press under the title, *The Deprived* (Q6), are a poignant and stirring collection of the faces and feelings of poverty. The particular utility of this collection is that it is mostly white poverty that is portrayed. For many urban city children, who in growing numbers tend to be Negro (and in some cities Puerto Rican, Mexican-American or Cuban), it is a new and startling idea that "white" people, too, can and do live in shacks and wear the hurt and bear the look of poverty.

It was distressing, when doing role-playing with a white group of girls from apparently affluent homes in Norfolk, Virginia, to be told that all Negroes in Norfolk lived in dreadful shacks and didn't care if their porches were falling to pieces. Yet, on the way to the center of the city from the airport one goes through an extensive middle-class Negro neighborhood, replete with picket fences, clipped hedges, and trimmed lawns. The white girls literally *did not see* this area of the city, yet they had driven through it many times. Similarly, a Negro child may not *see* any white person who is living in a slum, even though there may be many nearby.

It has been found helpful, too, for Negro youngsters to learn about the persecutions suffered by other minority groups; many of these young people are sure theirs is the only group that is "picked on." The poignant book of children's drawings and poems, *I Never Saw Another Butterfly*,[32] brings to heart breaking attention the fate of children killed by the Nazis. Also, children from other groups will be helped if they realize that, in man's troubled history, almost every group has at one time or another been the oppressed, and the oppressor. This view does not condone such practices, but it may be helpful to gain perspective on the contemporary scene. Pictures can bring this reality vividly into the classroom.

The inexpensive sets of pictures produced by UNESCO, *Schools Around the World, Children Around the World, UNESCO Around the World* (Q30), are valuable aids to the teacher in demonstrating the common experiences of all people. As bulletin board displays they can speak many silent lessons to the observing children. An excellent guide for teachers utilizing pictures to evoke creative writing is provided by Leavitt and Sohn (N111).

What is *not* helpful are the "colored brown" pictures developed by several leading publishers of children's books as part of reading readiness programs. The saccharine quality and "pretty" look of these pictures are educationally shameful. Faked photographs of historical events such as the landing of the *Mayflower* are also deplorable.

The teacher can also make her own collection of pictures. The pictures found in *Look, Life, Ebony,* or *Photographic Annual* are often very closely related to the many ideas and themes teachers will want to discuss with children. The students may write or tell stories about the pictures; they may arrange their own "picture book" from a selection they or the teacher may make; they may discuss a group of pictures in terms of how "near" or "far" the content of the picture feels to them. It goes without saying that children should at all times be encouraged to make their own pictures, and write and illustrate their own stories, feelings, and ideas.

Though not traditionally utilized in this fashion, the pictures in a standard text could be examined to see how true to life they are. Do they portray people as we know them? Who is in the picture? Who is left out? What difference would it make? What difference should it make?

[32] *I Never Saw Another Butterfly: Children's Drawings and Poems from Theresienstadt Concentration Camp, 1942-44* (New York: McGraw-Hill Book Company, 1966).

Children may do their own documentary picture taking. The ever-present camera could be a tool of student study and evaluation. This kind of assignment would be most appealing to students. The pictures in *Two Blocks Apart* (Mayerson, N122) were made by Harlem youth. It is possible that some of the less verbally minded youngsters would respond to the challenge of taking pictures to illustrate or demonstrate a theme or idea developed out of a discussion of intergroup relations. A photographic contest might inspire them to make an extra effort.

Teachers report (Webster, K43a) the great value of taking pictures of children in their own rooms. We each need to "see" ourselves in the picture. With care, a teacher (or an aide) can take pictures of "bad" children doing "good" things. These can be posted and labeled: "Bobby helped put the chairs away"; "Jane showed Sally where the cups were." Or just a sensitive and honest picture of each child; and why not ask the high school students for help?

A very interesting program conducted under the Seattle Public Schools' Title I Project includes providing for each designated school a special set of photographs made in and around *that* school. The children then discuss the pictures, in some of which they themselves may appear; the pictures are an immediate invitation to discussion. The Title I Curriculum Coordinator writes:

> Our discussion pictures are designed to develop attitudes in selected areas (school behavior, health, safety, respect for authority) and promote language skills. A set of 20 pictures were prepared for each of our 18 Title I elementary schools consisting of illustrative activities in that particular school. The pictures would have meaning for youngsters attending that school and would provide a basis for meaningful discussion. The production cost was slight because we utilized students in our high school photography classes to take, develop, and mount the photographs. . . . Sets of the pictures are not available outside of the district. The guide is currently in tentative form and will be revised and expanded during the summer.
>
> We are presently developing a similar project for home-school use. We are producing pads of 8½" by 11" local discussion pictures on inexpensive paper. Each picture will illustrate a school or community activity. On the back of each picture is a set of discussion questions aimed at parents for use with their children in developing language skills through the home. The primary student will bring the picture home and mother will channel discussion through the questions on the back.
>
> Our minority materials will be issued in the form of a kit for teacher use. Materials will deal with Negroes, Japanese, Chinese, Northwest In-

dians and Hispano-Americans from three points of view: historical data; cultural activities; and suggestions for developing intergroup relations in school and the community. Commercial books, filmstrips and tapes will be included in the kit.[33]

One possibility that teachers could explore is the use of the instant photographs possible with polaroid cameras. On a trip into the neighborhood, for instance, a series of pictures could be taken by the teacher, by an aide, by an interested parent, by one of the children, or by a child from a higher grade. Then this series could be mixed up by the teacher, and, on return from the trip, the class would be asked to put the pictures back into sequence. Such a procedure would help in guiding children to develop the left-to-right sequence necessary in learning to read, and also help focus attention on details as well as events. Again, the intrinsic interest in *themselves* as subjects can be utilized for maximizing student interest. Student-made movies have always been a source of great interest; it is unfortunate that today, with the heavy Federal investment in technology, teachers have not made more creative use of these aids in developing student talents.

5. *Affective Materials*

Some of the materials we use in teaching have more power to move us emotionally than others. These we can group under a general label of "affective materials," since they produce an impact over and beyond mere intellectual recognition. Many of the items and methods listed previously, such as open-ended situations, role-playing, selected photographs, have an implicit affective impact.

There are numerous reports of teachers using many kinds of books to evoke similar responses. The deliberate use of books to "educate" emotions is called *bibliotherapy*. In this instance, books are selected which aid the individual in gaining insight into his own personal situation.

In the intergroup area we have a large resource to draw upon. One source, autobiography, is particularly effective with adoles-

[33] Donald Bask, Title I Curriculum Coordinator, Seattle Public Schools, Seattle, Washington, in letter dated February 14, 1968 to Jean D. Grambs, College of Education, University of Maryland. (author)

cents. Such books as Richard Wright's *Black Boy* (O28), Sammy Davis Jr.'s *Yes, I Can* (O5), Althea Gibson's *I Always Wanted to Be Somebody* (O9), Dick Gregory's *Nigger* (O10), the *Autobiography of Malcolm X* (O16), Ethel Waters' *His Eye Is on the Sparrow* (O27), *Manchild in the Promised Land* (Brown, O3), the autobiographical essays of James Baldwin (N7, N8, N9, N10, N11), and the nostalgic report of Erskine Caldwell [34] provide an immediate sense of the world of the Negro (see also Redding, O21; Clark, A8; Sterne, N162). What it means to be on the forefront in the fight for equality is vividly and authentically reported by Trillin (E48), Belfrage (E3), Barrett (E2), Huie (E27), Ehle (E18), the Fayette County Volunteers (E21), and Friedman (E23). The personal struggles of members of other ethnic groups are likewise useful sources for autobiography and history (Handlin, N78, N79, N80). Few books have attained the popularity of the *Diary of Anne Frank* (O8) among young people. The art and poems of children doomed to die, such as *I Never Saw Another Butterfly* (see page 48), brings the hurt of the Nazi terror close to home. Even such a straightforward account of what it means to try to eat within a welfare diet as reported by Spalding (F29), can be a source of new insight for many an adolescent who has no notion of hunger.

It is obvious that fiction is also a pathway toward emotional insight into the world of others. Currently, only a few books for children deal directly with the intergroup area through fiction without glossing over the pain and hurt and providing a "nice" ending. Such current book lists as those provided by the American Jewish Committee (Wolfe, T31), the New York City Library (Baker, T4), and *Reading Ladders for Human Relations* (Crosby, T49), provide many suggestions for the teacher. The introduction to *Reading Ladders for Human Relations* includes excellent suggestions for teachers on the use of literature. The lists of source material in the *Study Guide to Urban Education Studies* (Q29) is also useful, although the publication dates for many items are missing.

The excellent bibliography by Kircher (T17) provides a guide to children's books based on the behavior patterns of children, with books grouped under such categories as "Moving to a New Home," "Understanding Those Who Are Different," "Fitting in at School," and "Acceptance of a Step-Parent." From the American Library

34 Erskine Caldwell, *In Search of Bisco* (New York: Pocket Books, Inc., 1966).

Association one can obtain a report which lists those books found to be most popular among disadvantaged youth.

Novels such as *Lost Boundaries* (White, N192), *Where Were You That Year?* (Strachan, N174), *The Learning Tree* (Parks, N136a), *To Kill a Mockingbird* (Lee, N112), *A Different Drummer* (Kelley, N105), *Invisible Man* (Ellison, N58), *Native Son* (Wright, N198), *Durango Street* (Bonham, N18), *The Empty Schoolhouse* (Carlson, L27), bring some of the intergroup problems of today into vivid focus. However, one must not assume that just because a student is a Negro or a Puerto Rican he prefers books in which his race is portrayed. Some students will; some will not. Like most other adolescents, he will respond to a good story *first,* but it is also true that many good stories featuring characters of minority group identity are not made readily available to all young people.

Many of the current best sellers are in paperback, and the secondary school teacher may well find that her students have already read them. What is essential is *the intellectual reflection upon the content and meaning of the material* (Loban, G19). It is even possible that an obviously biased and bitter novel can provoke discussion and argument so that the students are able to obtain a more realistic picture of themselves, others, and the world of the school.

For younger children, fourth through sixth grade, some particularly useful books of fiction are *Roosevelt Grady* (Shotwell, L152), *The Empty Schoolhouse* (Carlson, L27), *Sal Fisher's Fly-Up Year* (Gardner, L57), and *The Treasure of Green Knowe* (Boston, L15a). The primary-grade reader will find *Fun for Chris* (Randall, L140) a useful way to introduce the question of why we choose certain people for friends. A number of primary-grade books, such as *The Snowy Day* (Keats, L92), *A Special Place for Jonny* (Haas, L70), *Who's in Charge of Lincoln?* (Fife, L50), introduce Negro characters or focus on a Negro child, without making a point of the fact. The main character may be a Negro, in other words, just as he may be a white child, or any other kind. Such books help young children see that children of all races have similar problems and similar feelings.

Drama has always been a source of emotional education. We have already mentioned open-ended films. The plays of the American Theater Wing (Stirling, N164-170) require minimal production needs and focus on the recurrent problems of human relationships. A recent publication of this group, *Fences* (Stirling, N166), could be effective for showing the delusions of prejudice. High school drama groups could produce the plays to show in elementary schools and at PTA programs. The University of Maryland Drama Department has for a number of years successfully toured the area putting on one of these plays each season. Doubtless other college or university drama departments and local little theater groups could also cooperate.

Recent plays, such as *Blues for Mister Charlie* (Baldwin, N7), *In White America* (Duberman, N56), and *A Raisin in the Sun* (Hansberry, N81), can be read and/or produced by high school groups. The early plays of Paul Green about the South provide a vivid picture of the kind of society that preceded the current civil rights protest (Green, N71).

An inventive teacher can also "trap" students into wanting to read books that they might otherwise consider remote and irrelevant to them. A teacher in an *Upward Bound* program, designed for nonmotivated high school students from poverty-level homes, found an intriguing way to bring the play, *Billy Budd,* adapted from the Melville novel, to his group so that they became keenly involved in the moral issue:

> Earlier in the summer the class had read and written on Shirley Jackson's *The Lottery,* and this had provided a great deal of material for discussion. On Monday morning, the day we were to begin on *Billy Budd,* I came into class looking very grim. I distributed slips of paper and asked each student to write his name on the paper and fold it into four parts. Then I had the slips collected in a box. The students were puzzled, and perhaps nervous. I heard one or two suggest that this was to be a lottery. When I took my place at the front of the classroom again, I announced in the longest face I could pull that something so serious had occurred over the weekend that we had to consider closing the program two weeks early. The staff, however, had thought about the problems this would entail and had decided that, since everyone was involved equally in the problem, we would make examples of people, not on the basis of their involvement, but on the basis of names chosen at random. Each English class was therefore choosing two people who would be sent home early, simply as object lessons to the entire group. I then picked two names out of the box and asked my tutor to arrange with these two students to pack

their bags to leave. (I had alerted the tutor to explain to the students immediately on their leaving the classroom what the plot was.)

After the students left, I asked the class whether they had any questions. People who ordinarily spoke with the greatest reluctance began to raise questions about the justice of what I had done. One student asked if they might know what the offense was, and I replied that I did not want to talk about it. This made them even more indignant with me and the program. After a few minutes I asked whether they would prefer to have me call back the students, if I could find them, and discuss another way of solving the problem, and this they agreed to. The students came back, having been instructed to look unhappy, and the discussion continued on for a few more minutes. Finally, I announced that this had all been a trick and, over the indignant noises of the class, asked them to take the situation as I had structured it and their reaction to what I had done before they knew that it was a trick, and examine the problem of justice in *Billy Budd* from this perspective. The problem of justice, or as one student put it, the question of whether one person should suffer for many, engaged us for the rest of that hour. When we had talked about *The Lottery,* one of the issues that engaged us for two days and formed the basis for a writing assignment was whether it was ever appropriate to use a scapegoat, and—related to this in a tangential way—the ethical responsibility of the person who is ordered to kill another. The way this question was finally phrased owed something to our reading of some of the essays in John Hersey's *Here to Stay:* whether one man to save his own life should obey an order to kill five hundred. One student, talking about the issue of justice in *Billy Budd,* looked back to this earlier discussion and suggested that the reverse problem came to us here: whether it was ever appropriate to kill one—in this case Billy—to save many—in this case, to prevent future mutinies.

On the next day I decided to continue the discussion on a different basis. I divided the class into three groups. Half the high school students were to constitute themselves a prosecuting team, the other half the defense team. The pre-freshmen, our tutor aides, were to be the judges in the case. The two teams were to examine the play in as much detail as possible and be prepared to reopen the trial of Billy Budd before an appeal court sitting in 1966, taking into account the precedents established since the events of the play in the 1790's. The preparation for the retrial took all of that class hour and much of the study hall that day. The trial itself ran for most of a three-hour period covering two class meetings.

Although it has little to do with the way the discussion went, it is probably worth describing one other event that occurred during the week we were working on *Billy Budd.* While my class was divided into the teams to re-try the case, I noticed that my two biggest boys, usually good friends, seemed to be having some trouble with one another. This went on until about the middle of the class hour, when suddenly they leaped to their feet, grabbed each other and began to wrestle. I jumped up, ran over to their side of the room and tried to separate them. This went on for a short time, but long enough to have me worrying about this totally unprecedented happening. Just as I was convinced that this was going to get completely out of hand, the boys dropped their hands and one turned to the other, pointed at me and said, "We got him, Slim." The entire class, looking for a chance to get back at me for the trick I had pulled the day before, had been in on the plot, and they all agreed that I had deserved the trick which was played on me. I got a horse laugh, and then they went back to work.

The spokesman for the prosecution retried the case in pretty much the same terms established by the play. He would call people to the stand, identifying them as characters in the play and would then ask them for testimony, referring them to the appropriate pages of the play. The defense spokesman, following a hint offered him by my tutor, pleaded his case not simply on the circumstances surrounding Billy Budd's striking of Claggart, but also on the question of the morality of the Articles of War. He cited as a precedent of importance to a modern court the Nuremberg Trials, and argued that the Captain's insistence that the officers could not follow their private consciences but must obey the law and orders was unacceptable after the Nuremberg Trials, and where the law or orders to be followed were evil, not to follow one's conscience makes one responsible for the evil. This line of defense was supported by the direct testimony from the characters in the play, with the defense attorney citing the pages and passages to which he was referring. Captain Vere's insistence that his sailors were no longer citizens but parts of one weapon whose job was to fight and to obey, his insistence that no sailor had rights as a citizen, and his testimony to Billy regarding the Articles of War that were all wrong, provided strong support for the defense's case.

The prosecution, countering this argument in its summation, made two strong pleas. One was that, even where particular laws could not seem to mete out justice to individuals, the law was important for preserving society. The spokesman for the prosecution had gone to the library and found more information on the Admiralty Act under which Billy Budd had been tried, and had introduced this material, taken from the scholarly edition of Melville's story, *Billy Budd,* as evidence. Billy was tried under the appropriate act, by a court martial, in time of war. The decision of the Court of Appeals, the prosecution further argued, could not find Billy innocent without condemning the officers who, following their best understanding of the law, had found him guilty. It was not fair, he argued, to try those men for following what they believed to be right.

The case then went to the judges, some of whom had done research meanwhile in the Admiralty Laws of the time and the precedent of the Nuremberg Trials. They had also read the play with a great deal of care. This group of students met several times during the weekend before the verdict was to be rendered. They examined the two aspects of the case: the evidence and the law. Although some of the six judges were deeply concerned with the problem of Billy's innocence, they were also committed to the values of protection of the majority by strong laws. The evidence was all in Billy's favor, but the law was all against him. The result was a split decision, with the majority wishing to find Billy not guilty, with a dissent entered by two judges, strongly arguing for the need of society to protect itself. Appended are copies of those two opinions, with the dissenting opinions beginning with a dictionary definition of society.

What was the value of this treatment of *Billy Budd?* First of all, there was the value of knowing a play in very great detail. As my tutor said, the students had probably never read anything with as much care and knowledge as they read *Billy Budd.* There was, moreover, an understanding not only of what was happening in the play, but also of its relevance to them. They were able to generalize from the events in this play to some understanding of the problems of justice. Valid generalization is difficult for many people, but it is especially so for these students. This retrying of the case and acting out of the problem of Billy Budd in a contemporary setting helped some of the students to see how one generalizes from a few specific cases. Certainly an added bonus in this treatment of *Billy Budd* was the chance to relate previous discussions, on German Concentration Camps as described in John Hersey's *Here to Stay,* and the problems of scapegoating and obeying law or tradition in Shirley Jackson's *The Lottery.* Several different experiences with literature came alive as direct experience as we worked with *Billy Budd.* (Lacey, M16)

Although an increasing number of films illustrate the dilemma of the minority-group individual, these may not be available for school use or may distort more than they assist. The UNESCO listing of documentaries (de Heusch, R25) from many parts of the world suggests an unused source for authentic materials, though again the problem of procurement is a major barrier. Educational use of such a film as *Twelve Angry Men* (R113a) can demonstrate the power of influence, as well as the power of prejudice. The film made from the TV program, *The Eye of the Beholder* (R31a), is also a valuable educational device to illustrate the perceptual distortions that we unconsciously practice. A recent publication of the National Council of Teachers of English, *The Motion Picture and the Teaching of English* (Sheridan, R96), is of value in showing how teachers may utilize this medium creatively. Hoban (R45) provides an excellent overview of what is now known about how movies "teach" and gives some guidelines for the educator.

Other media, such as recordings of plays or music, are also avenues for affective education. The scripts of *The Ways of Mankind* (Goldschmidt, N68), available on records, are a valuable introduction not only to the field of anthropology but to the "feel" of social data. Folkways Records, Inc. (S7) has specialized in authentic music of cultures here and abroad, and in contemporary and historical material as well. The recording of *In White America* (Duberman, N56) can be effectively used with or without the reading of the script itself. Often the spoken word comes through more clearly than that which is read. Teachers of primary grades know the value of reading aloud; this technique should also be utilized by teachers at other grade levels. The major pitfall is that training and practice are required for effective oral reading. A teacher might be well advised to tape a reading, then play it back to hear herself, before inflicting a reading upon children or youth. The short anecdotal stories in the book by Sproel (L157) are designed for reading aloud, followed by group discussion.

Just as a documentary film has a special kind of impact, so does authentic history have an effect unlike paraphrased history. The original oral history, *Lay My Burden Down* (Botkin, C8), can be extremely valuable because of the genuineness of the source material, as can the several-volume anthology edited by Meltzer, *In Their Own Words* (D19).

History provides ample source material. An English publisher has put together in a packet called a "Jackdaw," *The Slave Trade and Its Abolition,*[35] a set of original documents and related data about the slave trade in the eighteenth century. The material is particularly impressive because it comes directly to the student from out of the past: for example, there is a slave auction poster and a drawing to show a shipbuilder how he can "store" the slave cargo. Distributors of historical posters of American origin are similarly valuable (*Posters of the Past,* Q17). However, much of history is beyond the intellectual grasp of young people unless it is carefully selected and in some cases translated into contemporary English (Cieciorka, D7; Cuban, D8; Archibald, D3; Hughes and

[35] John L. Davies, *The Slave Trade and Its Abolition,* Jackdaw Kit #JD6 (Inglewood, Calif.: Social Studies School Service, n.d.).

Meltzer, D16). The problems to be encountered in utilizing such source material have been discussed in connection with the developments of the junior high school program of Educational Services Incorporated (Patterson, M21). The dangers of unexamined history, based wholly on textbooks or secondary sources, are everywhere apparent (Billington, P9) and in no instance have been quite so damaging as in the mythology surrounding the story of the American Negro (Herskovits, C27). In attempting to undo past damage and produce more authentic history, there may be a tendency to err in the opposite direction.

It would be valuable for the teacher to turn to accepted sources of authentic reporting, such as the issues of *Hi Neighbor* (U11), describing the member nations of the United Nations, for contemporary material. Journals such as the *UNESCO Courier* (U31) or *Atlas* (U3), the world press in translation, are valuable for comparative studies. Often the foreign bias will be as apparent as that of the United States; this is a useful perspective for young people to gain.

Intergroup education is not the exclusive domain of history or literature. Stendler and Martin (K35, p. 116) provide an interesting commentary in relation to arithmetic:

> When the children studied Roman numerals, she saw to it that both the numerals and the people who originated and used them were appreciated. We think this is a particularly significant example because arithmetic does not seem to be an area of the curriculum in which we could accomplish much in intergroup education. Yet this third-grade teacher succeeded in identifying for her children the part that each of the many groups of people played in the development of our number system.

SUMMARY

Intergroup education can permeate every sector of the educational scene. Indeed, through the interactions of children with other children, through the education of children via nonschool influences, intergroup education is taking place all the time for all of us. The educational task is to recognize contemporary needs and to develop deliberate programs of education and re-education about the many groups that make up America, its history, and the world in which we live.

APPENDICES

APPENDIX A

The first two stories that follow were written for junior or senior high school students as discussion openers or for classroom role-playing.

The author has found one very successful way to use the first story, "Junior Prom," as a starter for role-playing. First, the teacher selects four people to play the roles. She seats them as they would be in the scene: the "teacher" behind a table, and the three "students" facing her. The role-players are given their names and instructed to take their seats in front of the class. They are told that they will hear themselves described in the story, which will present a typical high school problem, and then they will continue the discussion on their own as the characters in the story. The teacher then proceeds to read aloud to all the class the story, "Junior Prom." When each character is first mentioned, it is helpful to point to the person already designated to play that role, so that both the individual role-player and the other members of the class have it clearly in mind who is who. When the story ends, the teacher merely motions to the group and leaves the question hanging in the air. The role-players then take over.

This story has been very interesting when used with prospective student teachers. It has served to make more realistic the kinds of teaching situations they may encounter, and also brings out their own awareness of ethnic or racial stereotyping.

The second story, "The People's Choice," might be used only for starting class discussion. Or the teacher could select a student to play the role of Bud. Again, he would be asked to stand in front of the class—or sit in a chair for more ease—and when the story ends he can proceed to do a "monolog." He can proceed with the arguments as presented in the story, can evaluate them in light of his own school experience, or can finally turn to the class for help. The teacher, if she wants, can intervene by going into the role-play herself. For instance, if Bud sits there immobilized, the teacher can enter, obviously as someone else's teacher, and ask Bud, "My, you certainly look serious. What's on your mind?" Then the teacher can assist Bud in articulating the thoughts about the problems posed by the story.

JUNIOR PROM*

By Jean D. Grambs

Mrs. Richardson looked at the three serious faces watching her from across her desk. There was Tiny Johnson, president of the junior class—a good, hard-working president, not the brightest thing in the world, but honest and likable. Next to him was Janet Scanlon, secretary of the junior class, blonde, fluffy, but sharp as a whip. Maybe a little too sure of herself, and perhaps rightly so, with a father who was an Eminent Man, president of the State College, no less. Next to her was Eloise Ladas, chairman of the Junior Prom committee. Her dark eyes and smooth olive complexion showed her Greek inheritance. Her father, Pete Ladas, was a history teacher in the high school who made a particular point of dwelling on the glories of ancient Greek history both in class and out.

"It isn't that I want to interfere with your plans," Mrs. Richardson started to say. "Well, perhaps that is exactly what I do want to

* Written under the auspices of The Lincoln Filene Center for Citizenship and Public Affairs, Tufts University, 1966. Reprinted by permission of the author.

do . . ." and she smiled at the rather grim 17-year-olds facing her. They did not smile back. None of them seemed on the verge of saying anything.

A little urgently, Mrs. Richardson continued: "Now the Junior Prom isn't just a dance for our own school. It is something everyone in town hears about. It is one of our biggest occasions in the spring. Of course we all want it to be a big success. And I know you have already worked a long time on your plans and getting committees started on decorations and all that." She looked hopefully at Eloise; maybe she would say something, but her dark eyes just looked at Mrs. Richardson without a flicker of warmth.

"It wasn't just my idea to ask you to reconsider your plans," Mrs. Richardson went on, beginning to feel that the task ahead was going to be a harder one than she had thought. "Of course, as sponsor for the junior class, I am in a way responsible for what you do. I didn't think I had to oversee your work, because I know all three of you very well. I know that you are conscientious and responsible." A little flattery might, just might, bring a responsive smile from the three students. But they still didn't respond.

"Mr. Perkins, who is as fine a principal as any in this district, was the one who first mentioned the problem to me this morning, you know, when your posters advertising the dance were put up. He felt that we should talk about it and see what is to be done." Mrs. Richardson stopped. She leaned back in her chair. It was time for one of the students to say *something*. She wasn't going to do all the talking.

Tiny Johnson straightened his six-foot-three length and glanced at the two girls. He was pretty sure they were waiting for him to speak first.

"I don't get it, Mrs. Richardson," Tiny said. "Here we go, making our plans, we have everything fixed up for the best Junior Prom this place has seen, and then someone starts talking about 'prejudice' and 'stereotypes' and 'hurting people's feelings.' Honestly, Mrs. Richardson, they just miss the point."

"They sure do," said Eloise, a little breathlessly. "I guess I know a bit about prejudice and stereotypes, because we are Greeks, and you should hear some of the things people say sometimes. But just because we pick a fiesta theme for our dance and have some Mexicans with sombreros over their faces sleeping under a cactus for our poster, then we get put on the carpet and accused of all kinds of things."

"We thought it was a real cute idea," Janet spoke up. "With a Mexican fiesta theme, we can have real gay decorations and play a lot of rhumba music and that sort of thing. It's something different. We even thought we might have enchiladas and tamales for sale at the refreshment stand, if we can get some of the Mexicans to cook it for us." She looked triumphantly at the other two, and they nodded in agreement; these had been their ideas, and they liked them very much.

"That's exactly the point," Mrs. Richardson said. "The Mexican students—and they really aren't any more Mexican than Eloise is Greek; you are all Americans, you know—object to having posters with Mexicans depicted as lazy and always sleeping in peasant clothes under a cactus. It isn't any more true of modern Mexico than it is of the Americans of Mexican descent who live here in town."

"But heck, Mrs. Richardson," said Tiny, "there aren't more than ten or a dozen Mexican kids in our school; most of them go to the San Angelo High School. I don't see why they should care. No one's making fun of them. It's just a good idea for a dance is all."

"And *all* the posters are made, and all the programs are ordered and due from the printers today—why, we have already spent all the money we have for the dance. We couldn't possibly work up another theme!" Janet's voice rose shrilly as she made her devastating points.

"Why do they have to be so sensitive, anyway? Are we going to let a few kids spoil the fun for all the rest of us—why, we expect about two hundred at our dance if it is a good one, and this one *was* going to be a good one." Tiny glared at Mrs. Richardson as he began to realize the full import of what she was saying.

"But, Mrs. Richardson," Janet implored, "isn't there anything we can *do?*"

And that, thought Mrs. Richardson to herself, is exactly what she wanted to know, too.

THE PEOPLE'S CHOICE*

By Jean D. Grambs

"Hey, Bud, who you going to vote for?"

"What do you mean, who am I going to vote for?"

"Just what I said, man, who are you going to vote for?"

Bud hadn't wanted to stop and talk with Jerry. He knew that Jerry, with his loud insistent voice and his loud insistent opinions, would soon have him pushed in a corner, at least verbally. And Bud had not made up his mind whom to vote for in the coming student body election at Barksdale Senior High School.

"Aw, come on, Bud, don't be in such a rush. All you got to go to is another dreary class, and it's still ten minutes before the warning bell." Jerry had caught up with Bud now and his voice was loud in Bud's ear. Wearily, Bud slowed his pace and they both walked across the parking lot towards the school building.

"Quite an election campaign," Bud said, hoping he could bring up a slightly different topic and keep Jerry off his own decision on the candidates. But Jerry was never one to be deterred from his objective, and his objective at this point was to get Bud to commit himself to a candidate.

"After all, Bud," Jerry roared in his ear, "as star basketball player for our team and one of the top men on the principal's honor roll people are going to want to know who you are going to vote for. You know all the people running pretty well, I guess."

Yes, Bud thought to himself, I do know all of them pretty well—maybe too well. Maybe that is why I don't know whom to vote for myself. "Well, Jerry," Bud said slowly, "I really haven't made up my mind."

"You haven't made up your mind!" Jerry literally screamed. "Why the election's tomorrow practically!! Look, man, what's eating you? Don't you think any of them are any good?"

"Now let me tell you this," Jerry went on before Bud could answer, even if he had wanted to, "I found out just yesterday what was really wrong with that guy Bill Cohen they are pushing for

* Written under the auspices of The Lincoln Filene Center for Citizenship and Public Affairs, Tufts University. Reprinted by permission of the author.

president. He's Jewish, for one thing, but I never let things like that bother me—I'm not prejudiced for or against anyone—but they tell me he's promised to make Sally Blickstein, she's Jewish too, chairman of the Senior Prom committee, and put all his other friends in top positions. And I think that's going a little too far."

Bud looked at Jerry with distaste. "Well, I haven't heard that and I don't know who is spreading the story. So what if Bill Cohen puts his friends on the good committees—it's just what you and I would do, isn't it?"

"Yeah, but who wants the school run by a bunch of Jews," Jerry whined. "Mind you, I haven't anything against one or two of them, but you just let one of them in, and by golly they take over everything. Pretty soon they'll be calling this the kike school, and then what would you think of it?"

The bell rang, and Bud and Jerry increased their pace as they joined streams of other students headed for the nearest open door.

"Well, remember what I told you," Jerry called as he turned away from Bud and down the corridor, disappearing into an open door.

Bud went on, troubled by what Jerry had said as much as by what he hadn't said. Maybe Bill Cohen wouldn't be such a good choice. But then, would George O'Brien be any better? As though reading his mind, George himself materialized beside him.

"Going my way, Bud?" George asked with a genial, politician's smile. Bud couldn't help smiling in spite of himself.

"George, you already sound like a Congressman," Bud said.

"Now don't besmirch the fair name of our fine leaders, sweating away in the jungles of Washington," George grinned happily. "Not that I am campaigning, old boy, but I just wanted you to remember me when the old election box is in front of you," said George, as he moved on down the hall.

"Now, there's someone I like," a light familiar voice spoke up at Bud's elbow.

"Hey, Louise, quit sneaking up on a guy like that." Bud turned, smiling at Louise Henry, who was one of the Big Wheels at Barksdale High. "Now what would you see to like in O'Brien—a politician if I ever saw one. I thought you liked the egghead type, like Bill Cohen!"

Louise ignored the bait. "I like George, oh, well, because for one thing he is a real smooth dancer. And besides, his father is Vice-President at the Barksdale State Bank. But really, I think he represents the better element in town. He is a Catholic, and maybe some people would hold that against him. I don't. I think this school has been run too long by kids who don't come from very cultured homes. And George's father—why he just bought a new electric organ, I saw it myself." Louise was getting more enthusiastic about her favorite candidate every minute, and Bud found it amusing.

"And I suppose the Delta Chi's are for him, and all the rest of the bunch," Bud said, with just the slightest edge of sarcasm in his voice.

"Why of course," said Louise, her blue eyes open and innocent. "All the clubs are for him."

So, Bud thought to himself, I shouldn't vote for Bill Cohen because he is Jewish and might put all his friends on committees, and I should vote for George O'Brien because his father has lots of money, bought an electric organ, and the snooty clubs are for him. Are these the reasons for voting for a student body president?

"Frankly, Louise, I'm confused," Bud said. He moved into the classroom and opened his book. The door closed and the school day began.

He couldn't keep his mind off Louise's remarks about George O'Brien. Sure, he knew George's family were pretty rich. They lived in a large house with beautiful trees and flowers and a lawn so smooth and green you could tell there was a gardener somewhere in the shrubbery.

Bud's father drove a truck. He was a driver for the Dy-Dee Wash, a baby diaper service. The truck was a *lovely* pale blue with a fat rosy pink infant on top, with a jaunty golden crown. "Babies are Kings in Our Business" was the slogan that ran around the truck on a baby-pink streamer. Bud had never told his friends what company his father worked for, and he was glad that Grove City was large enough so no one had found out—yet. His father wore a natty pale blue uniform, too, with "Dy-Dee Wash" in pink on the back. At least, he didn't have to park the repulsive truck at the house, or wear his monkey suit home.

What a distance between Bud's father and George O'Brien's. "They like me just because I am good at basketball," Bud told himself angrily. He had never accepted a pledge to join any of the secret clubs because he would have to tell about his father's job. Louise's remarks made him realize more than ever that he didn't really belong with The Crowd.

The third candidate for student body president was just getting up to recite. Sue Halliday was a serious, smart, ambitious girl, and pretty, too. Bud listened to her give her usual excellent recitation. "Now why should she want to be student body president?" Bud asked himself. No girl had ever been elected president; in fact, it seemed unlikely that any had ever run for the office before. She hadn't a chance, Bud told himself, and he was rather sorry that she would be hurt by the defeat. But who was going to vote for a girl for president, anyway?

Though he should have been following the class lesson, Bud's mind, like a stuck phonograph needle, kept going round and round the problem of the three candidates for president. What exactly did he know about them, anyway? Bill Cohen had been editor of the paper, and had put out the best paper the high school had ever had; everyone knew him as an energetic, talkative, friendly, and determined fellow. "The junior executive type," Bud labeled him in his own mind. Certainly someone who would be a good president, unless . . .

Then George O'Brien. Well, Bud wasn't so sure about Catholics. Hadn't he heard some things about how they put religion before loyalty and stuff like that? Though it probably wouldn't make much difference in such small time as a student body job. And George sure could get anything out of the faculty; he had been chairman of the Spring Carnival, and had not only raised lots of money, but had gotten everyone on the faculty and many parents to work with the students in building booths and getting things to sell. Yes, a born politician, an organizer, one who already had a way with him, maybe too much of a way . . .

What about Sue? Bud knew her, too, from being in a number of classes with her. They were both top students scholastically. Sue could always be counted on as chairman of a committee to see that the work was done, and done well. Perhaps she wasn't as popular as, say, Louise, but she could certainly hold her own on the student council, where she had served for three terms. She knew student government, that was sure, and if anyone could see that things ran smoothly, she probably could. She spoke well, too, which was not one of the talents of either Bill or George, and could represent the school at public dinners and that sort of thing. But a girl presiding, well . . .

At lunch, Bud's best friend, Snicker Williams, met him as usual at the back table in the cafeteria. "So, who are you going to vote for?" Snicker asked, stuffing half a sandwich into his mouth.

"Gosh," Bud said, "everyone's been pestering me about that today. Doesn't a guy have a right to any privacy? I thought a person's vote was his own business in a democracy."

"Yeah, sure, but who says this is a democracy. This is *school,* man, and besides, no one is trying to take away your precious privacy. I just asked a civil question and you bite my head off. OK, what have we got? There's Bill Cohen, and all the Jews are for him; there's George O'Brien, and all the sorority and fraternity crowd are for him—he just smells of money; and then there's Sweet Sue, and who wants a woman?"

And that, thought Bud, was exactly his dilemma. Who *would* he vote for?

The following three short open-ended stories are examples of the material developed by the Shaftels for use with classroom groups of children and young people. The techniques for using the stories are developed in the book by the Shaftels (J22), which also includes a number of other short examples as well as some much longer stories.

BUT NAMES WILL NEVER HURT ME?*

Lorna had just left the apartment and was walking into the playground behind the housing project when she saw her sister, Ellie. *Heard* her, too. Ellie was crying. Loudly.

Lorna hurried toward her and brushed Ellie's matted blond hair out of her eyes and put her arm about Ellie's shoulders.

"What happened?" Lorna demanded. "Why're you crying?"

* Fannie R. Shaftel and George Shaftel, *Role-Playing for Social Values: Decision-Making in the Social Studies,* © 1967. Reprinted by Prentice-Hall, Inc., Englewood Cliffs, New Jersey.

Ellie was a third grader, eight years old. Lorna, who was eleven and big for her age, was a sixth grader.

"They slapped me!" Ellie wailed. "They t-tore my dress!"

"Who did? Show me!"

Ellie turned, and led Lorna toward a group of three small colored girls playing hopscotch in a corner of the playground. They looked up, and grew silent, their eyes big, as they saw Ellie approaching with her angry big sister.

"They did it!" Ellie shrilled. "They hit me and kicked me and tore my dress!"

They stood stiff and silent as Lorna's outraged glance swept their faces.

"Three of you," she said scornfully, "ganging up on one kid! I ought to slap your faces. Maybe I will."

"She called us names," one child said.

"Yeah," another said. "She called me a monkey. A black monkey."

Lorna caught a sharp breath. She looked at Ellie.

"Did you?"

Ellie nodded, her eyes filling with tears.

"B-but they were doing it too! I just said what they were saying. Lucille called Betty a—what they said."

Lorna looked at the three girls.

"Is that true?"

They nodded.

Lucille burst out, "But *she* can't call us that!"

Lorna turned.

"Come on, Ellie."

Ellie stood stubbornly in her tracks, her small face ugly with anger.

"Ain't you going to hit them back?" she demanded. "Go on—hit them!"

EENY-MEENY-MINEY-MO*

Martha asked, "You kids ever play Duck-on-a-Rock?"

"No."

* Fannie R. Shaftel and George Shaftel, *Role-Playing for Social Values: Decision-Making in the Social Studies,* © 1967. Reprinted by Prentice-Hall, Inc., Englewood Cliffs, New Jersey.

"What's that?"

"Let's play, let's play!"

"Hold on. You can't play a game until you know what it is. Listen."

The faces of the third graders were respectful and eager. Martha, a big seventh grader, felt very grown-up and important. This was a new kind of arrangement being tried by the city schools—using some responsible seventh graders to help with primary-grade children. The six- and seven-year-olds were delighted to have big eleven- and twelve-year-olds thinking up games for them, playing with them, helping with their lessons.

Martha explained. "You take four of these wooden blocks and pile them up straight, like this," she said, building a straight column. She did not explain that when boys played Duck-on-a-Rock on a vacant lot or in a back alley, they did not use wooden blocks but half-bricks. "Then, everybody stands back here, back of a line, and takes turns throwing a block at the pile. When the pile is hit and knocked down, everybody runs and hides—except the kid who is It. He has to run to the blocks and stack them up straight again—and count to thirty. [Then] he starts hunting the others. Everybody who can run past him and touch the pile without his tagging them is free. But if he tags someone, that person is It for the next game."

"That'll be fun!"

"Who's It?"

"John's It!"

"No, Lena's It!"

"No," Martha said. "We'll draw lots."

"Too many," Lucy said. "I know! Everybody stand in a circle. We'll find out who's It." And as the kids grouped around her, she started chanting, "Eeny, meeny, miney, mo—" and as she spoke each word, she pointed to a different child, moving around the circle, "Catch a nigger by the toe—If he hollers, let him *go!*—You're It, Sammy!"

But then something happened.

Toby Jones smacked Lucy's face.

For a startled moment, the group stood frozen in shock. Then Lucy burst out crying, and a chorus of angry words exploded from the rest.

"You crazy? Why'd you do that?"

"Why'd he hit her?"

"You can't play with us!"

"Martha, don't let him play with us!"

Toby had turned away from the group. He was leaving, his dark face set and defiant.

"Wait, Toby!" Martha called.

"Oh, let him go, Martha!"

"But why did he slap her?"

"We don't want him around."

"Wait," Martha called. "Toby, don't go!"

"What got into him?"

"Hitting a girl!"

Dora, the other Negro child in the group, had run after Toby and put her arm around his shoulder and was going off with him.

"Why did he hit me?" Lucy was wailing.

Martha said, "Wait here," to the group, and started to go after Toby and Dora.

The other children said, "Oh, let him go!"

"We don't care—we can play without him."

Martha said:

SEED OF DISTRUST*

Betty was all excited when she ran into the apartment.

"Mother, will you iron my green dress tonight?"

"I was planning to do it Saturday night, honey, so you'd have it for Sunday School."

"But I'll need it!"

"What's the rush?"

"Nora's invited me to a party tomorrow after school."

"Oh, I see," her mother said slowly, as if thinking hard. "Nora's the little girl on the second floor?"

"Yes. She's real nice."

Betty's sister Lucy, who was a sophomore in high school, asked, "Does her mother know?"

* Fannie R. Shaftel and George Shaftel, *Role-Playing for Social Values: Decision-Making in the Social Studies*, © 1967. Reprinted by Prentice-Hall, Inc., Englewood Cliffs, New Jersey.

"Know what?" Betty asked.

"Nora's white, isn't she?"

"Sure!"

"Does her mother know she's invited you?"

"Of course! I m-mean, I guess so."

"Does her mother know you're Negro?" [Or Mexican, or Puerto Rican, etc.]

"Sure!"

"You mean—you *think* so?"

"Y-yes," Betty stammered.

"Better make sure," Lucy said, and turned back to the math she was studying.

"I'll iron your dress, honey," Betty's mother said reassuringly. "You'll look real nice."

"Uh-huh," Betty said dully. "Thanks, Mom."

And then, next day, after lunch, the thing happened—

Nora met Betty in the hall, outside the fifth-grade room.

"Betty, I've been hunting for you," Nora said urgently. "Listen. My Aunt Dorothy phoned last night. She's arriving today for a visit. My grandma's coming over to see her, and mother's making a dinner for the whole family, cousins and all. You see? We've got to postpone my party. Until next week, maybe. I'll let you know!"

Betty looked at her, blank-faced.

"Don't bother," Betty said. "Don't bother at all." And Betty turned and walked away, her back very straight.

For an instant Nora just stood and stared. Then she ran. She caught Betty's arm and stopped her.

"Betty, what's the matter? Why're you talking like that?"

APPENDIX B

OPEN-ENDED SCRIPTS

The following two scripts were prepared for use as discussion starters or for role-playing. The first script was sponsored by the Southern Region YWCA, as one of a series of such scripts on problems facing young women today. They were to be used as the clubs might decide as the basis for club programs. "The Case of the Possible Member" was based on a tape recording of a role-playing session with a group of Y-Teen girls in Norfolk, Virginia, in 1959. While sentiments may have changed in some parts of the country, the views expressed by these girls are, in many instances, still quite prevalent. At least, using the script might tell the group leader or teacher whether the group he or she is working with does or does not hold to these or similar opinions! How far have we come since 1959?

The technique for developing the script may interest some teachers: A situation was developed with the participating girls. The characters to be played were outlined on the board—the president, secretary, etc. Their attitudes and positions regarding the situation of a possible Negro member of their club were discussed and decided upon. Then the girls went through the role-play. In this instance, the discussion got so heated that it went far beyond the time allotted for the role-playing. However, in preparing the other scripts in the series, about five or seven minutes were taped, then the scene was cut, the tape was played back to the girls, they criticized their own roles and how the problem had been stated, and then they went through it again. Usually only one replaying was done. Then the author undertook, on the basis of the tape transcriptions, to tighten up the interchange, using the girls' own words and phrases as much as possible, but pointing toward a dramatic and "open end." This procedure worked very well and is recommended to anyone who would like to try his hand a developing similar materials which are, indeed, highly effective with youth groups.

The second script, "Some of My Best Friends . . . ," is designed to show the problem of intergroup understanding in a family setting. The *design* of this role-playing script is particularly significant. Although there are only four role-players, everyone in the class is assigned to one of the four persons as his "back-up" man. When the role-playing "breaks," each role-player goes to "his" group for advice as to how to proceed next to break the impasse. He gets new arguments and ammunition from his colleagues, who are, in a sense, also then playing the role. This device is extremely effective in providing for total group involvement, and also in exploring new strategies which might not otherwise have been in the repertoire of the individual. This procedure might also be useful in completing the role-playing for the unfinished story "Junior Prom" in Appendix A.

It is urgently recommended that students do not memorize the scripts. The most effective way to use these scripts is to select the role-players immediately before they are to go through the script before the class. Give the role-players just enough time to read through the entire script and, if necessary, to mark their own lines so they come in without undue fumbling. But the time should be too short to permit them to begin to speculate about what they will do in the role-playing; thus one can obtain maximum spontaneity. In no sense are these "plays," and they should not be staged or considered as such. It has been found that even reading them completely "cold" will work with older students (such as student teachers). These particular scripts may not be effective with younger students.

It is possible to tape the scripts ahead of time and, using the technique suggested for "Junior Prom," have the "real" role players sit in appropriate positions in front of the class as they listen to the tape which gives them their roles and their characters, and then let them go on from there.

THE CASE OF THE POSSIBLE MEMBER*

By Jean D. Grambs

Cast

ALICE — President of the Southern City High School Y-Teen Club. Calm, tries to be fair; a good chairman. Has been in Y-Teens the longest.

LAURIE — Vice-President. Well liked, popular with the boys, does not have very set opinions of her own.

KATHY — Program Chairman. Efficient, good organizer. Knows exactly what she thinks and is not afraid to tell you. Spends a great deal of time on club.

ANN — Worship Chairman. Quiet type.

LINDA — Secretary-Treasurer. Gets top grades, works very hard for club.

* Written for the Southern Region YWCA, June, 1959. Reprinted by permission of the author.

Scene

It is after school. The five people above are meeting in a special session as the Executive Committee of their Y-Teen Club. Their club advisor, Mrs. Robinson, could not meet with them, unfortunately. However, she wants the girls to make their own decisions about the club and its activities and it is not unusual for her to give the Executive Committee full responsibility. Today they have a very urgent problem to discuss.

(Before the script is read, the Director, a student, will read the following to the rest of the club members, or say essentially the same thing.)

DIRECTOR: Today we are going to see how a club tries to reach a decision. I guess we know our own club pretty well; we know some of the problems we have been up against, some of the good things as well as not so good things about the way we try to run our club. Sometimes it is helpful to see how others like us act when faced with a problem to solve.

It is after school at Southern City High School. The Y-Teen (a YWCA-sponsored organization) Executive Committee is meeting. There is only one Y-Teen Club in this school. It is an active club. It has been going for a number of years. It has a membership of about 35, but about 15 girls regularly come to meetings—sounds familiar, doesn't it? So of course the club is always seeking strong members to help in the projects and parties that the club sponsors. Mrs. Robinson, a teacher in the school who is the club advisor, could not come to this special meeting but told the girls to go ahead without her as she was sure they could handle any problems that came up.

The members of our cast are:

Alice, the club president, played by ____________________
Laurie, club vice-president " " ____________________
Kathy, program chairman " " ____________________
Ann, worship chairman " " ____________________
Linda, secretary-treasurer " " ____________________

This is not like a regular play. The cast will read from a script. We are going to see the problem this club faces —but the solution to the problem—well, that is going to be up to us! Following the reading of the script, our discussion will be led by ____________ (*Introduce discussion leader, if you have planned for one*), who may want to say something to you now.

. . . . .

Our scene opens, then, on a familiar place—a high school classroom after school is out; quiet, waiting

. . . . .

(*Cast enters, takes chairs in a circle.*)

. . . . .

Just so you will remember, here again are the officers of the Y-Teen Club of Southern City High School: (*Repeat list of names and point out each girl in cast so audience can remember who each represents.*)

* * * * *

LINDA What's the special meeting for, Alice? You sure sounded mysterious about it.

LAURIE Yeah, what's it all about? Bill's waiting for me so let's make it quick, huh?

KATHY So it's Bill today, Laurie? I thought it was Steve or was that yesterday?

LAURIE O.K. O.K., you're just jealous.

ALICE Well, I'll tell you why I thought we ought to have a special meeting if you'll just shut up and quit talking about your boy friends.

ANN I've got to get home, Alice.

ALICE I guess you have heard that one of the new colored girls in school wants to join our club. I think we ought to have a little discussion on it before we decide.

KATHY I am definitely against it. I don't think she ought to be able to come in.

ANN Why?

KATHY Because there's been an awful lot of trouble this year because of the colored students coming to school and I for one think it is partly her fault for all the trouble.

LINDA That's true. They say they want to come just for the education but I don't think it's all the way true.

ALICE Yes, there is a lot of feeling about it and maybe in a year or two people won't feel this way. But since she's applied now . . .

ANN Has she really applied, Alice?

ALICE Well, I don't know. Mrs. Robinson did say that she had come up to her after class and asked her about our Y-Teen Club, as she knew Mrs. Robinson was the sponsor. She said she belonged to the Y-Teen Club at Dunbar High School.

LINDA Well, she can still belong to that; she doesn't have to come spoil our club, does she?

LAURIE But she can't still belong over at Dunbar. You belong to the club that is in your high school. And ours is the one here at school. So if she wants to join, this would be it.

ALICE That's right.

KATHY O.K., and you let one in this year, next year there will be 20 and pretty soon where's our club?

ANN It's bound to come. It's bound to happen sometime.

LINDA Well, it doesn't have to be while I'm a member of the club. Maybe in three or four years.

ALICE I wonder what our club advisor would say. Or the school principal? Maybe the Y-Teen Director down at Central could tell us what to do.

KATHY Look, we're old enough to decide a few things for ourselves. And who we let in our club is our business, isn't it? We're the officers!

LAURIE This girl seems pretty good—I mean she's got nice clothes and I imagine she's clean. She's a higher class one, but when they start letting just anyone come . . .

ALICE She's in my homeroom and one day when she wasn't in there my homeroom teacher gave a nice talk about her and I think it helped some of the boys who were against her. She said that Ruthann was here and whether some of us liked it or not, she was going to stay here and go to school and that the least we could do was to be friendly to her or to ignore her—either way we chose but not to make a public spectacle of her. And I think it's difficult for anyone. I know, I thought about it for a long time when I found out she was going to be in my homeroom and all. But I don't see why that so long as she is in our school why she can't be a member of our club if she's the right type of girl.

KATHY Well, that's just it, she isn't on the same social level and colored people just aren't up to us. I'm not saying we're so much better, but they just don't try, they're satisfied with being like they are.

LINDA Yeah, they are just satisfied to sit in their little houses and rot.

ANN But, they do try; that's the reason they want to come to our school because it does have things they don't have at Dunbar.

LINDA Then why don't they get them over at Dunbar; they don't have to push in here—and probably they got paid to try to come here anyway.

KATHY I know the colored maids, like ours, and all those people who have talked to their maids say the same things. They're not interested in going to our school. They want to stay where they are. There are Communists behind it anyway.

ALICE You've got to realize your maid is older, a different generation.

LINDA So what. I bet the kids don't want to come either. What kind of fun can they have anyway? I know the only people who talk to her are the Jewish people. She doesn't have any friends—and she won't either.

LAURIE Look, I'm not a Jew and she's in my geometry class and I talk to her and I just don't see anything wrong with just talking to her. I mean if she asks me something I'll answer her.

KATHY Well, all right but that doesn't mean you have to be bosom pals with her.

LAURIE Who said anything about being bosom pals with her?

LINDA Well, let's face it. If she joins the club that's what you'll have to do. After all it's a fellowship, a social group, and she'll be a member of this group.

KATHY If you have a pajama party you'll have to invite her to the pajama party and I can just see my father now! And if you have a dance she'll bring her friends to the dance.

ANN I guess we would have to give up dances.

KATHY And I'm program chairman and guess who'd be blamed if we didn't do some things that were fun. Beach parties. Dances.

LINDA I can just see the club when we can't even have Y-Teen dances! I for one wouldn't be interested.

LAURIE I can just see Bill's face if he came to a dance and they were there, or Steve or Dave or any of the fellows.

ALICE I thought they were all members of the Hi-Y?

KATHY What's that got to do with it?

ALICE Well, look, there's our club motto, right there on the wall. It says—well, just read what it says. Well, we have fun together but I don't think it's purely a social club like you have in some schools.

LINDA But we do have social things—we had a tea, and a pajama party and a dance and most of that would be cut out because of our parents—I could just see my father. Why I'd be put right out of the house if I went to a pajama party with one of them.

ANN Maybe she wouldn't want to come if she was the only one.

LINDA Then why did she come to our school when she's about the only one?

KATHY She was paid, that's why!

ALICE How do you know?

LAURIE I've heard that too. I'm not so sure I believe it.

ALICE Anyway, you're getting way off the subject.

ANN What are we going to do about this one girl? It seems to me that if we are a Christian club and like our purpose says . . .

KATHY Too many people bring religion into it. I mean, I can't see their point about why religion comes into it. And then they go back to the Constitution and other things like "all men are created equal." And you are—you all have five fingers on one hand and five fingers on the other hand and five toes on each foot. But you're white and they're black and that's different and I don't see where religion comes into it.

ALICE I saw a picture in a magazine just yesterday that showed a little Negro boy walking down the street with his arm around the shoulders of a white boy and it said down at the bottom of the picture, "They're still too young to know the hate that's in some men's hearts."

LAURIE You can say those things, Alice, because you just haven't been here long. You don't know what it is like here in the South.

KATHY I've lived in the North and the South, too. And it is different. I've gone to school with them since I was in the sixth grade. I've had them sit in front of me, in back of me, beside me and I've taken gym with them and I don't love them any more than the day I started.

LINDA I don't think that's quite fair, Alice, either. I don't hate them. Well, I do hate what they've done to our school and all. All this trouble and everyone getting upset, and all, just because they want to come to our schools. I just am sick and tired of it all. I wish they'd stay where they belong and try to make their own schools good, or something. I don't think they try one little bit. They want everything done for them!

ALICE How do you know they aren't trying? Have you talked to them? Have you talked to Ruthann?

LAURIE Come on, Bill's waiting for me. This discussion could go on forever.

ANN The trouble with you, Kathy, is that you just echo everything your parents say. Why can't you think for yourself on something like this?

KATHY That's not true at all. My parents have nothing to do

with it. Anyway, my mother and father don't agree on this integration thing.

LINDA I told my father one day that I didn't like colored people and he nearly knocked me off my feet. It's not my parents that have influenced me. It's my own beliefs and the things I have seen and that's the way I feel.

LAURIE Me, too. But I'm not quite sure what I think. Sometimes I think one way and sometimes another. I mean as a Christian you're supposed to like all kinds of people. And if I saw a colored person who really needed help I could help them and feel it in my heart to help them. But when I see them lying around the street and living in filthy shacks and then driving big flashy cars, it just doesn't make me want to help them.

ALICE And I suppose you don't think there aren't a lot of white people who do the same things. Have you ever seen a white slum?

LAURIE Well, I haven't really. And I'd want to help a white person who really needed it, too, I suppose . . .

LINDA Well, people who can't get up and help themselves—I don't feel sorry for them one little bit.

ALICE Then why complain when they do show some initiative like wanting a better education, coming to our school!

LINDA That's not the same thing at all!

ANN Oh, it isn't?

LAURIE It is hard to think straight about this sort of thing.

KATHY Well, I know how I feel!

ANN I really don't know, Alice. I really don't know.

ALICE Are we ready to have a vote on it?

LAURIE Hey, wait a minute . . . !

* * * * *

(ad lib *from here*)

SOME OF MY BEST FRIENDS . . .

By Jean D. Grambs

How to produce this role-play:

What follows is a script of a family argument. The argument focuses on a problem which is familiar to many American families. The problem in this argument is not solved in the script. Its solution is left either to those reading the script, to the audience, or to both.

The following suggestions are made for using the script:

1. Assign parts to four members of the class, and arrange the classroom as described under "Setting."
2. To involve the rest of the class, divide it into four listening groups—one for each of the characters. The members of each group are to listen to the argument as though they were the characters themselves.
3. If possible, tape the *ad lib* (final) argument of the family, so that the class can refer to it during its discussion of the issues raised in the role-play.
4. When the script ends, each of the listening groups should meet with their cast member and advise him on what strategy to take next.
5. After consultation, resume the role-play to see if the family can work out a solution to the problem. To allow more students to participate, other members of the class may be asked at this time to take parts in the play.
6. The role-play ends either when the family agrees on a solution or when the members acknowledge they cannot solve the problem.
7. After the role-play, the class must consider the argument and decide:
   a. What issues were raised in the argument?
   b. Why is it difficult to solve such family problems?

Setting: Although no sets or props are needed, chairs and tables are to be arranged so that we can imagine that we are seeing a cross-section of a house; the living room is on the left, the dining room is in the middle, and the kitchen is on the right. To signify the living room, two chairs are placed on the side; the kitchen also has two chairs. The dining room has a table with four chairs around it. The arrangement will look something like this:

Living Room *Dining Room* *Kitchen*

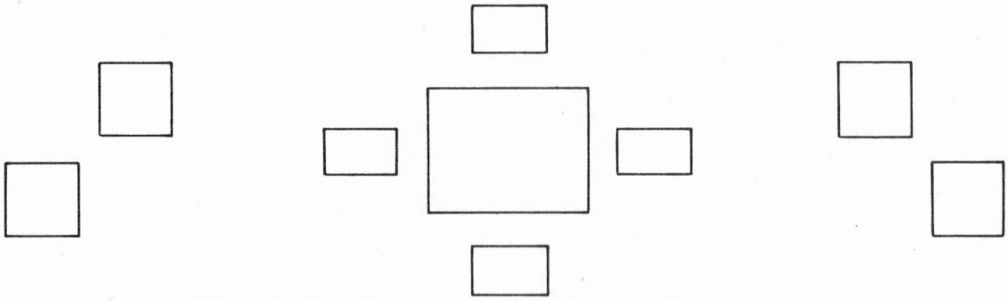

Characters: JUNIOR (age 16)
SISTER (a year or so younger than Junior)
MOTHER
FATHER

(At the opening, Junior and Sister are in the living room, Mother and Father in the kitchen. Each side will talk alternately for a few minutes; as in a real house, they cannot hear what the other group is saying.)

JR: You know, I just can't understand adults.

SIS: You mean parents! Now what has gone wrong?

JR: Well, wouldn't you say we had had a good Christian upbringing?

SIS: Yeah, what's that got to do with what?

JR: Well, here we go to Sunday School half the days of our lives, and we belong to Boy Scouts—I mean I do—and all sorts of stuff, and they really drill it into you.

SIS: Drill what into you? That perhaps you ought to have better manners and not be such a slouch?

JR: Aw, come off it. This is serious. I've got a problem.

SIS: Ok, ok. I've had the Sunday School bit myself, you know, and I've even been President of the Youth Group. So what?

JR: Well, I thought they meant it, I mean, I thought it was all for real.
(They freeze: switch to parents.)

DAD: I can't understand what's gotten into the boy.

MOM: What's Junior gone and done now?

DAD: We've given him the best of everything; set a good example. We have seen they got to Sunday School—why, I can hardly remember what it's like to sleep in on a Sunday morning, what with getting the kids up and cleaned and off to church . . .

MOM: Except when you went to play golf and I got them off to church.

DAD: (*glares*) So what. The point is, we've been good parents. We've given the kids a chance, a sense of values. Then what does he want to do!

MOM: I don't know, for heaven's sake; I never find out what he's up to till it's all over!

DAD: Yeah, that's the truth of it. Well, that group he goes with, sort of a fraternity I guess it is, has gone and pledged a Negro!

MOM: So?

DAD: So! You don't think anything of it! Well, for one thing, Junior's behind it. It was his idea in the first place!

MOM: And now?

DAD: Are you just forgetting one little thing, Mother, that we are host and hostess for the annual spring dance that the group gives, and it will be at *our* house, and that black boy will be coming, with a black date no doubt! In *our* house!

MOM: Oh!

DAD: Yeah, Oh is right!

(*Freeze: back to Sis and Jr.*)

SIS: Well, what's the big thing now?

JR: Jack, you know, Jack Thompson, the vice-president of our class, and a real nice kid. . . .

SIS: Oh, that nice-looking Negro boy.

JR: Yeah, he's Negro all right. Well, we pledged him to our club—you know, the one that anyone who is a "wheel" belongs to, and it means you can make the top fraternity at State, or almost any other university that has a chapter—well, we pledged him.

SIS: Is he the first one?

JR: You know, I guess he is. I hadn't thought of it. I like the guy. He's, well, just like the rest of us—any of us. So I sponsored him. The other fellows took my word for it, and he's in.

SIS: Oh—now it all comes clear—the big dance, and at our house—and Dad!

JR: (*gloomily*) That's it. Dad hit the roof. You should have heard what he said. And I thought he'd be on the *right* side.

SIS: Mom's calling us to dinner. No doubt we will hear more of it very, very, soon.

(*All four gather around table in the middle. Pantomime eating. Artificial silence.*)

JR: Ok, Dad, let's have it. I know what you're thinking.

DAD: Oh, so now you know what I'm thinking? I guess pretty soon you'll think you have a right to tell me what to think? ? ?

MOM: For heaven's sake, Father, don't get upset.

DAD: Who's upset? (*getting upset*) I just wish this young fellow here had some plain decent common sense, is all.

SIS: What did Junior do now, Father?

DAD: (*glaring*) As though you don't know about it already. Probably put him up to it too. You've been seeing too much of that Goldstein girl, if you ask me.

SIS: What's Sylvia got to do with it? Can't I have my own friends, for gosh sake.

MOM: Dad means, dear, that he thinks you should choose among your nice *Christian* friends, because girls like Sylvia Goldstein—and I'm not saying she isn't nice, and she has a very nice home, and her mother seems very nice though I do think she dyes her hair—

JR: Look who's talking!

MOM: (*glares at him*) But she does have sort of advanced ideas, just like most Jewish people.

SIS: Mom, you really are the limit!

DAD: Now don't you talk to your mother that way. She's just looking out after your best interests. You keep going around with a Goldstein and pretty soon that's the only kind that will ask you out for a date, and then what, young lady?

JR: Well, I want to know what's wrong with that.

DAD: I'll tell you what's wrong with it, and I'll tell you why you aren't having that colored boy and his date at the dance at our house, either, next week, or there will be no dance!

JR: Oh, so that is the way you'll keep your prejudices, eh Dad?

DAD: That's getting pretty close to being insulting, son, and I'm not taking insults off of my own children. Now you just listen to me. I'm not any more prejudiced than the next fellow—we're all prejudiced. . . .

SIS: Yeah, I don't like dumb jerks.

DAD: What's that? (*ignores her*) Why, some of my best friends are colored, and even some of the Jewish fellows at the office I play golf with—it's just that the world isn't made that way.

JR: So how is the world made? I was told at church . . .

MOM: (*sweetly*) And in church of course we don't mix; we go to our church and they go to theirs.

SIS: There are several colored families in our church, Mom, remember?

MOM: I meant the Jewish people.

DAD: What I want to say—if you will just *listen,* is that your future depends on your friends. We live in this neighborhood so you can meet the right people; people who will help you later in life. We go to the best church. When it's time to go to college, you will pledge the top fraternity because of your club you're in now. And let me tell you, young man, that fraternity doesn't take in anything but good Christian white boys. And it's these boys and these connections that are going to *count.*

JR: Aw, Dad, sure, I know it helps to have friends in the right places.

DAD: It sure does help. Why, if it hadn't been for my old fraternity brother who tipped me off to the opening at the office, why I'd be another pencil-pusher down the line, instead of top-dog in my division. It's the people you meet in school who count. And I don't want any son or daughter of mine to get known as those radicals, or people who run around with the wrong bunch.

SIS: (*getting bored*) Nice lecture, Dad, but that's old-fashioned stuff. No one goes for that nowadays.

DAD: (*getting purple*) Listen young lady, you keep your notions to yourself, just you come down to my office any day and you'll find out how the people who make the decisions think—and it is just what I said! (*pause*) And finally, I mean it, there will be *no dance at this house* if that colored boy comes. I've already talked to your sponsor, Mr. Jones, who just happens to think it was a mistake all along to let the boy get in, and he agrees with me.

JR: (*shocked*) Mr. Jones!

DAD: Yeah, your precious Mr. Jones. Sort of dumb, I'd say, letting you pledge a colored boy. He should have known how the rest of the parents would feel. He told me he'd just pass the word quietly to the boy—whatever his name is—and he'll understand. He wouldn't want to come where he wasn't wanted.

JR: Well, if that's how you feel, if you're going to go behind my back—let me tell you—I'm resigning from the club, I'll never join that old fraternity, I'll, I'll—why I think I'll go to Mississippi and register voters, so there. . . .
(*Stamps out of room. Sis follows.*)

MOM: Oh dear me. Do you think he means it?

DAD: He knows what I think and I'm not about to change my mind!

* * * * *

Each member of the cast meets with his listening group. Each group is to give the cast member advice on what to do next, presumably when the family meets for dinner again the next day. After a brief discussion in each group, the cast reassembles around the dinner table and the discussion continues, *ad lib,* until the family agrees on a solution or admits it cannot solve the problem.

Part III

BIBLIOGRAPHY

The bibliography that follows has been compiled with the patient help of many people. In most instances the annotations are based on a personal review of the item, but in some instances I have depended on the recommendation of reviewers, colleagues, and others familiar with the material. I wish to acknowledge a special debt to Mrs. Barbara Glancy who provided guidance in the selection of items in the category of children's literature. Assistance in preparation of the bibliography was also given by Gail Adams, Dorothy Hodges, Denece Feldman, M. Lucia James, and numerous students and colleagues who, knowing of my interest, pointed out items I might otherwise have missed.

The bibliography is not exhaustive; many items have been omitted because they either appeared too late to include, were not considered of sufficient general interest for the educator, or were not considered useful or of adequate quality. An effort has been made to identify the best items available in each category. Some good and valuable references have undoubtedly been overlooked. It is hoped that the categories will be of maximum help to the busy educator in locating material he needs. The reader is urged to consult the first part of this book, where suggestions are given for utilization of material in each of the categories.

A. RACE, ETHNIC, AND RELIGIOUS ASPECTS OF AMERICAN LIFE: GENERAL BACKGROUND

(A1) Ashmore, Harry S., *The Other Side of Jordan*. New York: W. W. Norton & Company, Inc., 1960. Re Negroes outside the South; originally newspaper articles.

(A2) Ausubel, David P., *The Fern and the Tiki: An American View of New Zealand National Character, Social Attitudes, and Race Relations*. New York: Holt, Rinehart & Winston, Inc., 1965. An interesting cross-cultural study.

(A3) Baltzell, E. Digby, *The Protestant Establishment: Aristocracy and Caste in America*. New York: Random House, Inc., 1964. Witty and informed report of the ascendancy of white Anglo-Saxon Protestant values in American life.

(A4) Benedict, Ruth, and Gene Weltfish, *The Races of Mankind*. New York: Public Affairs Pamphlets, 1961. One of the clearest, simplest, and most direct analyses of race, by two outstanding anthropologists.

(A5) Berelson, Bernard, and Gary A. Steiner, *Human Behavior: An Inventory of Scientific Findings*. New York: Harcourt, Brace & World, Inc., 1964. A very valuable reference which summarizes the major research findings about behavior.

(A6) Brink, William, and Louis Harris, *Black and White: A Study of U.S. Racial Attitudes Today*. New York: Simon and Schuster, Inc., 1967.

(A7) Brophy, William A., and Sophie D. Aberle, *The Indian: America's Unfinished Business*. Norman, Okla.: University of Oklahoma Press, 1966.

(A8) Clark, Kenneth B., *Dark Ghetto*. New York: Harper & Row, Publishers, 1965. Educational sections of particular pertinence for teachers and administrators.

(A9) Coser, Lewis A., "Race Relations," *Sociology Through Literature*, Section 13, pp. 300-27. Englewood Cliffs, N.J.: Prentice-Hall, Inc., 1963.

(A10) Domnitz, Myer, *Educational Techniques for Combating Prejudice and Discrimination and for Promoting Better Intergroup Understanding*. Hamburg, Germany: UNESCO Institute for Education, 1965. Report on an international meeting held May 25–30, 1964.

(A11) Dunbar, Ernest, "The Negro in America Today," *Look*, April 10, 1962.

(A12) *Ebony* Magazine Editors, *The Negro Handbook.* Chicago: Johnson Publishing Co., Inc., 1967. Concise and accurate reference work documents the history and contemporary status of the American Negro.

(A13) Elman, Richard M., *Ill-at-Ease in Compton.* New York: Pantheon Books, Inc., 1967. A study of the industrialized lower-middle-class suburb nearest to Watts in the Los Angeles area. Superior sociological report of a critical aspect of interracial attitudes.

(A14) Flannery, Edward H., *The Anguish of the Jews: Twenty-Three Centuries of Anti-Semitism.* New York: The Macmillan Company, 1965.

(A15) Foster, G. W., Jr., "The North and West Have Problems, Too," *Saturday Review,* April 20, 1963.

(A16) Glazer, Nathan, and Daniel P. Moynihan, *Beyond the Melting Pot: The Negroes, Puerto Ricans, Jews, Italians and Irish of New York City.* Cambridge, Mass.: The M.I.T. Press and Harvard University Press, 1963. Tracing the role of ethnicity in New York City, which has not become a melting pot, according to the authors.

(A17) Goffman, Erving, *Stigma: Notes on the Management of Spoiled Identity.* Englewood Cliffs, N.J.: Prentice-Hall, Inc., 1963. Brilliant discussion of the ways in which overt as well as covert stigmata affect behavior and relationships.

(A18) Gordon, Milton M., *Assimilation in American Life: The Role of Race, Religion and National Origins.* New York: Oxford University Press, Inc., 1964. Reviews the cultural and social history of the "melting pot" concept.

(A19) Gottleib, David, "Teaching Students: The Views of Negro and White Teachers," *Sociology of Education,* XXXVII, Summer, 1964, 345-53. Research report which identifies the different perceptions of Negro and white teachers viewing Negro students.

(A20) Hapgood, Hutchins, *The Spirit of the Ghetto,* ed. Moses Rischin. Cambridge, Mass.: Harvard University Press, The John Harvard Library, 1967. Originally issued in 1902, this classic tells the story of the immigrant Jew, reported by a New England Yankee.

(A21) Harleston, Bernard W., "Higher Education for the Negro," *The Atlantic,* November, 1965, pp. 139-44.

(A22) Henry, Jules, *Culture Against Man.* New York: Random House,

Inc., 1963. A cultural anthropologist examines American society and institutions, including the elementary and secondary school.

(A23) Isaacs, Harold R., *The New World of Negro Americans* (paperback). New York: The John Day Company, Inc., 1963.

(A24) Lisitzky, Gene, *Four Ways of Being Human.* New York: The Viking Press, Inc., 1956. An introduction to anthropology for the layman.

(A25) Montagu, Ashley, ed., *The Concept of Race.* New York: The Free Press, 1964. Leading anthropologists, zoologists, and biologists focus a major attack on the biological concept of race.

(A26) ———, *What We Know About Race.* New York: The One Nation Library, Anti-Defamation League of B'nai B'rith, 1967.

(A27) Morris, Willie, ed., *The South Today,* New York: Harper & Row, Publishers, 1965. Collection of essays, the dominant theme being the need for more humane leadership and for acceptance of the fact that the problem of the South is the problem of the North, the tragedy of the Negro is the tragedy of the white.

(A28) "The Negro American," 1 and 2, *Daedalus,* VIC, No. 4 (Fall, 1965), pp. 743-1166; Winter, 1966, pp. 1-445.

(A29) *New Voices of the Southwest.* Washington, D.C.: National Education Association, 1967. Report of a symposium on the Spanish-speaking child in the schools of the Southwest. Includes a good bibliography for the educator.

(A30) Northwood, L. K., and Ernest A. T. Barth, *Urban Neighborhoods in Which Negro Families "Pioneered."* Seattle: University of Washington Press, 1965.

(A31) Osofsky, Gilbert, *Harlem: The Making of a Ghetto.* New York: Harper & Row, Publishers, 1966. Traces the forces in a large city which produce a slum.

(A32) Parker, Seymour, and Robert J. Kleiner, *Mental Illness in the Urban Negro Community.* New York: The Macmillan Company, 1966.

(A33) Pettigrew, Thomas F., *A Profile of the Negro American* (paperback). Princeton, N.J.: D. Van Nostrand Co., Inc., 1964. The best summary to date of the sociological research on the Negro.

(A34) Redding, J. Saunders, *On Being Negro in America* (paperback). Indianapolis: The Bobbs-Merrill Company, Inc., 1951. A moving personal record of a sensitive Negro author of an older generation.

(A35) Rohrer, John H., *et al., The Eighth Generation: Cultures and Personalities of New Orleans Negroes.* New York: Harper & Row, Publishers, 1960.

(A36) Rosenberg, Stuart E., *The Search for Jewish Identity in America.* New York: Doubleday & Company, Inc., 1965.

(A37) Rowan, Carl T., "We Tell Our Children," *Saturday Evening Post,* August 22, 1959, pp. 18ff. A noted Negro author describes how he has explained the racial situation to his children.

(A38) Rubel, Arthur J., *Across the Tracks: Mexican-Americans in a Texas City.* Austin: University of Texas Press, 1966. The reasoning behind the attitudes and behavior of Mexican-Americans in a city along the Texas-Mexican border, and a description of life as they see it. A publication in the Hogg Foundation Research Series.

(A39) Drake, St. Clair, "The Social and Economic Status of the Negro in the United States," *Daedalus* VIC, No. 4 (Fall, 1965), 771-814.

(A40) Silberman, Charles E., *Crisis in Black and White.* New York: Random House, Inc., 1964. Two skilled reporters vividly describe the confused and conflicting feelings of Southerners in a time of social change.

(A41) Stember, Charles H., *Jews in the Mind of America.* New York: Basic Books, Inc., Publishers, Institute of Human Relations Press of the American Jewish Committee, 1966. Author analyzes changing public attitudes toward Jews as revealed in the findings of nationwide public opinion polls spanning a 25-year period from 1937 onward.

(A42) Terkel, Studs, *Division Street: America.* New York: Pantheon Books, Inc., 1967. Autobiographical reflections of a cross-section of Chicagoans, reported by a radio-journalist. Fascinating and revealing.

(A43) Travers, Robert, "The Transmission of Information to Human Receivers," *Audio-Visual Communication Review,* XII, No. 4 (Winter, 1964), pp. 373-85.

(A44) Vogt, Evon, and Ethel M. Albert, eds., *The People of Rimrock. A Study of Values in Five Cultures.* Cambridge, Mass.: Harvard University Press, 1965. In the Rimrock area of New Mexico five distinct cultures come together in a complex network that is the subject of a major study by a group of outstanding scholars. The Navahos, Zuni Indians, Spanish-Americans, Mormons, and "Anglos" (Texan dirt farmers) are described.

(A45) Wakefield, Dan, *Island in the City*. New York: Corinth Books, 1957. A vivid and searing report on Spanish Harlem.

(A46) White, Mary Alice, and June Cherry, eds., *School Disorder, Intelligence, and Social Class*. New York: Teachers College Press, Columbia University, 1966. A research study which shows clearly a different interpretation of school misbehavior as against mental illness, as related to socio-economic status.

B. PREJUDICE AND ITS BY-PRODUCTS

(B1) Allport, Gordon W., *The Nature of Prejudice*. Cambridge, Mass.: Addison-Wesley Press, 1954. A classic summary of research to date, plus superb analytic insight.

(B2) Anglund, Joan W., *What Color Is Love?* New York: Harcourt, Brace & World, Inc., 1966. As in her many previous little books, Mrs. Anglund shows in delicate prose and drawings the fact that love is "color-blind."

(B3) Alsop, Stewart, "Portrait of a Klansman," *Saturday Evening Post*, April 9, 1966, pp. 23-27. A reporter tries to find out why a person would belong to the Ku Klux Klan.

(B4) Barzun, Jacques, *Race: A Study in Superstition*. New York: Harper & Row, Publishers, Harper Torchbooks, 1964. Reprint of an earlier classic analysis. $1.95.

(B5) Bettelheim, Bruno, and Kurt Lewin, *Securing Our Children Against Prejudice* (paperback). New York: Community Relations Service, 386 Fourth Avenue, n.d.

(B6) Black, Algernon, *Fair Play in Housing: Who's My Neighbor?* New York: Public Affairs Pamphlets, 381 Park Ave. South, N.Y. 10016, 1966, Pamphlet #396. The effects of prejudice and discrimination on housing patterns.

(B7) Brody, Eugene B., "Color and Identity Conflict in Young Boys," *Psychiatry*, XXVI, No. 2 (May, 1963), 188-201. Psychiatric report on how skin color influences personality development.

(B8) Caughey, John, and Laree Caughey, *School Segregation on Our Doorstep: The Los Angeles Story*. Los Angeles: Quail Books, 304 Riverside Drive, 1966. A UCLA American history professor and his wife document the segregation crisis that has built up in Los Angeles.

(B9) Clark, Kenneth, *Prejudice and Your Child* (rev. ed.). Boston: Beacon Press, 1955. A useful short pamphlet for parent and teacher education.

(B10) "The Crime of Being Married," *Life,* March 18, 1966, pp. 85-91. A Virginia couple fights to overturn an old law against miscegenation.

(B11) Dykeman, Wilma, and James Stokley, *Neither Black Nor White.* New York: Holt, Rinehart & Winston, Inc., 1959. Two skilled journalists report on the South. Excellent background on a personal level.

(B12) *Ebony* Magazine Editors, *The White Problem in America.* Chicago: Johnson Publishing Co., Inc., 1965. *Ebony*'s special issue of August, 1965; now in hardcover form are the articles by *Ebony* staff writers and by such authors as James Baldwin, Kenneth B. Clark, and Dr. Martin Luther King, Jr.

(B13) Flannery, Edward H., *The Anguish of the Jews: Twenty-Three Centuries of Anti-Semitism* (paperback and hardbound). New York: The Macmillan Company, 1965.

(B14) Flowers, Richmond, "Southern Plain Talk About the Ku Klux Klan," *Look,* May 3, 1966, pp. 36-44.

(B15) Forster, Arnold, and Benjamin R. Epstein, *Report on the Ku Klux Klan.* New York: Anti-Defamation League of B'nai B'rith, n.d.

(B16) Goffman, Erving, *Stigma: Notes on the Management of Spoiled Identity.* Englewood Cliffs, N.J.: Prentice-Hall, Inc., 1963. Masterful and insightful discussion of the many ways in which deviance, whether it be blindness, a prison record, or being a Negro, affects behavior. Highly recommended; adult.

(B17) Griffin, John H., *Black Like Me.* Boston: Houghton Mifflin Company, 1961. A white man disguises himself as a Negro and reports what it feels like and what things happen to him as he travels through the South in this role. A good opening book for persons who have never considered the impact of race discrimination in personal terms. High school and adult.

(B18) Gross, Ronald, and Judith Murphy, *The Revolution in the Schools.* New York: Harcourt, Brace & World, Inc., Harbinger Books, 1967.

(B19) Hulse, Frederick S., *The Human Species.* New York: Random House, Inc., 1964. Of special interest is Chapter 14, "Problems of Race, Language, and Culture–Some Theories of Racial Superiority."

(B20) Kardiner, Abram, and Lionel Ovesey, *The Mark of Oppression.* New York: W. W. Norton & Company, Inc., 1951. (Available in paperback.) Psychoanalytic research report on how being Negro affects people. Very important data.

(B21) Kraus, Sidney, "Modifying Prejudice: Attitude Change as a Function of the Race of the Communicator," *Audio-Visual Communication Review,* Vol. 10 (No. 1, Jan.–Feb., 1962), pp. 14-22.

(B22) Olson, Bernhard E., *Faith and Prejudice: Intergroup Problems in Protestant Curricula.* New Haven: Yale University Press, 1963. Examines the teaching materials used by three different denominations.

(B23) Pettigrew, T., and E. Campbell, *Christians in the Racial Crisis: A Study of Little Rock's Ministry.* Washington, D.C.: Public Affairs Press, 1959. Where did the church stand? This field research study is extremely illuminating.

(B24) Randel, William P., *The Ku Klux Klan: A Century of Infamy.* Philadelphia: Chilton Books, 1965. Shows that the Klan is more than a historical curiosity spawned by the hate and fear of the conquered South. For an entire century the Klan has been a specter menacing those who would claim that law must prevail and justice must triumph.

(B25) Rosen, Harry, and David Rosen, *But Not Next Door* (paperback). New York: Avon Books, 1962. Interracial housing problems presented.

(B26) Slawson, John, "Mutual Aid and the Negro," *Commentary,* April, 1966, pp. 43-50. An analysis of why it has been more difficult for Negroes to "pull themselves up by their own bootstraps" than for other groups, it also shows how many efforts Negroes have made to help each other.

(B27) Smith, Lillian, "The Day It Happens to Each of Us," *McCall's,* November, 1964, pp. 124ff. The recognition of the harm and futility of prejudice.

(B28) Smith, M. Brewster, *Determinants of Anti-Semitism: A Social-Psychological Map.* New York: Anti-Defamation League of B'nai B'rith, 1966. Pamphlet.

(B29) Stember, Charles H., *Jews in the Mind of America.* New York: Basic Books, Inc., Publishers, Institute of Human Relations Press of the American Jewish Committee, 1966. Author analyzes changing public attitudes toward Jews as revealed in the findings of nationwide public opinion polls spanning a 25-year period from 1937 onward.

(B30) Stewart, Maxwell, *The Negro in America.* New York, Public Affairs

Pamphlets, 381 Park Ave. South, N.Y. 10016. Pamphlet #95, 1950. Based on Gunnar Myrdal's *An American Dilemma*. The classic study of the Negro in America during the 1940's. Basic to understanding today's problems.

(B31) Vander Zanden, James W., *American Minority Relations—The Sociology of Race and Ethnic Groups* (2nd ed.). New York: The Ronald Press Company, 1966. This book examines current developments in American minority relations within the context of the latest theoretical advances in the field.

(B32) Westie, Frank R., "Race and Ethnic Relations," *Handbook of Modern Sociology*, Chapter 16. Skokie, Ill.: Rand McNally & Co., 1964. A summary of sociological theory and research.

C. BACKGROUND AND HISTORY OF THE NEGRO IN AMERICA: AFRICAN HISTORY: CONTEMPORARY AFRICA

(C1) Aptheker, Herbert, ed., *A Documentary History of the Negro People in the United States, Vols. I and II*. New York: The Citadel Press, 1962 and 1964. Good source material.

(C2) ———, *American Negro Slave Revolts*. New York: Columbia University Press, 1943. A part of history usually omitted from history courses.

(C3) Balandier, Georges, *Ambiguous Africa! Cultures in Collision*. New York: Pantheon Books, Inc., 1965. The author's double aim is to portray the development of African traditions and to present the depth of the disturbance modern civilization has caused the African societies.

(C4) Barrett, Russell H., *Integration at Ole Miss*. New York: Quadrangle, 1965. Tells what happened when the first Negro student enrolled at the University of Mississippi.

(C5) Bennett, Lerone, Jr., *Before the Mayflower*. Chicago: Johnson Publishing Co., Inc., 1962. A history of the Negro. Very readable.

(C6) Bone, Robert A., *The Negro Novel in America* (rev. ed.) (paperback). New Haven: Yale University Press, 1965.

(C7) Bontemps, Arna, and Jack Conroy, *Any Place But Here*. New York: Hill and Wang, 1966. An updated revision of *They Seek a City;* the exploits of the Negro explorers and wanderers across the American continent and the Negro migrations that followed them.

(C8) Botkin, B. A., ed., *Lay My Burden Down: A Folk History of American Slavery*. Chicago: University of Chicago Press, 1945. Oral history as told to WPA interviewers by the last of the ex-slaves. Excellent primary source material.

(C9) Carawan, Guy, and Candie Carawan, *Ain't You Got a Right to the Tree of Life?* New York: Simon and Schuster, Inc., 1967. In picture and prose the Carawans describe the people of Johns Island, South Carolina, where an isolated group of Negroes has developed a unique culture.

(C10) Curtin, Philip D., ed., *Africa Remembered: Narratives by West Africans From the Era of the Slave Trade.* Madison, Wisc.: Wisconsin University Press, 1967. Presents a dramatic view of eighteenth- and nineteenth-century West Africa as it looked to ten men caught up in the slavery machine.

(C11) Davis, David Brion, *The Problem of Slavery in Western Culture.* Ithaca, N.Y.: Cornell University Press, 1966. The moral problem posed by slavery from classical Greece and Rome to the period immediately preceding the rise of militant abolitionist movements in England and the U.S. The author summarizes the historical arguments for and against slavery.

(C12) Dollard, John, *Caste and Class in a Southern Town.* New Haven: Yale University Press, 1937 (paperback reprint, 1963). Classic social-psychological study of a small Southern town. Revealing insights, still accurate today.

(C13) *Ebony* Magazine Editors, *The Negro Handbook.* Chicago: Johnson Publishing Co., Inc., 1966. This volume brings together hard-to-locate facts and figures about the Negro. A text of 18 sections, each devoted to a different aspect of Negro-American life, supplemented by tables of statistics on Negro population, education, socio-economic groups, libraries, crime, professional and other employment, etc.

(C14) Elkins, Stanley M., *Slavery: A Problem in American Institutional and Intellectual Life.* Chicago: University of Chicago Press, 1959.

(C15) Evans, Lancelot D., ed., *Emerging African Nations and Their Leaders, Vol. II.* New York: Educational Heritage, Inc.

(C16) Faris, Robert E. L., ed., *Handbook of Modern Sociology.* Skokie, Ill.: Rand McNally & Co., 1964. See especially Chapter 16, "Race and Ethnic Relations," for up-to-date summary of the most recent research and theory.

(C17) Fordham, Paul, *The Geography of African Affairs.* Baltimore: Penguin Books, Inc., 1965.

(C18) Franklin, John Hope, *From Slavery to Freedom, A History of American Negroes* (rev. ed.). New York: Alfred A. Knopf, Inc., 1968. Discusses the distinguished personalities and the nameless millions, slave and free, whose activities make up the history of American Negroes. Commences with record of the Negro from medieval kingdoms of Africa to contemporary life in the West Indies, Latin America, Canada, and the U.S.

(C19) Genovese, Eugene D., *The Political Economy of Slavery*. New York: Random House, Inc., Pantheon Books, Inc., 1965. Discusses the economic basis for slavery.

(C20) Ginsberg, Eli, with James K. Anderson, Douglas W. Bray, and Robert W. Smuts, *The Negro Potential*. New York: Columbia University Press, 1956. Presents data to show the contribution the Negro could make if equal opportunity were available.

(C21) Ginsberg, Eli, and A.S. Eichner, *The Troublesome Presence*. New York: The Free Press, 1964. The history of the Negro's struggle for equality. Scholarly and well written.

(C22) Gossett, Thomas F., *Race: The History of an Idea in America*. New York: Schocken Books, 1965.

(C23) Green, Constance McLaughlin, *The Secret City*. Princeton, N.J.: Princeton University Press, 1967. The history of the Negro in Washington, D.C., written by a Pulitzer Prize winning historian.

(C24) Gross, Seymour L., and John Edward Hardy, *Images of the Negro in American Literature*. Chicago: University of Chicago Press, 1966. This collection deals with traditions and conventions in the literary depiction of the Negro and with individual authors, both Negro and white.

(C25) Harlan, Louis, *The Negro in American History*. Publication No. 61 (paperback). Washington, D.C.: Service Center for Teachers of History. A summary of changing historical interpretations.

(C26) Herskovits, Melville J., *The American Negro*. Bloomington: Indiana University Press, 1966. Herskovits attempts to establish grounds, based on physical measurements and a study of the genealogies of several hundred representative Negroes, for determining the new "racial" composite he believes the American Negro is forming.

(C27) ———, *The Myth of the Negro Past*. Boston: Beacon Press, 1958. An anthropologist reviews historical distortions regarding Negro background.

(C28) ———, *The New World Negro: Selected Papers in Afro-American Studies,* ed. Frances S. Herskovits. Bloomington: Indiana University Press, 1966. Bringing together for the first time selected articles by the distinguished anthropologist, a pioneer in studies on the Negro. This volume presents a comprehensive survey of Herskovits' exhaustive study of the Negro in the Western Hemisphere.

(C29) Hill, Herbert, *Anger and Beyond: The Negro Writer in the United States.* New York: Harper & Row, Publishers, 1966. A dozen articles illuminate the situation of the Negro in America, past and present.

(C30) *History of the Negro People* (*Viewer's Handbook*) (paperback). New York: National Educational Television, 1965. Supplement to N.E.T.'s nine-program series of the same name. A brief overview of Negro history.

(C31) Kalven, Harry, Jr., *The Negro and the First Amendment.* Chicago: University of Chicago Press, 1966.

(C32) Klein, Herbert S., *Slavery in the Americas: A Comparative Study of Virginia and Cuba.* Chicago: University of Chicago Press, 1967. How the English and the Spanish systems differed in their treatment of slavery.

(C33) Klineberg, Otto, *The Human Dimension in International Relations.* New York: Holt, Rinehart & Winston, Inc., 1964. Treats such related questions as the reasons for war, how public opinion is shaped, the nature of leadership, and the racial problem.

(C34) Larsson, Clotye M., ed., *Marriage Across the Color Line.* Chicago: Johnson Publishing Co., Inc., 1965. A series of essays, reports, and studies of several interracial marriages.

(C35) Leckie, William H., *The Buffalo Soldiers: A Narrative of the Negro Cavalry in the West.* Norman, Okla.: University of Oklahoma Press, 1967. Negro soldiers who wished to remain in the U.S. Army after the Civil War were organized into the Ninth and Tenth Cavalry Regiments—and their service in controlling Indians on the Great Plains was as invaluable as it was unpraised. Commanded by white officers and operating under intense disadvantages, they were remarkable fighting units during the extensive engagements on the Southwestern plains.

(C36) Leiserso, Avery, *The American South in the 1960's.* New York: Frederick A. Praeger, Inc., 1965. A useful report of the current situation.

(C37) Litwack, Leon F., *The Negro in the Free States, 1790–1860.* Chicago: University of Chicago Press, 1961.

(C38) Logan, Rayford W., *The Betrayal of the Negro.* New York: Collier Books, 1965. An angry book which points out how the Negro has been consistently deprived of his rights.

(C39) Lord, Walter, *The Past That Would Not Die.* New York: Harper & Row, Publishers, 1965. History of freedom and the Negro.

(C40) McKitrick, Eric I., *Slavery Defended: The Views of the Old South.* Englewood Cliffs, N.J.: Prentice-Hall, Inc., 1963.

(C41) McPherson, James M., *How the Negro Felt and Acted During the War for the Union.* New York: Pantheon Books, Inc., 1965. A collection of speeches, letters, articles, and official documents written by and about Negroes who at the time were as divided as the white people but, when fundamental principles were involved, spoke out with amazing unanimity.

(C42) Mannix, Daniel P., with Malcolm Cowley, *Black Cargoes: A History of the Atlantic Slave Trade.* New York: The Viking Press, Inc., 1962. The story of the gigantic commercial operation, from 1518 to 1865, that changed the history of the world.

(C43) Meier, August, and Elliot M. Rudwick, *From Plantation to Ghetto: An Interpretive History of the American Negro.* New York: Hill and Wang, Inc., 1966. In chronological fashion, the authors report events, ideologies, institutional developments, and protest movements throughout the Negro's history in America.

(C44) Myrdal, Gunnar, *The American Dilemma.* New York: Harper & Row, Publishers, 1944. This study is the basic document for understanding the Negro today. Superbly written and documented.

(C45) Nye, Russel B., *Fettered Freedom: Civil Liberties and the Slavery Controversy, 1830–1860.* East Lansing, Mich.: Michigan State University Press, 1963. Historical background of interest to the specialist.

(C46) Quarles, Benjamin, *The Negro in the Making of America.* New York: Collier Books, The Macmillan Company, 1964. An excellent history.

(C47) Record, Wilson, *Race and Radicalism, The NAACP and the Communist Party in Conflict.* Ithaca, N.Y.: Cornell University Press, 1966. Sociological and historical reference to political issues in race movements.

(C48) Reimers, David M., *White Protestantism and the Negro.* New York: Oxford University Press, Inc., 1965. The author discusses the Protestant churches' involvement with the anti-slavery crusade and their activities during Reconstruction to aid and educate southern Negroes.

(C49) Shinner, Margaret, *Ancient African Kingdoms.* London: Edward Arnold Publishers, Ltd., 1965. Was Africa really the "Dark Continent"?

(C50) Smith, Elbert B., *The Death of Slavery: The United States, 1837–65.* Chicago: University of Chicago Press, 1967. Historical study of the forces that lead to the outlawing of slavery.

(C51) Spock, Benjamin, "Children and Discrimination," *Redbook Magazine,* October, 1964. Reprint available from Anti-Defamation League of B'nai B'rith. A simple and penetrating analysis of prejudice and children.

(C52) Sterling, Dorothy, *Forever Free.* Garden City, N.Y.: Doubleday & Company, Inc., 1963. Chronicles the long, continuing struggle for freedom and puts in perspective the Negro's role in history.

(C53) Thomas, John L., *Slavery Attacked: The Abolitionist Crusade.* Englewood Cliffs, N.J.: Prentice-Hall, Inc., 1964.

(C54) Walker, Margaret, *Jubilee.* Boston: Houghton Mifflin Company, 1966. Views the plantation South, Civil War, and Reconstruction through the eyes of Negro slaves. Interesting to contrast the same era with the picture presented in *Gone With the Wind.*

(C55) Wish, Harvey, *The Negro Since Emancipation.* Englewood Cliffs, N.J.: Prentice-Hall, Inc., 1964.

(C56) Woodson, Carter G., and Charles H. Wesley, *The Negro in Our History.* Washington, D.C.: The Associated Publishers, Inc., 1962.

(C57) Wynes, Charles, ed., *The Negro in the South Since 1865.* University, Ala.: University of Alabama Press, 1965. Selected essays on American Negro history.

Selected State Histories: The Negro and Slavery

(C58) Franklin, John Hope, *The Free Negro in North Carolina 1790–1860.* Chapel Hill: University of North Carolina Press, 1943.

(C59) McManus, Edgar J., *A History of Negro Slavery in New York.* Syracuse, N.Y.: Syracuse University Press, 1966.

(C60) Strother, Horatio T., *The Underground Railroad in Connecticut.* Middletown, Conn.: Wesleyan University Press, 1966.

(C61) Wagandt, Charles L., *The Mighty Revolution: Negro Emancipation in Maryland, 1862–1864.* Baltimore: Johns Hopkins University Press, 1964.

(C62) Wallace, John, *Carpetbag Rule in Florida.* Gainesville: University of Florida Press, 1964. The author rose from slavery to serve in the Florida Senate; covers Florida government 1865–1876.

(C63) Zilversmit, Arthur, *The First Emancipation: The Abolition of Negro Slavery in the North.* Chicago: University of Chicago Press, 1967. Was it economic necessity or idealism that led the North to abolish slavery? This book helps resolve the question.

D. HISTORY OF THE NEGRO ADAPTED FOR SCHOOL USE

(D1) Adams, Russell L., *Great Negroes Past and Present.* Chicago: Afro-American Publishing Co., 1964. Pictures for bulletin board.

(D2) American Oil Company, *American Traveler's Guide to Negro History* (rev. ed.) (paperback). Chicago: American Oil Company, 910 South Michigan Avenue, 1966. A state-by-state guide to historical landmarks that point up phases of Negro history all over the United States.

(D3) Archibald, Helen A., ed., *Negro History and Culture: Selections for Use With Children.* Chicago: Department of Curriculum Development, Chicago City Missionary Society, n.d. Selected source materials such as poems, sayings, factual material, short essays, which a teacher can use with children.

(D4) Bittle, William E., and Gilbert Geis, *The Longest Way Home: Chief Alfred C. Sam's Back-to-Africa Movement.* Detroit, Mich.: Wayne State University Press, 1964. When Oklahoma was settled, Negroes tried to make of Boleby a genuinely American community enterprise. As the whites successfully whittled them down to second-class citizenry, a group sought to salvage human dignity by resettling the Gold Coast. The episode is here recited with a telling restraint.

(D5) Board of Education of the City of New York, *The Negro in American History* (paperback). Curriculum Bulletin, 1964–1965 Series, No. 4. New York: The Board of Education, 1965.

(D6) Bontemps, Arna, *Story of the Negro.* New York: Alfred A. Knopf, Inc., 1955. Popular and well written.

(D7) Cieciorka, Bobbi and Frank, *Negroes in American History: A Free-*

dom Primer. The Student Voice, Inc., 1965. Designed for use in the freedom schools staffed by the Student Nonviolent Coordinating Committee. Simplified account of Negroes in America for younger children or poor readers.

(D8) Cuban, Larry, *The Negro in America.* Glenview, Ill.: Scott, Foresman & Co., 1964. Written particularly for high school youth by a master teacher.

(D9) Dannett, Sylvia, ed., *Profiles of Negro Womanhood,* Vol. I. New York: Educational Heritage, Inc., n.d.

(D10) Davidson, Basil, *A Guide to African History,* Garden City, N. Y.: Doubleday & Company, Inc., 1965.

(D11) Davis, John P., *The American Negro Reference Books,* Vols. I and II. Englewood Cliffs, N.J.: Prentice-Hall, Inc., 1966.

(D12) Detroit Public Schools, *Struggle for Freedom and Rights: The Negro in American History.* Detroit: The Board of Education, 1964. Supplement text for Grade 8. 52 pp.

(D13) *Ebony* Magazine Editors, *The Negro Handbook.* Chicago: Johnson Publishing Co., Inc., 1967. Concise and accurate reference work documents the history and the contemporary status of the American Negro.

(D14) Friedman, Leon, ed., *Southern Justice.* New York: Random House, Inc., 1965. Nineteen lawyers report judicial cases. Good source for senior high school students.

(D15) Hall, Wade H., *The Smiling Phoenix: Southern Humor from 1865 to 1914.* Gainesville: University of Florida Press, 1965. Study of post-Civil War humor that reveals the attitudes of the South toward the War, Reconstruction, reconciliation with the North, the Negro, the poor white, and politics.

(D16) Hughes, Langston, and Milton Meltzer, *A Pictorial History of the Negro in America* (rev. ed.). New York: Crown Publishers, Inc., 1963. Contains more than 1,000 illustrations along with a simple text. Very valuable for classroom reference.

(D16a) Lincoln, C. Eric, *The Negro Pilgrimage in America.* New York: Bantam Books, 1967 (paperback). The many illustrations will appeal to the younger reader. Some of the historical material may be more authentic than that in other sources.

(D17) Lively, Robert A., *Fiction Fights the Civil War.* Chapel Hill, N.C.: University of North Carolina Press, 1957. Useful in relating literature to history. Will provide students a new view of the novel.

(D18) McRae, Norman, and Jerry Blocker, *The American Negro, A History in Biography and Pictures.* Skokie, Ill.: Rand McNally & Co., 1966.

(D19) Meltzer, Milton, ed., *In Their Own Words: A History of the American Negro, 1865–1916.* New York: Thomas Y. Crowell Company, 1965. Volume II of a series. Letters, speeches, memoirs, and testimony in which Negroes describe the dreams and disappointments following Emancipation. Volume I, published in 1964, covers 1619–1865. Vol. II, 1865–1916, pub. 1965; Volume III, published in 1967, covers 1916–1966. Available in paperback: Princeton, N.J.:

(D20) Mendelsohn, Jack, *The Martyrs: Sixteen Who Gave Their Lives for Racial Justice.* New York: Harper & Row, Publishers, 1966. Dramatic story of martyrs for justice.

(D21) Oliver, Roland, and J. D. Page, *A Short History of Africa.* Baltimore: Penguin Books, Inc., 1964.

(D22) Stewart, Maxwell, *The Negro in America.* New York: Public Affairs Pamphlets, 381 Park Avenue South, N.Y. 10016. Pamphlet #95, 1950. Based on Gunnar Myrdal's *An American Dilemma.* Brief, readable pamphlet.

(D23) Wagley, Charles, and Marvin Harris, *Minorities in the New World.* New York: Columbia University Press, 1958. Six case studies.

(D24) Woodson, C. G., and C. H. Wesley, *The Story of the Negro Retold.* New York: Associated Press, Inc., 1959.

E. BACKGROUND MATERIAL AND DISCUSSION OF THE CONTEMPORARY CIVIL RIGHTS MOVEMENT AND SCHOOL DESEGREGATION

(E1) Anderson, Margaret, *The Children of the South.* New York: Farrar, Straus & Giroux, Inc., 1964. A teacher's report of what it felt like to live through one of the first bitter desegregation crises: Clinton, Tennessee.

(E2) Barrett, Russell H., *Integration at Ole Miss.* Chicago, Ill: Quadrangle Books, Inc., 1965. Report of the turmoil that occurred when the first Negro (James Meredith) enrolled at the University of Mississippi.

(E3) Belfrage, Sally, *Freedom Summer.* New York: The Viking Press, Inc., 1965. Perceptive report of the work of "outsiders" in Mississippi attempting to reach the disfranchised Negro.

(E4) Bennett, Lerone, Jr., *Confrontation: Black and White.* Chicago: Johnson Publishing Co., Inc., 1965.

(E5) ———, *The Negro Mood.* Chicago: Johnson Publishing Co., Inc., 1964. Controversial collection of essays which analyze and consider contemporary Negro discontent.

(E6) Berman, Daniel M., *It Is So Ordered.* New York: W. W. Norton & Company, Inc., 1966. Detailed examination of the strategy of both the plaintiffs and the defendents in the Supreme Court case on school desegregation, *Brown v. Board of Education,* 1954.

(E7) Blossom, Virgil T., *It Has Happened Here.* New York: Harper & Row, Publishers, 1959. Contributes to an understanding of what happened in Little Rock, why it happened, and how its repetition may be avoided; by the man who was the school superintendent during the turmoil.

(E8) Bring, William, and Louis Harris, *The Negro Revolution in America* (paperback). New York: Simon and Schuster, Inc., 1964. Reports changes in Negro attitudes and aspirations.

(E9) Broderick, Francis L., and August Meier, eds., *Negro Protest Thought in the Twentieth Century* (paperback). Indianapolis: The Bobbs-Merrill Company, Inc., 1965. Selections, some abridged.

(E10) Carter, Hodding, III, ed., *Mississippi Black Power.* New York: Random House, Inc., 1965. Affidavits on police brutality.

(E11) Clayton, Edward T., *The Negro Politician.* Chicago: Johnson Publishing Co., Inc., 1964. Written for the layman; talks politics at the family level. The impotence of the Negro politician in the past; also his future potential. Introduction by Dr. Martin Luther King, Jr.

(E12) Coles, Robert, *Children of Crisis: A Study of Courage and Fear.* Boston: Little, Brown And Company, 1967. Dr. Coles sums up in this volume his many studies of the process of integration of the South, both Negro and white. A very useful and important study. Beautifully and humanely written.

(E13) ———, "When I Draw the Lord He'll Be a Real Big Man," *Atlantic,* CCXVII (May, 1966), 69-75. A psychiatrist reports his study of the Negro and white children who were involved in the "pioneer" desegregation in New Orleans. He also reports on their parents and their attitudes.

(E14) Conot, Robert, *Rivers of Blood, Years of Darkness.* New York:

Bantam Books, 1967. The story of the Watts disaster and what it meant to the people who were involved. Dramatic and pitiless.

(E15) *A Conversation with LeRoy Collins: Civil Rights and The Community Relations Service.* New York: Anti-Defamation League of B'nai B'rith, 1965.

(E16) *Daedalus,* Journal of the American Academy of Arts and Sciences, Fall, 1965; Winter, 1965. Two issues devoted to "The Negro American." Scholars focus on the current civil rights struggle and its background.

(E17) *Ebony* Magazine Editors, *The White Problem in America.* Chicago: Johnson Publishing Co., Inc., 1965. Hardcover edition of *Ebony*'s special issue of August, 1965.

(E18) Ehle, John, *The Free Men.* New York: Harper & Row, Publishers, 1965. Civil Rights in Chapel Hill, N.C., in 1964.

(E19) Fager, Charles, E., *White Reflections on Black Power.* Grand Rapids, Mich.: William B. Erdsmans Publishing Company, 1967. Brief paperback exploration of the meaning of black power advocates for white liberals.

(E20) Farmer, James, *Freedom—When?* New York: Random House, Inc., 1966. A leader of the civil rights movement discusses issues of the movement and his experiences in it.

(E21) Fayette County Project Volunteers, *Step by Step.* New York: W. W. Norton & Company, Inc., 1965. A Cornell University student civil rights group and the project they worked with in Tennessee in the summer of 1964. Includes photographs.

(E22) Freeman, Harrop A., *et al., Civil Disobedience.* Santa Barbara, Calif.: Center for the Study of Democratic Institutions, 1967. Pamphlet based on a series of discussions at the Center.

(E23) Friedman, Leon, ed., *Southern Justice.* New York: Random House, Inc., 1965. A series of careful reports by lawyers presenting the biased justice which prevails in many Southern jurisdictions.

(E24) Haselden, Kyle H., *The Racial Problem in Christian Perspective.* New York: Torchbooks, 1964. Statement on the racial problem by a leading Protestant minister.

(E25) Hentoff, Nat, *The New Equality* (rev. ed.) (paperback). New York: The Viking Press, Inc., 1966. A perceptive reporter writes of the Negro from close association, particularly with civil rights leaders, musicians.

(E26) Holt, Len, *An Act of Conscience.* Boston: Beacon Press, 1965. The author, a lawyer, chronicles the oppression and legal battles which ensued from civil rights demonstrations in Danville, Virginia, in 1963.

(E27) Huie, William Bradford, *Three Lives for Mississippi.* New York: Trident Press, 1965. A reporter gathers all known facts about the three young men who were murdered because of their civil rights activities.

(E28) Jones, LeRoi, *Home: Social Essays.* New York: William Morrow & Co., Inc., 1966. A famous and angry Negro author.

(E29) Kennedy, John F., *Time to Act.* An address to the American people, June 11, 1963. New York: Anti-Defamation League of B'nai B'rith. Rights, equality, and the Negro.

(E30) Keppel, Francis, *Freedom Is More Than Academic.* New York: Sidney Hillman Foundation, reprint department, 1964. Number 26 in the Sidney Hillman Reprint Series.

(E31) Killens, John Oliver, *Black Man's Burden.* New York: Trident Press, 1966.

(E32) Killian, Lewis, and Charles Grigg, *Racial Crisis in America, Leadership Conflict.* Englewood Cliffs, N.J.: Prentice-Hall, Inc., 1964. Florida State University sociologists analyze various interrelated roles (e.g., the Negro, the white liberal, the segregationist) in the face-to-face drama of today.

(E33) King, Martin Luther, Jr., *Stride Toward Freedom.* New York: Harper & Row, Publishers, 1958. The Nobel Prize winner tells the story of the Montgomery, Alabama, bus boycott and the birth of the nonviolent action civil rights movement.

(E34) Klein, Woody, "The Press Wrongs Civil Rights," *Pageant,* November, 1965, pp. 60-73. Does the press provide an accurate report?

(E35) Kunstler, William M., *Deep in My Heart.* New York: William Morrow & Co., Inc., 1966. The experiences of a New York attorney in defending civil rights workers in Southern courts.

(E36) Leiserson, Avery, ed., *The American South in the 1960's.* New York: Frederick A. Praeger, Inc., 1965. A balanced and penetrating review of the various aspects of Southern life today.

(E37) Lynd, Staughton, ed., *Nonviolence in America: A Documentary History.* Indianapolis: The Bobbs-Merrill Company, Inc., 1966. Part of the American Heritage series.

(E38) Miller, Loren, *The Petitioners: The Story of the Supreme Court of the United States and the Negro.* New York: Pantheon

Books, Inc., 1966. A leading Negro lawyer reviews the legal story of civil rights. Available in paperback from Meridian, a division of The World Publishing Company, Cleveland, Ohio.

(E39) National Commission on Professional Rights and Responsibilities, NEA, *Detroit, Michigan: A Study of Barriers to Equal Educational Opportunity in a Large City*. Washington, D.C.: The Commission, March, 1967. A revealing and significant objective report of urban educational opportunity for all.

(E40) ———, *Wilcox County, Alabama: A Study of Social, Economic and Educational Bankruptcy*. Washington, D.C., June, 1967. No one, after reading this, can doubt the need for forceful intervention to ensure the rights of all students to adequate education. A shameful indictment of "professional" educators and bigoted or apathetic community leaders.

(E41) Parsons, Talcott, and Kenneth B. Clark, *The Negro American*. New York: Houghton Mifflin Company, 1966. These 30 essays constitute the most complete summary available of today's racial crisis. (Reprints the 2 issues of *Daedalus* devoted to the Negro American in 1965.)

(E42) Peltason, J. W., *Fifty-Eight Lonely Men: Southern Federal Judges and School Desegregation*. New York: Harcourt, Brace & World, Inc., 1961.

(E43) Pope, Liston, *Millhands and Preachers*. New Haven, Conn.: Yale University Press, 1966. A brilliant criticism of the relationship between textile mills and churches in industrial areas of Gaston County, N.C., with implications for today's civil rights efforts.

(E44) Stahl, David, Frederick B. Sussman, and Neil J. Bloomfield, eds., *The Community and Racial Crises*. New York: Practising Law Institute, 20 Veasey Street, 1966. Laws governing demonstrations and other forms of protest.

(E45) Strickland, Arvath E., *History of the Chicago Urban League*. Chicago: University of Illinois Press, 1966. Provides a detailed organizational history of one of the League's leading local branches, the Chicago Urban League.

(E46) Sutherland, Elizabeth, *Letters From Mississippi*. New York: McGraw-Hill Book Company, 1965. Letters from 650 volunteers who went South in the summer of 1964 to work with the civil rights movement.

(E47) Thompson, Era Bell, and Herbert Nipson, eds., *White on Black*. Chicago: Johnson Publishing Co., Inc., 1963. Twenty-two essays by famous white Americans on various aspects of relations between whites and Negroes in America.

(E48) Trillin, Calvin, *An Education in Georgia: The Integration of Charlayne Hunter and Hamilton Holmes.* New York: The Viking Press, Inc., 1964. First appeared as a series in *The New Yorker.* Sensitive and informative.

(E49) Tucker, Shirley, *Mississippi from Within.* New York: Arco Publishing Co., 1965. Covers the period from July 2, 1964, to May, 1965, including excerpts from Mississippi daily papers, with photographs taken there at the same time. Dramatic, bitter, revealing.

(E50) U.S. Commission on Civil Rights, *Equal Employment Opportunity Under Federal Law.* Clearinghouse Publication Number 5. Washington, D.C.: The Commission, June, 1966.

(E51) ———, *Federal Rights Under School Desegregation Law.* Clearinghouse Publication Number 6. Washington, D.C.: The Commission, June, 1966.

(E52) Waskow, Arthur I., *From Race Riot to Sit-In, 1919 and the 1960's: A Study in the Connections Between Conflict and Violence.* Garden City, N.Y.: Doubleday & Company, Inc., 1966.

(E53) Weltner, Charles L., *Southerner.* Philadelphia: J. B. Lippincott Co., 1966. A leading Southern politician describes what it means to be a Southerner and also a person of conscience.

(E54) Wright, Nathan, Jr., *Black Power and Urban Unrest.* New York: Hawthorn Books, Inc., 1967. Author contends that Black Power can be the force that brings genuine solutions to the nation's current racial crisis. He presents Black Power as a movement vital to the growth, development, and peace of the entire nation. Discusses why the movement for Negro equality in America may be meaningless unless led by Negroes.

(E55) Zinn, Howard, *The Southern Mystique.* New York: Alfred A. Knopf, Inc., 1964. An account of the author's experiences on an integrated faculty of a Southern Negro college. Somewhat overstated.

F. POVERTY AND EDUCATION

(F1) Agee, James, and Walker Evans, *Let Us Now Praise Famous Men.* Boston: Houghton Mifflin Company, 1941. An excellent writer and photographer report on Alabama tenant farmers during the Depression; still applicable in many ways today. A classic.

(F2) Ausubel, David P., "The Effects of Cultural Deprivation on Learning Patterns," *Audiovisual Instruction.* Washington, D.C.: Department of Audiovisual Instruction, National Education Association, January, 1965, pp. 10-12.

(F3) ———, *Maori Youth: A Psychoethnological Study of Cultural Deprivation.* New York: Holt, Rinehart & Winston, Inc., 1965 (paperback).

(F4) Bloom, Benjamin, Allison Davis, and Robert Hess, *Compensatory Education for Cultural Deprivation.* New York: Holt, Rinehart & Winston, Inc., 1965.

(F4a) Chein, Isadore, *et al., The Road to H.* New York: Basic Books, Inc., Publishers, 1964. An excellent report on young drug addicts in New York and what can be done about the problem.

(F5) Duhl, Leonard J., *The Urban Condition.* New York: Basic Books, Inc., Publishers, 1963. A collection of papers originally presented at the annual meeting of the American Orthopsychiatric Association in 1962. Many excellent discussions.

(F6) Dunn, Nell, *Up the Junction.* Philadelphia, J. B. Lippincott Co., 1967. Sixteen brief episodes bring to life the slums of Battersea, England. An interesting comparison to the similar reporting pattern and subjects in Terkel's *Division Street: America.*

(F7) Eddy, Elizabeth, *Walk the White Line: A Profile of Urban Education* (paperback). Garden City, N.Y.: Doubleday Anchor Original, 1967. A publication growing out of *Project True,* Hunter College. An excellent discussion of what urban education is like.

(F8) *Education and Poverty:* A portfolio of the major addresses delivered at the Second Annual Conference of the National Committee for Support of the Public Schools. Washington, D.C.: National Committee for Support of the Public Schools, 1964.

(F9) Fichter, Joseph H., *Neglected Talents: The Careers of Negro College Graduates.* Chicago: Aldine Publishing Company, 1966.

(F10) Frost, Joe L., and Glenn R. Hawkes, eds., *The Disadvantaged Child: Issues and Innovations.* Boston: Houghton Mifflin Company, 1966.

(F11) Gordon, Edmund W., and Doxey A. Wilkerson, *Compensatory Education for the Disadvantaged.* Princeton, N.J.: College Entrance Examination Board, 1964. The result of a study sponsored by the College Entrance Examination Board and the National Scholarship for Negro Students.

(F12) Grimes, Alan P., *Equality in America: Religion, Race, and the Urban Majority*. New York: Oxford University Press, Inc., 1964. From their roots in colonial times, the author traces the religious, racial and political manifestations of the American concept of equal rights.

(F13) Janowitz, Gayle, *Helping Hands: Volunteer Work in Education*. Chicago: University of Chicago Press, 1965. This handbook for volunteers describes the organization of after-school study centers for children from poverty-stricken backgrounds and offers valuable advice on the kind of approach needed for successful tutoring. Available in paperback.

(F14) Jeffers, Camille, *Living Poor*. Ann Arbor, Mich.: Ann Arbor Publishers, 1967. The insightful report of a woman who, with her children, lived as a participant-observer in an urban renewal project. Many myths and preconceptions about persons living in poverty are dispelled.

(F15) Kovach, Bill, and Nat Caldwell, "The Plight of the Rural Poor," *The Reporter*, April 21, 1966, pp. 27-32. Not all poverty is restricted to the urban slum.

(F16) Krosney, Herbert, *Beyond Welfare—Poverty in the Supercity*. New York: Holt, Rinehart & Winston, Inc., 1966. This presents an indictment of New York's war on poverty—why it has failed and why it will continue to fail—with a suggested program that could succeed.

(F17) Lanning, Frank W., and Wesley A. Many, eds., *Basic Education for the Disadvantaged Adult: Theory and Practice* (paperback). Boston: Houghton Mifflin Company, 1966. Collection of articles dealing with: overview of basic education; social and psychological implications; preparing for basic education; reading, a basic curricular area; and programs, past and present.

(F18) Lewis, Oscar, *La Vida:* A Puerto Rican Family in the Culture of Poverty—San Juan and New York City. New York: Random House, Inc., 1966. Relates the similarities and differences in the reaction to poverty in two settings.

(F19) ———, "The Culture of Poverty," *Scientific American*, 1966. The author, a social anthropologist, presents his summary of years of field experiences in exploring the meaning of poverty.

(F20) Liebow, Elliott, *Tally's Corner*. Boston: Little, Brown And Company, 1967. A participant observer reports on a year spent with inner-city citizens.

(F21) Loretan, Joseph O., and Shelley Umans, *Teaching the Disadvantaged.* New York: Teachers College Press, Columbia University, 1966.

(F22) Moynihan, Daniel P., *The Negro Family: The Case for National Action.* Washington, D.C.: U.S. Department of Labor, March, 1965. A controversial report on the Negro family in America.

(F23) ———, "The Discarded Third," *Look,* May 17, 1966, pp. 27-35. Discusses the one-third of the nation's Negro families with one or both parents absent.

(F23a) Prentice-Hall Editorial Staff, *Educators' Complete ERIC Handbook,* Phase I. Englewood Cliffs, N.J.: Prentice-Hall, Inc., 1967.

(F24) *Project True.* New York: Hunter College, 1966–1967. A number of significant publications are available reporting this project on education of slum children and their teachers. Contact Dr. Marjorie Smiley, Hunter College, New York, New York, for further information. See volumes by Eddy (F7) and Moore (K28).

(F24a) Bagdikian, Ben H., *In the Midst of Plenty: A New Report on the Poor in America* (paperback). New York: Signet, 1964.

(F25) Riese, Hertha, *Heal the Hurt Child.* Chicago: University of Chicago Press, 1962. An approach through educational therapy with special reference to the extremely deprived Negro child. Poignant and impressive.

(F26) Riessman, Frank, *The Culturally Deprived Child,* New York: Harper & Row, Publishers, 1962. Particularly valuable for discussion of the values and uses of role-playing with children considered nonverbal. One of the most often cited books in the field.

(F27) ———, Jerome Cohen, and Arthur Pearl, eds., *Mental Health of the Poor: New Treatment Approaches for Low Income People.* New York: The Free Press, 1965. Contains suggestions for adaptations and modifications of traditional treatment approaches, representing virtually all of the major work on the subject in the last ten years, including a group of papers designed to provide new directions for the therapeutic aspects of the "war" on poverty.

(F28) Ritz, Joseph P., *The Despised Poor: Newburgh's War on Welfare.* Boston: Beacon Press, 1966. In 1961 the small city of Newburgh, New York, became a center of national attention because of the campaign by its controversial city manager, Joseph M. Mitchell, to reduce public welfare costs through unsympathetic handling of applications and public embarrassment of aid recipients.

(F29) Spalding, Alice B., "Eating Low on the Hog," *Harper's* Magazine, March, 1965. What a poverty-level budget is like.

(F30) Stern, Phillip M., *The Shame of a Nation.* New York: Ivan Obolensky, Inc., 1965. A stirring report on the impact of poverty.

(F31) Stringfellow, William, *Dissenter in a Great Society.* New York: Holt, Rinehart & Winston, Inc., 1966. A frontal attack on the complacency of the American consensus. Stringfellow explores the relationship between poverty and property in the U.S., the ideological crisis in U.S. politics, and the continuing war between the races.

(F32) Strom, Robert D., *Teaching in the Slum School* (paperback). Columbus, Ohio: Charles E. Merrill Books, Inc., 1965. A general overview of the problems to be met, with particular emphasis on administrative and staffing needs. Good bibliographies, but not too much on specific teaching methodology.

(F33) Tenbroek, Jacobus, ed., *The Law of the Poor* (paperback). San Francisco: Chandler Publishing Company, 1966. Is justice dependent on income?

(F34) Webster, Staten W., ed., *Knowing the Disadvantaged* (paperback). San Francisco: Chandler Publishing Company, 1966.

(F35) ———, ed., *Understanding the Educational Problems of the Disadvantaged Learner* (paperback). San Francisco: Chandler Publishing Company, 1966.

(F36) ———, ed., *Teaching the Disadvantaged Learner.* San Francisco: Chandler Publishing Company, 1966. All three titles by Webster available in one book or as three. Excellent material of practical help to the classroom teacher.

(F37) Weisbrod, Burton A., ed., *The Economics of Poverty: An American Paradox.* Englewood Cliffs, N.J.: Prentice-Hall, Inc., 1966. (Available in paperback.)

(F38) Weller, Jack E., *Yesterday's People.* Lexington, Kentucky: University of Kentucky Press, 1965. Study of contemporary life in Appalachia.

(F39) Wright, Richard, *Black Boy.* New York: New American Library of World Literature, Inc., 1945. A talented Negro author describes his poverty-ridden childhood.

G. LANGUAGE AND CULTURALLY DIFFERENT STUDENTS

(G1) Bernstein, Basil, "Social Class and Linguistic Development: A Theory of Social Learning," in *Education, Economy and Society,* pp. 288-314, eds. A. H. Halsey, Jean Floud, and C. Arnold Anderson. New York: The Free Press of Glencoe, Inc., 1961. Language differences related to class; Bernstein proposes two linguistic codes, formal (for school) and public.

(G2) Brown, Charles T., and Charles Van Riper, *Speech and Man* (paperback). Englewood Cliffs, N.J.: Prentice-Hall, Inc., 1966. Ranging widely through the social sciences, the authors show how speech is the device whereby man seeks mastery over his environment and himself.

(G3) Chreist, Fred M., *Foreign Accent.* Englewood Cliffs, N.J.: Prentice-Hall, Inc., 1964. For the culturally disadvantaged, standard English is a new language. This book shows what the special characteristics of English are, what an accent is, and what teaching is needed to eradicate accent or dialect.

(G4) Corbin, R., and Muriel Crosby, *Language Programs for the Disadvantaged.* Champaign, Ill.: National Council of Teachers of English, 1963. Outlines some of the main syntactical features of Negro folk "sociolect."

(G5) Evertts, Eldomma, *Dimensions of Dialect.* Champaign, Ill.: National Council of Teachers of English, 1967.

(G6) Francis, W. N., *The Structure of American English.* New York: The Ronald Press Company, 1958. Contains an excellent chapter on regional and social dialects. This work is also well known as one of the structural grammars of the so-called "revolution in grammar" in the U.S.

(G7) Golden, Ruth I., *Improving Patterns of Language Usage.* Detroit, Mich.: Wayne State University Press, 1960. Provides help in dialect remediation exercises for the inner-city child.

(G8) Gunderson, Doris V., *Research in Reading Readiness.* U.S. Department of Health, Education, and Welfare, Office of Education. #OE-30013, Bulletin 1964, No. 8. Washington, D.C.: Government Printing Office, 1964.

(G9) Hall, Edward T., *The Silent Language* (paperback). New York: Fawcett Publications, Inc., 1961. A leading anthropologist reveals how people communicate without words and how behavior reflects a nation's influence on world affairs.

(G10) Hayakawa, S. I., ed., *The Use and Misuse of Language* (paperback). New York: Fawcett Publications, Inc. Selected essays from ETC: *A Review of General Semantics.* Exploring the problem of communication in contemporary life.

(G11) Hess, Robert D., and Virginia Shipman, "Early Blocks to Children's Learning," *Children,* XII, No. 5 (September-October, 1965), 189-94.

(G12) Holbrook, David, *English for the Rejected.* New York: Cambridge University Press, 1964. Based on the author's work with literacy programs in the lowest level of English secondary schools. Creative and helpful.

(G13) Hurst, Charles G., Jr., *Psychological Correlates in Dialectolalia: Cooperative Research Project No. 2610.* Washington, D.C.: Howard University Press, 1965. "Dialectolalia" is Dean Hurst's coined designation of what we have termed "Negro folk speech" or "folk sociolect." The title is indicative of the contents—the book is worth reading for background.

(G14) *Improving English Skills of Culturally Different Youth.* Washington, D.C.: U.S. Department of Health, Education, and Welfare, 1964. Includes many practical suggestions as well as a summary of research.

(G15) "Language Arts (excluding reading)," *IRCD Bulletin on Curriculum.* New York: Project Beacon, Ferkauf School of Education, Yeshiva University, 1966. Special bulletin on language only; includes tips on where to go for more information.

(G16) Kurath, Hans, *A Word Geography of the Eastern United States.* Ann Arbor, Mich.: University of Michigan Press, 1966. Paperback reprint of the original edition. Kurath identifies the major dialect areas, cites key words which characterize each region, and discusses the historical significance of regional speech patterns; 268 pages, 164 maps.

(G17) *Language Programs for the Disadvantaged:* Report of the NCTE Task Force on Teaching English to the Disadvantaged. Champaign, Ill.: National Council of Teachers of English, 1965. Excellent summary of what is known to date about promising programs and practices, with recommendations and selected annotated bibliography.

(G18) Lee, Dorris M., and R. V. Allen, *Learning to Read Through Experience* (2nd ed.). New York: Appleton-Century-Crofts, 1967. Excellent guide to developing all the skills that go into learning to read.

(G19) Loban, Walter, *Literature and Social Sensitivity.* Champaign, Ill.: National Council of Teachers of English, 1954. This research report provides valuable help for teachers who wish to discuss materials which they read aloud to children in order to achieve insight.

(G20) McDonald, James B., and Robert R. Leeper, eds., *Language and Meaning.* Washington, D.C.: Association of Supervisor and Curriculum Development, National Education Association, 1966. See especially the paper by Walter Loban, "What Language Reveals."

(G21) Maelstrom, Jean, and Armabelle Ashley, *Dialects, U.S.A.* Champaign, Ill.: National Council of Teachers of English, 1967.

(G22) Munkres, Alberta, *Helping Children in Oral Communication.* New York: Teachers College Press, Columbia University, 1959.

(G23) "Providing School Library Services for the Culturally Disadvantaged," *Bulletin,* American Library Association, June, 1964; January, 1965. A reprint of articles that appeared in *ALA Bulletin,* June, 1964–Jan., 1965.

(G24) *The Reading Teacher.* Journal of the International Reading Association.

(G25) Research and Development Center for the Study of Social Organization of Schools, *The Learning Process.* Baltimore: The Johns Hopkins University. A first series of research reports, including James Fennessey's "An Exploratory Study of Non-English Speaking Homes and Academic Performance," May, 1967.

(G26) Sirios, L. M., *Elementary Good American Diction.* Kankakee, Ill.: Imperial Products, 1967. Consists of tape and student manual, Grades 7-12, to aid in correction of speech, with taped drills.

(G27) Stewart, William A., *Non-Standard Speech and the Teaching of English.* Washington, D.C.: Center for Applied Linguistics of the Modern Language Association of America, 1964. See especially the chapter on speech problems of American Negroes.

H. HUMAN RELATIONS EDUCATION: BACKGROUND AND SUGGESTED PRACTICES

(H1) Ashmore, Harry S., *The Negro and the Schools.* Chapel Hill: University of North Carolina Press, 1954. A scholarly report of Negro educational deficiencies up to the time of the 1954 Supreme Court decision in *Brown v. Board of Education.*

(H2) Ashton-Warner, Sylvia, *Teacher*. New York: Bantam Books, 1963. Presents two ideas about teaching the disadvantaged: cultural differences must be recognized and utilized, and the teacher must be committed to the child and teaching.

(H3) Bennis, Warren G., *et al.*, eds., *The Planning of Change: Readings in the Applied Behavioral Sciences*. New York: Holt, Rinehart & Winston, Inc., 1961.

(H4) Corey, Stephen M., *Helping Other People Change*. Columbus, Ohio: Ohio State University, 1963. Why change is difficult but possible.

(H5) Crosby, Muriel, *An Adventure in Human Relations*. Chicago: Follett Publishing Co., 1965. The story of the Wilmington, Delaware, program to improve education through a focus on human relations.

(H6) Crow, Lester D., Walter I. Murray, and Hugh H. Smythe, *Educating the Culturally Disadvantaged Child*. New York: David McKay Co., Inc., 1966.

(H7) Dean, John P., and Alex Rosen, *A Manual of Intergroup Relations*. Chicago: University of Chicago Press, 1955. Although designed for community groups, this volume provides excellent material for the educator.

(H8) Ebersole, Eleanor, *Christian Education for Socially Handicapped Children and Youth* (paperback). Philadelphia: United Church Press, 1964. Includes some sound advice for church-related workers dealing with those in institutions or from handicapped areas.

(H9) Entwistle, Doris R., "Developmental Sociolinguistics: Inner-City Children." Baltimore: The Johns Hopkins University Center for the Study of Social Organization of Schools, May, 1967.

(H10) ———, "Subcultural Differences in Children's Language Development." Baltimore: The Johns Hopkins University Center for the Study of Social Organization of Schools, May, 1967.

(H11) *Experiences in Citizenship for Elementary School Children*. New York: Bureau of Publications, Teachers College, Columbia University, 1953. A series of four pamphlets that describe procedures teachers can use in developing insight into human relations problems as they relate to the concept of citizenship. Useful suggestions for role-playing.

(H12) Fox, Robert, Margaret B. Luski, and R. Schmuck, *Diagnosing Classroom Learning Environments*. Chicago: Science Research Associates, 1966. Aids assessment of climate of learning.

(H13) Gillham, Helen L., *Helping Children Accept Themselves and Others.* New York: Bureau of Publications, Teachers College, Columbia University, 1959. Practical suggestions for classroom human relations practices.

(H14) Grambs, Jean D., *Group Process in Intergroup Education.* New York: National Conference of Christians and Jews, 1953. Utilizing the need to affiliate to promote better education and acceptance.

(H15) ———, *Report of the Leadership Conference on Institutes.* Washington, D.C.: Government Printing Office, #OE-20074, 1964. Suggestions for workshops and institutes in desegregation and human relations.

(H16) ———, "The Self-Concept: Basis for Re-education of Negro Youth," in William Kvaraceus, ed., *Negro Self-Concept.* New York: McGraw-Hill Book Company, 1965. How children, especially Negroes, learn to value or disvalue themselves.

(H17) "Human Relations in Education," *Review of Educational Research,* XXIX (October, 1959), 315-90.

(H18) Hunnicutt, C. W., ed., *Urban Education and Cultural Deprivation.* Syracuse, N.Y.: Syracuse University Press, 1964. A series of original papers read at a conference. Several specific descriptions of school programs and problems.

(H19) *Inventory of Classroom Study Tools for Understanding and Improving Classroom Learning Processes.* Ann Arbor, Mich.: Institute for Social Research, University of Michigan, 1962. (Mimeographed.) Describes a number of tools for teachers to use in assessing the awareness of children in human relations situations.

(H20) Landes, Ruth, *Culture in American Education.* New York: John Wiley & Sons, Inc., 1966. Report of an experimental teacher-training program in areas with minority group students. Anthropological and social work approach makes this an unusual contribution.

(H21) *Learning Together:* A Book on Integrated Education. Chicago: Integrated Education Associates, 343 So. Dearborn St., 1964. A 222-page paperback which reprints the major articles from the first year's issue of *Integrated Education.*

(H22) Maher, Trafford P., S.J., "The Catholic School Curriculum and Inter-group Relations," *Religious Education,* March–April, 1960.

(H23) Mead, Margaret, *The School in American Culture.* Cambridge,

Mass.: Harvard University Press, 1951. This short volume helps define the social function of education.

(H24) Moore, G. Alexander, *Realities of the Urban Classroom: Observations in Elementary Schools* (paperback). New York: Doubleday Anchor Original, 1967. A look inside typical classrooms in the inner city.

(H25) Noar, Gertrude, *The Disadvantaged,* What Research Says to the Teacher Series, No. 33. Washington, D.C.: National Education Association, Department of Classroom Teachers, 1967. A pamphlet which interprets research findings and explains implications for day-to-day classroom practice.

(H26) ———, *The Teacher and Integration.* Washington, D.C.: Student National Education Association, NEA, 1966. Excellent specific advice for teachers in integrated situations.

(H27) "Problems of Urban Education," *Phi Delta Kappan,* XLVIII (March, 1967), 305-73, and whole issue. Excellent series of articles on many issues involving urban education.

(H28) *Review of Educational Research,* "Education for Socially Disadvantaged Children," XXXV, No. 5 (December, 1965). Summarizes current research.

(H29) *The Role of the Educator in Decreasing Racial Tension.* Bloomington, Ind.: Phi Delta Kappa Publications, 1964.

(H30) Stendler, Celia B., and William E. Martin, *Intergroup Education in Kindergarten-Primary Grades.* New York: The Macmillan Company, 1953. Although of older vintage, the insights and recommendations of this volume by two eminent child psychologists are relevant today.

(H31) Taba, Hilda, *et al., With Focus on Human Relations; Elementary Curriculum in Intergroup Relations; Curriculum in Intergroup Relations: Secondary School; Reading Ladders for Human Relations; Sociometry in Group Relations; Literature for Human Understanding; With Perspective on Human Relations; Leadership Training in Intergroup Education: School Culture; Intergroup Education in Public Schools.* Washington, D.C.: American Council on Education, 1947–1955. Many publications in this series have material of considerable current interest.

(H32) Taba, Hilda, and Deborah Elkins, *Teaching Strategies for the Culturally Deprived.* Skokie, Ill.: Rand McNally & Co., 1966. Based on the authors' earlier work, with new insights gained from current experience. Highly recommended.

(H33) "U.S. Appeals Court Judge Skelly Wright's Decision of the District of Columbia's Track System," *Congressional Record—House,* June 21, 1967, pp. H7655-H7697. Washington, D.C.: Government Printing Office, 1967. Contains the complete record of the decision of Judge Wright in *Hobson v. Hansen, et al.* The data presented resulted in the decision that many policies pursued by the D.C. schools resulted in unequal educational opportunity, but that the track or ability grouping procedure itself was a prime factor in low achievement. This decision will be a major event in subsequent interracial school policies.

(H34) "The Urban School," *National Elementary Principal,* XLVI (January, 1967), 6-40, and whole issue. Describes many programs and summarizes research and issues; includes selected bibliography.

(H35) Warner, W. Lloyd, Robert J. Havighurst, and Martin B. Loeb, *Who Shall Be Educated?* New York: Harper & Row, Publishers, 1944.

(H36) Williams, Robin M., *The Reduction of Intergroup Tensions.* New York: Social Science Research Council Bulletin 57, 1947. (Reprinted, 1965.) Basic theorems derived from research to guide practices in integrating different groups.

(H37) Wright, Betty A., *Educating for Diversity.* New York: The John Day Company, Inc., 1965. Covers familiar territory in developing ideas of practical value in the classroom.

(H38) ———, *Teachers Guide,* to accompany *Urban Education Studies.* New York: The John Day Company, Inc., 1966.

I. CITY AND STATE GUIDES AND REPORTS

(I1) Chicago Public Schools, *Curriculum Guide for the Social Studies for Kindergarten, Grades 1, 2.* Chicago: Chicago Public Schools, 1964. Social Studies course adapted to fill the needs of urban life in a multi-cultural society.

(I2) Detroit Board of Education, *The Struggle for Freedom and Rights.* Detroit: Board of Education, 1964.

(I3) District of Columbia Public Schools, *The Negro in American History:* A Curriculum Resource Bulletin for Secondary Schools. Washington, D.C.: District of Columbia Public Schools, 1964.

(I4) Florida State Department of Education, *Education for All.* Tallahassee: The State Department of Education, 1966. Report of a state conference, with excerpts from main addresses, outlining goals for the state in educating disadvantaged children.

(I5) Los Angeles City Schools, Council in Human Relations, *Improving Inter-Group Relations:* A Handbook for Teachers, Publication No. 4. Los Angeles: City Schools, 1965.

(I6) Michigan Department of Public Instruction, *The Treatment of Minority Groups in Textbooks.* Lansing, Mich.: Department of Public Instruction, 1965.

(I7) New York City Board of Education, "Policy Statement on Treatment of Minorities in Textbooks." New York: Board of Education, 1962. (Mimeographed.)

(I8) ———, *Puerto Rican Profiles:* Resource Materials for Teachers, Curriculum Bulletin, 1964–1965, Series No. 5. New York: Board of Education, 1964.

(I9) ———, *The Negro in American History,* Curriculum Bulletin, 1964–1965, Series No. 4. New York: Board of Education, 1964.

(I10) Pennsylvania Department of Public Instruction, *Guidelines for Textbook Selection—the Treatment of Minorities.* Harrisburg, Pa.: Department of Public Instruction, 1964.

(I11) ———, *Our Greatest Challenge:* Human Relations, Curriculum Development Series No. 6. Harrisburg, Pa.: Department of Public Instruction, 1962. A state committee on human relations prepared this guide covering resources and techniques for elementary and secondary grades. A particularly outstanding list of film and filmstrip resources.

(I12) San Francisco Unified School District, Division of Instruction Materials, *The Whole of Us:* Selected Bibliographies on Human Relations. San Francisco: Unified School District, 1963.

(I13) University of the State of New York, *Intergroup Relations:* A Resource Handbook for Elementary School Teachers, Grades 4, 5, and 6. Albany, N.Y.: University of the State of New York, State Education Department, 1964. Material to help the teacher provide children with meaningful information about Negro life in various subject areas throughout the school year.

J. ROLE-PLAYING, GAMES, SIMULATIONS

(J1) Alexander, Jean E., *Let's Get Down to Cases.* New York: Anti-Defamation League of B'nai B'rith, 1957. Provides role-playing guide for use with teenagers.

(J2) Amidon, Edmund, and Elizabeth Hunter, *Improving Teaching: The Analysis of Classroom Verbal Interaction* (paperback). New York: Holt, Rinehart & Winston, Inc., 1966. Provides numerous vignettes of classroom interactions, with analysis for discussion, including many suggestions. Useful for teacher education at all levels.

(J3) Bernard, E. J., "Teach Retail Selling Through Role-Playing," *Journal of Business Education,* XXXIX (November, 1963), 61-62.

(J4) Braddock, Clayton, "Sociodrama Does a Job at Nashville's East High," *Southern Educational Report,* II (January–February, 1967). Southern Education Reporting Service, P.O. Box 6156, Nashville, Tenn., 37212. A brief description of values of role-playing as an aid to youth adjustment.

(J5) Carlson, Elliot, "Games in the Classroom," *Saturday Review,* April 15, 1967. Describes classroom games now available, some in experimental stages, and claims made for them by users of games.

(J6) Carlton, Lessie, and Robert H. Moore, "The Study of the Effects of Self-Directive Dramatization on the Progress in Reading Achievement and Self-Concept of Culturally Disadvantaged Elementary School Children." Cooperative Research Project S-190. Washington, D.C.: Office of Education, 1965. (Unpublished report.) Describes a method of teaching reading through self-directed dramatization.

(J7) Chase, Stuart, *Roads to Agreement: Successful Methods in the Science of Human Relations.* New York: Harper & Row, Publishers, 1951. An early but still valid account of how role-playing can be used with adults.

(J8) Chesler, Mark, and Robert Fox, *Role-Playing Methods in the Classroom.* Chicago: Science Research Associates, 1966. A short but useful guide to classroom role-playing. Excellent brief introduction to role-playing, with an appendix of typical problem situations for various grade levels. Included are some human relations situations with interracial and interreligious problems. Brief annotated bibliography.

(J9) Corsini, Raymond J., Malcolm F. Shaw, and Robert R. Blake, *Role-playing in Business and Industry.* New York: The Free Press, 1961. Introduction to and manual for a technique with potentialities for business and industry. Annotated bibliography.

(J10) Duberman, Martin B., *In White America* (paperback). Boston:

Houghton Mifflin Company, 1964. A documentary play given off-Broadway with great success. Also available as a recording. Based on authentic sources, with related music. Excellent for creating mood and empathy, as well as reporting some often-evaded facts.

(J11) *Experiences in Citizenship for Elementary School Children:* Citizenship Education Project. New York: Teachers College Press, Columbia University, 1953. Four "sociodramatic" teaching situations, one using picture identification, all using unfinished stories and class discussion. Each pamphlet, a manual for the teacher, describes an adaptable procedure, developed and tested in cooperation with intermediate classroom teachers.

(J12) Graham, G., "Sociodrama as a Teaching Technique," *Social Studies,* LI (December, 1960), 257-59.

(J13) Grambs, Jean D., *Discussion Scripts,* A Preliminary Series. Atlanta, Ga.: YWCA, 1958. For information write YWCA, Southern Region, 17 Exchange Place, S.E., Atlanta, Georgia. Open-ended scripts on problems facing teenage girls; designed for role-playing.

(J14) ———, "Dynamics of Psychodrama in the Teaching Situation," *Sociatry,* I, No. 4 (March, 1948), 383-99.

(J15) Jennings, Helen H., "Sociodrama as Educative Process," *Fostering Mental Health in Our Schools,* pp. 280-85. Washington, D.C.: Association for Supervision and Curriculum Development, 1950. An excellent description of role-playing by one of the leaders in the field.

(J16) Klein, A. F., *How to Use Role-Playing Effectively.* New York: Association Press, 1959. One of the best guides for using this technique with adults.

(J17) Lippitt, Rosemary, "The Auxiliary Chair Technique," *Group Psychotherapy,* I, No. 1 (March, 1958), 8-21. A device which frees the leader from needing to use "live" actors for effective role-playing.

(J18) Nichols, Hildred, and Lois Williams, *Learning About Role-Playing for Children and Teachers.* Washington, D.C.: Association for Childhood Education International, 1960.

(J19) Reissman, Frank, and Jean Goldfarb, "Role-Playing and the Poor," *Group Psychotherapy,* XVII, No. 1 (March, 1964), 36-48. Describes why role-playing is useful and gives some situations in which it can be used with the poor.

(J20) Shaftel, Fannie, and George Shaftel, *Building Intelligent Concern for Others Through Role-Playing*. New York: National Conference of Christians and Jews, 1967.

(J21) ———, *Role-Playing the Problem Story*. New York: National Conference of Christians and Jews, 1952.

(J22) ———, *Role-Playing for Social Values*. Englewood Cliffs, N.J.: Prentice-Hall, Inc., 1967. Provides fundamental basis for use of role-playing in education on theoretical and research grounds. Also has original and stimulating unfinished stories in episodes designed (and tested) for classroom use. The best current source. Complete bibliography.

(J23) ———, *The Words and Action Program: Role-Playing Photo Problems for Young Children*. New York: Holt, Rinehart & Winston, Inc., 1967. Twenty pictures accompanied by a teacher's manual to assist the teacher in helping children talk and/or role-play the common problem situation presented. Urban setting; interracial.

(J24) "Simulation Games and Learning Behavior," *American Behavior Scientist,* X, No. 2 (October, 1966), 3-32.

(J25) Smith, M. Brewster, and Irving L. Janis, "Effects of Education and Persuasion on National and International Images," in *International Behavior: A Social Psychological Analysis,* ed. N. C. Kelman. New York: Holt, Rinehart & Winston, Inc., 1965. Describes research findings particularly relevant to role-playing in attitude change.

(J26) Williams, Elizabeth, "Helping Children Feel Like Someone Else —and Talk Like Someone Else," *Elementary English,* XLIV (January, 1967), 57-58. Describes role-playing especially for students with language and behavior problems.

(J27) Zeleny, Leslie D., *How to Use Sociodrama,* The How to Do It Series, No. 29. Washington, D.C.: National Council for the Social Studies, NEA, 1955. A brief useful guide for the classroom teacher. Good bibliography.

K. ELEMENTARY EDUCATION: BACKGROUND

(K1) Ambrose, Edna, and Alice Miel, *Children's Social Learning*. Washington, D.C.: Association for Supervision and Curriculum Development, National Education Association, 1958. Summarizes research to date with implications for classroom practice.

(K2) Amidon, Edmund, and Elizabeth Hunter, *Improving Teaching:*

The Analysis of Classroom Verbal Interaction. New York: Holt, Rinehart & Winston, Inc., 1966. Shows classrooms in action, with guides to improved self-analysis of teaching style.

(K3) Bonney, Merl E., and Richard S. Hampleman, *Personal-Social Evaluation Techniques.* Washington, D.C.: The Center for Applied Research in Education, Inc., 1962. Authors set forth a wide selection of techniques which teachers can use to study better and to guide more effectively the individual students and groups of young people.

(K4) *Chandler Language-Experience Readers.* San Francisco, Calif.: Chandler Publishing Co., 1964. This series emphasizes photographs for reading readiness, in the form of large illustrations plus pictures that are loose in a slip-jacket. Children are of various races and in urban settings.

(K5) Clements, H. Millard, William R. Fielder, and Robert B. Tabachnick, *Social Study: Inquiry in Elementary Classrooms.* Indianapolis: The Bobbs-Merrill Company, Inc., 1965. The approach to teaching social studies described here would help improve intergroup understanding.

(K6) Coles, Robert, *Children of Crisis.* Boston: Little, Brown And Company, 1967. This book includes previously published articles and also new material on the impact of desegregation.

(K7) ———, "Children and Racial Demonstrations," *American Scholar.* Winter, 1964–1965. Do children suffer when there are racial incidents?

(K8) ———, "Some Children the Schools Have Never Served," *Saturday Review,* June 19, 1966, 58-60.

(K9) Crosby, Muriel, ed., *Reading Ladders for Human Relations* (rev. ed.). Washington, D. C.: American Council on Education, 1963. A superior bibliography of books for children, annotated and grouped according to human relations areas.

(K10) Decatur Public Schools, *New Curricular Ideas for Helping Children Discover and Fulfill Their Potentialities.* Decatur, Ill.: Decatur Public Schools, 1965. (Mimeographed.) Particularly valuable because of the reading lists, films, and other aids in the area of individual differences.

(K11) "Education for Socially Disadvantaged Children," *Review of Educational Research,* XXXV, No. 5 (December, 1965), 375-442, and whole issue.

(K12) *The First Big Step: A Handbook for Parents Whose Child Will*

Soon Enter School. Washington, D.C.: National Education Association, 1967. (Spanish edition also available.) Excellent short pamphlet designed for parents to help them prepare their child for school life. Could be used in high school home economics classes and in Spanish language classes, as well as in adult education programs.

(K13) Fox, Robert, Margaret B. Luski, and Richard Schmuck, *Diagnosing Classroom Learning Environments.* Chicago: Science Research Associates, 1966. Provides valuable ideas to help the teacher assess the climate of learning in his own classroom.

(K14) Gillham, Helen L., *Helping Children Accept Themselves and Others.* New York: Bureau of Publications, Teachers College, Columbia University, 1959. Provides practical advice for the classroom teacher.

(K15) Goodman, Mary Ellen, *Race Awareness in Young Children.* Palo Alto, Calif.: Addison-Wesley Press, 1952. Research report regarding how pre-school children feel about racial differences.

(K16) Gottlieb, David, "Teaching and Students: The Views of Negro and White Teachers," *Sociology of Education,* XXXVII (Summer, 1964), 345-53. A study of elementary teachers showing how race differences affect perception.

(K17) Hechinger, Fred, ed., *Pre-School Education Today.* Garden City, N.Y.: Doubleday & Company, Inc., 1966. (Also available in paperback.) Special focus on problems of the urban pre-school child.

(K18) Hentoff, Nat, "The Principal," *The New Yorker,* May 7, 1966. A superb account of a Harlem principal who creates a climate of acceptance and learning, and a description of the way he works with the community as well as with school personnel. Also published as *Our Children Are Dying,* same author, New York, The Viking Press, Inc., 1966.

(K19) Hill, Wilhelmina, and Helen K. Mackintosh, *How Children Learn About Human Rights.* Bulletin 1951, No. 9. Washington, D.C.: U.S. Government Printing Office, 1958.

(K20) Kvarceus, William C., *et al., Negro Self-Concept: Implications for School and Citizenship* (paperback). New York: McGraw-Hill Book Company, 1965. Reviews research and spells out educational implications for the school.

(K21) Loban, Walter D., "What Language Reveals," in *Language and Meaning,* J. D. MacDonald and R. R. Leeper, eds. Washington, D.C.: National Education Association, Association for Supervision and Curriculum Development, 1966, pp. 63-73.

(K22) ———, *Literature and Social Sensitivity*. Champaign, Ill.: National Council of Teachers of English, 1954. Research report on the need to discuss material read aloud to get insight.

(K23) Mackintosh, Helen K., Lillian Gore, and Gertrude M. Lewis, *Administration of Elementary School Programs for Disadvantaged Children*. Disadvantaged Children Series No. 4. Washington, D.C.: U.S. Department of Health, Education, and Welfare, Government Printing Office, 1966.

(K24) ———, *Educating Disadvantaged Children in the Middle Grades*. Disadvantaged Children Series No. 3. Washington, D.C.: U.S. Department of Health, Education, and Welfare, Government Printing Office, 1965.

(K25) ———, *Educating Disadvantaged Children Under Six*. Disadvantaged Children Series No. 1. Washington, D.C.: U.S. Department of Health, Education, and Welfare, Government Printing Office, 1965.

(K26) Martin, Clyde I., *An Elementary Social Studies Program*. Austin, Texas: The University of Texas, 1963. Has some omissions and discrepancies in social studies education.

(K27) Miel, Alice, and Edwin Kiester, *The Short-Changed Children of Suburbia*. New York: Institute of Human Relations Press, The American Jewish Committee, 1967. Report of a research study on the attitudes of children in suburbia regarding racial and economic differences and school programs. A "must" item for suburban educators.

(K28) Moore, G. Alexander, *Realities of the Urban Classroom: Observations in Elementary Schools* (paperback). New York: Doubleday Anchor Original, 1967. Publication of Project *TRUE*. Reports actual observations of many classrooms.

(K29) N.E.A. Journal, *Unfinished Stories—For Use in the Classroom*. Washington, D.C.: National Education Association, 1966. A series, mostly at the elementary level, of short problem situations for class discussion or role-playing.

(K30) Nelson, Leslie W., *Instructional Aids: How to Make and Use Them*. Dubuque, Iowa: Wm. C. Brown Co., Pubs., 1958. Has an especially good chapter on how to make puppets.

(K31) Potter, David, J. Joel Moss, and Herbert F. A. Smith, *Photosituations: A Technique for Teaching*. Particularly useful in teacher education.

(K32) Robinson, Helen, *et al., Such Interesting Things to Do!* Curriculum Foundation Series, Language Arts Program. Glenview, Ill.: Scott, Foresman & Co., 1963. Suggestions regarding centers for work and play activities, prereading and reading activities, spelling and writing activities, and arts and crafts.

(K33) Smith, James A., *et al., Creative Teaching in the Elementary School.* Boston: Allyn & Bacon, Inc., 1967. A series of books focusing on creative teaching both in general and in the various subject fields, with profuse specific examples developed by teachers, particularly Dr. Smith.

(K34) Sproel, Dorothy T., ed., *Tensions Our Children Live With.* Boston: Beacon Press, 1959. Vignettes which describe typical problem situations facing children. To be read aloud to children.

(K35) Stendler, Celia B., and William E. Martin, *Intergroup Education in Kindergarten-Primary Grades.* New York: The Macmillan Company, 1953. Although of older vintage, the insights and recommendations of this volume by two eminent child psychologists are relevant today.

(K36) Stern, Virginia, "The Story Reader as Teacher," *Publications,* No. 24. New York: Bank Street College of Education Publications, 1966. (Reprinted from *Young Children,* October, 1966.) Shows the value of reading aloud to young children, with a list of stories of special interest and appeal.

(K37) Stevenson, Ian, "People Aren't Born Prejudiced," *Parents' Magazine,* February, 1960.

(K38) Taba, Hilda, *et al., Diagnosing Human Relations Needs* (paperback). Washington, D.C.: American Council on Education, 1951. Excellent guide for sociometric testing, open questions, and other procedures for gaining insight into the needs of children.

(K39) Taylor, Stanford E., *Listening.* Washington, D.C.: Department of Classroom Teachers, American Educational Research Association of the National Education Association, 1964. Author has drawn upon educational research materials that might be helpful to classroom teachers.

(K40) Thomas, Murray R., *Social Differences in the Classroom* (paperback). New York: David McKay Co., Inc., 1965. Excellent introduction to sociometrics and the meaning of group cleavage in the classroom, with practical guides for the teacher.

(K41) Thorpe, Louis P., *et al., Studying Social Relationships in the*

Classroom: Sociometric Methods for the Teacher. Chicago: Science Research Associates, 1959. A guide to sociometric techniques.

(K42) Trager, Helen G., and Marian R. Yarrow, *They Learn What They Live: Prejudice in Young Children.* New York: Harper & Row, Publishers, 1952. A classic research report on the impact of instructional materials, and teaching methods on how children learn about themselves and others.

(K43) *Urban Education Studies.* New York: The John Day Company, Inc., 1965. Large picture albums of value in elementary classrooms for the purpose of promoting discussion.

(K43a) Webster, Staten W., ed., *The Disadvantaged Learner.* San Francisco, Calif.: Chandler Publishing Co., 1966.

(K44) Wolf, Anna W. M., and Child Study Association of America, *A Reader for Parents.* New York: W. W. Norton & Company, Inc., 1965. The aim of the book is to persuade psychology-ridden parents that truths of youth have been told by imaginative writers in forms more palatable even than Gesell. Collection of stories, poems, and biographical fragments.

(K45) Young, Margaret B., *How to Bring Up Your Child Without Prejudice.* New York: Public Affairs Pamphlets, 381 Park Ave. South, N.Y. 10016, 1965, Pamphlet #373.

L. RESOURCES FOR ELEMENTARY STUDENTS: NOVELS, BIOGRAPHY, TEXTS

(L1) Agle, Nan Hayden, *Joe Bean.* New York: Seabury Press, 1967. Story of an eleven-year-old Negro boy who likes horses better than anything. He spends a summer with a family on their farm outside Baltimore.

(L2) Baker, Betty, *Walk the World's Rim.* New York: Harper & Row, Publishers, 1966. Of Esteban, the Negro slave who traveled with Cabeza de Vaca in 1527 from Cuba to Mexico and there gave his life—"the wisest, bravest man there ever was."

(L3) Ball, Dorothy Whitney, *Hurricane: The Story of a Friendship.* Indianapolis: The Bobbs-Merrill Company, Inc., 1965. Davey, a white boy, and Luke, a Negro, are best friends; they have problems but their loyalty to one another never wavers.

(L4) Bannon, Laura, *The Other Side of the World.* Boston: Houghton Mifflin Company, 1960. Children of East and West meet through pictures. Grades K-3.

(L5) Treviño, Elizabeth Borton de, *I, Juan de Pareja.* New York: Farrar, Straus & Giroux, Inc. (Bell books), 1965.

(L6) Baum, Betty, *Patricia Crosses Town.* New York: Alfred A. Knopf, Inc., 1965. A Negro girl goes to a white school. Integration here appears to be a great deal simpler than in real life, but a model may help some gain acceptance.

(L7) Beim, Lorraine, and Jerrold Beim, *Two Is a Team.* New York: Harcourt, Brace & World, Inc., 1945. One of the most popular books for young children, in which a Negro child is one of the team.

(L8) Benet, Stephen Vincent, *John Brown's Body.* New York: Holt, Rinehart & Winston, Inc., 1928. Pulitzer Prize winning epic poem of the Civil War. A favorite with youngsters.

(L9) Bishop, Claire Huchet, *Martin de Porres, Hero.* Boston: Houghton Mifflin Company, 1954. Story of a man who from early childhood, a childhood of poverty, prejudice, and mistreatment, devoted his life to ministering to the sick and the poor, the oppressed and the exploited, regardless of race, color, or creed. Grades 7-9.

(L10) Bond, Gladys, *Little Stories.* New York: Anti-Defamation League of B'nai B'rith, 1964.

(L11) Bonsall, Crosby, *The Case of the Cat's Meow.* New York: Harper & Row, Publishers, 1965. An "I Can Read Mystery," illustrated by the author. Only the illustrations indicate that one of the characters is Negro in this tale of boyish escapades.

(L12) ———, *The Case of the Dumb Bells.* New York: Harper & Row, Publishers, 1966. An "I Can Read Mystery," illustrated by the author.

(L13) Bontemps, Arna, *Chariot in the Sky.* New York: Holt, Rinehart & Winston, Inc., n.d. Land of the Free Series. Shows how the Negro spirituals grew out of slavery and how the Fisk Jubilee Singers made those songs known to the world.

(L14) ———, *Sad-Faced Boy.* Boston: Houghton Mifflin Company, 1937. A Negro boy and friends move to Harlem; a particularly poignant scene in a library. Grades 4-6.

(L15) ———, *We Have Tomorrow.* Boston: Houghton Mifflin Company, 1945. Biographical stories about the struggles and successes of twelve Negro Americans who have distinguished themselves in some art or profession.

(L15a) Boston, Lucy M., *The Treasure of Greene Knowe.* New York: Harcourt, Brace and World, Inc., 1958.

(L16) Bourne, Miriam Anne, *Emilio's Summer Day*. New York: Harper & Row, Publishers, 1966. Illustrated by Ben Shecter. Emilio explores ways of having fun in the city on a hot day in August.

(L17) Boyle, Sarah Patton, *For Human Beings Only*. New York: Seabury Press, 1964.

(L18) Brodsky, Mimi, *The House at 12 Rose Street*. New York: Abelard-Schuman Limited, 1966. Illustrated by David Hodges. Three-dimensional characters people this tale of the racial integration of a neighborhood and its impact on the local Boy Scout troop.

(L19) Brown, Jeanette Perkins, *Keikoo's Birthday*. New York: Friendship Press, 1954. Illustrated by Jean Martinez.

(L20) ———, *Ronnie's Wish*. New York: Friendship Press, 1954. Illustrated by Jean Martinez.

(L21) Brown, William A., and Lavinia Dobler, *Great Rulers of the African Past*. Garden City, N.Y.: Doubleday & Company, Inc., 1965.

(L22) Buckley, Peter, and Hortense Jones, *Holt Urban Social Studies Program*. New York: Holt, Rinehart & Winston, Inc., 1965, 1966, 1967. Illustrated with photographs, these readers are for primary-grade children in urban centers. They focus on the real-life problems of such children.

(L23) Buff, Mary, and Conrad Buff, *Hah-Nee*. Boston: Houghton Mifflin Company, 1956. Gives a fine portrayal of thirteenth-century American Indian life. Has added value in its explanation of how prejudice arises.

(L24) Burch, Robert, *Queenie Peavy*. New York: The Viking Press, Inc., 1966. A small-town Georgia girl growing up in the 1930's with a father in jail and a working mother.

(L25) Burchardt, Nellie, *Project Cat*. New York: Franklin Watts, Inc., 1966. Illustrated by Fermin Rocker. Subdued emphasis on conflicts.

(L26) Burden, Shirley, *I Wonder Why . . .* Garden City, N.Y.: Doubleday & Company, Inc., 1963. Also available as a film from the Anti-Defamation League of B'nai B'rith. Open-ended picture story of a Negro girl.

(L27) Carlson, Natalie S., *The Empty Schoolhouse*. New York: Harper & Row, Publishers, 1966. An intensely real story of ten-year-old Lullah and the change in her life and that of her family when school integration comes to their Louisiana town. Depth of characterization balances simple, though moving, treatment of the problem.

(L28) Carson, John F., *Twenty-Third Street Crusaders.* New York: Farrar, Straus & Giroux, Inc. (Ariel), 1958.

(L29) Caudill, Rebecca, *A Certain Small Shepherd.* New York: Holt, Rinehart & Winston, Inc., 1965. Illustrated by William Pene du Bois. A nativity play at school with a Negro cast.

(L30) Chandler, Ruth Forbes, *Ladders to the Sky.* New York: Abelard-Schuman Limited, 1959. Illustrated by Harper Johnson.

(L31) Chessman, Ruth, *Bound for Freedom.* New York: Abelard-Schuman Limited, 1965. Story of two young boys who were bondservants in eighteenth-century America. For ages 9-12.

(L32) Christopher, Matthew W., *Baseball Fly Hawk.* Boston: Little, Brown And Company, 1963. Lack of skill, plus being a Puerto Rican, are the themes disclosed. Grades 3-5.

(L33) Chu, Daniel, and Elliott Skinner, *A Glorious Age in Africa.* Garden City, N.Y.: Doubleday & Company, Inc. (Zenith Books), 1965.

(L34) Cieciorka, Frank, and Bobbi Cieciorka, *Negroes in American History: A Freedom Primer.* Atlanta, Ga.: The Student Voice, Inc., 360 Nelson St., 1965. A publication of the Student Voice, Inc., the communications organ of the Student Nonviolent Coordinating Committee, designed for use in the "freedom schools" in the South and in the Northern ghettos. The book has chapters on Negroes in the Civil War, Reconstruction, the Old West, and the current Freedom Movement. (Understandable to children.)

(L35) Colman, Hila, *Classmates by Request.* New York: William Morrow & Co., Inc., 1964. This story deals with school integration.

(L36) Colorado, Antonio, *First Book of Puerto Rico.* New York: Franklin Watts, 1966. A brief but informative discussion of the geography, history, and way of life of this island commonwealth, well illustrated.

(L37) Coombs, Charles, *Young Infield Rookie.* New York: Lantern Press, 1954. Ken, a white boy whose jaw was broken by a beanball, and Amos, a Negro boy, overcome their fear and join the Little League baseball group.

(L38) Courlander, Harold, and George Herzog, *The Cow-Tail Switch and Other West African Stories.* New York: Holt, Rinehart &

Winston, Inc., 1967. Holt Library. These 17 stories, mostly gathered in the Ashanti country, are told with humor and originality.

(L39) Courlander, Harold, and Wolf Leslau, *The Fire on the Mountain.* New York: Holt, Rinehart & Winston, Inc., 1950. A collection of Ethiopian folk tales.

(L39a) Davis, Christopher, *Sad Adam—Glad Adam.* New York: The Macmillan Company, 1966. It isn't that Adam doesn't want to learn to read, but he has a hard time; dejected because of his own ineptitude and because he hasn't been able to teach a younger child to whistle, Adam is sad. He is glad when he does learn.

(L40) DeAngeli, Marguerite, *Bright April.* Garden City, N.Y.: Doubleday & Company, Inc., 1946. A Philadelphia Negro girl joins an integrated Brownie Scout troop, encounters prejudice, and is later accepted.

(L41) Douglas, Marjory Stoneman, *Freedom River: Florida 1845.* New York: Charles Scribner's Sons, 1953. An Indian and a white boy become friends in the Everglades and share the plans of a Negro boy escaping to seek an education.

(L42) Durham, Philip, *The Adventures of the Negro Cowboys.* New York: Dodd, Mead & Co., 1966. Both Negro and white children will be fascinated to read that there were Negro cowboys. This one plays no favorites; there are scamps as well as heroes.

(L43) Eager, Edward, *The Well-Wishers.* New York: Harcourt, Brace & World, Inc., 1960. Some whimsical kids in the suburbs decide to welcome officially the first Negro family to their neighborhood.

(L44) Edell, Celeste, *A Present for Rosita.* New York: Julian Messner, 1952. Puerto Ricans in Spanish Harlem.

(L45) Estes, Eleanor, *The Hundred Dresses.* New York: Harcourt, Brace & World, Inc., 1944. A classic by now, this story helps children gain insight into social-class differences and the harm of ridicule directed at those who differ.

(L46) Eth, Clifford, and David Eth, *Your Face Is a Picture.* Indianapolis: E. C. Seale & Co., 1963. Evocative pictures of children's faces showing feelings that are pervasive, regardless of culture or ethnic differences.

(L47) Evans, Eva Knox, *All About Us.* New York: Golden Press, 1967. Excellent introduction to anthropology and differences among people; first published in 1947.

(L48) Fall, Thomas, *Canalboat to Freedom.* New York: The Dial Press, Inc., 1966. An immigrant boy and a former slave build a special relationship which brings meaning to their outcast lives. The canal is the Old Delaware and Hudson in upstate New York.

(L49) Farquhar, Margaret C., *Indian Children of America: A Book to Begin On.* New York: Holt, Rinehart & Winston, Inc., 1964. Daily life of Indian children from several tribes is colorfully recorded and vividly illustrated. A book to interest young children in the history of the American Indians.

(L50) Fife, Dale, *Who's in Charge of Lincoln?* New York: Coward-McCann, Inc., 1965. Primary-grade level book about Lincoln, a Negro boy who is left alone in New York and comes to Washington to find Lincoln.

(L51) Flory, Jane, *One Hundred and Eight Bells.* Boston: Houghton Mifflin Company, 1963. A gentle story of a forgetful little girl in present-day Tokyo who longs to become an artist like her father.

(L52) Franck, Frederick, *African Sketch Book.* New York: Holt, Rinehart & Winston, Inc., 1961. Impressions of people and places in Senegal, Cambia, Sierra Leone, Ghana, Nigeria, Kenya, Ethiopia, Sudan, the former Belgian Congo, and Gabon in prose and pen-and-ink drawings.

(L53) Friedman, Frieda, *Carol.* New York: Scholastic Book Services, 1950. For girls aged 8-13. What urban living can be like in a crowded area. Describes socio-economic problems well.

(L54) ———, *The Janitor's Girl.* New York: William Morrow & Co., Inc., 1956. Social-class differences in acceptance. Have *you* been the janitor's girl?

(L55) Friermood, Elizabeth H., *Whispering Willows.* Garden City, N.Y.: Doubleday & Company, Inc., 1964. Indiana in the 1900's—a white girl's friendship with a Negro girl who is her neighbor.

(L56) Fritz, Jean, *Brady.* New York: Coward-McCann, Inc., 1960. Illustrated by Lynd Ward. A sensitive story of a boy reaching maturity through understanding his abolitionist father in a pro-Southern town as he discovers his father is a conductor on the Underground Railroad.

(L57) Gardner, Lillian S., *Sal Fisher at Girl Scout Camp.* New York: Franklin Watts, Inc., 1959. Also *Sal Fisher, Brownie Scout,* 1953; *Sal Fisher's Fly-Up Year,* 1957. This integrated troop shares many friendly adventures through the years, covered by the three books.

(L58) Garst, Shannon, *The Golden Bird.* Boston: Houghton Mifflin Company, 1956. A story of a young Mexican Indian boy who gets lost on his first visit to the market city. The careful joining of the old with the new through the process of education is brought out.

(L59) Gates, Doris, *Little Vic.* New York: The Viking Press, Inc., 1957. Pony, whom the reader late in the book discovers is a Negro, devotedly follows a racehorse, Little Vic, from owner to owner to eventually prove the horse's worth.

(L60) Giles, Lucille H., *Color Me Brown.* Chicago: Johnson Publishing Co., Inc., 1965. Coloring book for children, picturing famous Negroes, with descriptive poems.

(L61) Gilstrap, Robert, and Irene Estabrook, *The Sultan's Fool and Other North African Folk Tales.* New York: Holt, Rinehart & Winston, Inc., 1958. Collection of folk tales from North Africa. Provides insight into Middle Eastern life.

(L62) Gipsour, Frederick, *Trail-Driving Rooster.* New York: Harper & Row, Publishers, 1955. Sam Goodall, a Negro trail cook, keeps a runty rooster as his mascot; the cowboys form a united front when they encounter prejudice along the trail.

(L63) *Golden Legacy.* Hollis, N.Y.: Fitzgerald Publishing Co. (Distributed by Diversified Distributors, Inc., 1444 Rhode Island Ave., N.W., Washington, D.C.) A comic book format used to tell the dramatic story of Negro heroes and heroines, with the purpose of planting pride and self-esteem in Negro young people, and respect in others. Each issue treats a different person.

(L64) Graham, Lorenz B., *North Town.* New York: Thomas Y. Crowell Company, 1966. A sequel to *South Town.* The convincing story of any boy in a strange community. For Dave Williams, the problems of newness are complicated by his color.

(L65) ———, *South Town.* New York: Thomas Y. Crowell Company, 1958. Focus on interracial situations at home and school in the South today. Authentic. (Paperback edition, New York: Signet Key, New American Library, Inc., 1965.)

(L66) Graham, Shirley, and George D. Lipscombs, *Dr. George Washington Carver, Scientist.* New York: Julian Messner, 1944.

(L67) Grifalconi, Ann, *City Rhythms.* Indianapolis: The Bobbs-Merrill Company, Inc., 1965. Colorful and meaningful pictures and text depicting a Negro boy discovering the sounds and rhythm of his city.

(L68) Guy, Anne Welsh, *William.* New York: The Dial Press, Inc., 1961. Sam, the hooky-playing Negro boy, may make some cringe, but this book deals sensitively with the embarrassment that Negroes sometimes feel toward their less aspiring brothers, when William realizes he, too, had erroneously assumed that Sam had taken some missing money.

(L69) Haas, Dorothy, *Everybody Has a Name.* Racine, Wisc.: Whitman Publishing Co., 1966. Maria is helped to learn English by her classmates and a friendly grocer. Provides insight into the dilemma of a bilingual child. The classroom is integrated.

(L70) ———, *A Special Place for Jonny.* Racine, Wisc.: Whitman Publishing Co., 1966. A short and delightful story of a little boy who is afraid to go to school the first day, but is helped to find his place. Jonny is a Negro and his school is integrated.

(L71) Hagler, Margaret, *Larry and the Freedom Man.* New York: Lothrop, Lee & Shepard Co., Inc., 1959. Some of the harshness of slave life is depicted in this book. The hero, Larry, learns much from his new friend, a Negro boy whom he helps to escape.

(L72) Hamilton, Virginia, *Zeely.* New York: The Macmillan Company, 1967. One reviewer states, "By the time you find out the Geeder and her younger brother Toeboy are Negro, it doesn't really matter anyway, although that fact is a part of their composite personalities."

(L73) Harnden, Ruth, *Summer's Turning.* Boston: Houghton Mifflin Company, 1966. A boy who has to stay home in summer to improve his reading learns many lessons. Good for those who have a reading problem, too.

(L74) Haugaard, E. C., *A Slave's Tale.* Boston: Houghton Mifflin Company, 1965. A slave girl in Viking times.

(L75) Hayes, Florence, *Alaskan Hunter.* Boston: Houghton Mifflin Company, 1959. The story of two Eskimo boys who leave their igloo village for a year and visit a more modern Eskimo community. Shows the adjustment of the Eskimo to the invasion of another culture.

(L76) ———, *Skid.* Boston: Houghton Mifflin Company, 1948. A Negro boy moves from Georgia to Connecticut, with many problems to be solved. Grades 4-6.

(L77) *Hi Neighbor.* New York: Hastings House, 1960–1965. A series of publications, of which eight are now available, showing the work of UNICEF. Four countries are described in each issue. Designed for elementary school children.

(L78) Hill, Elisabeth Starr, *Evan's Corner.* New York: Holt, Rinehart & Winston, Inc., 1966. Evan, a little Negro boy in Harlem, lives with seven other members of his family in a two-room flat. Text and illustrations present an engaging child, and the living conditions are shown matter-of-factly.

(L79) Hoffine, Lyla, *Jennie's Mandan Bowl.* New York: David McKay Co., Inc., 1960. A girl with Indian background learns that cultural differences can be advantageous. Grades 4-5.

(L80) Hogan, Bernice, *A Small Green Tree and a Square Brick Church.* Nashville: Abingdon Press, 1967. An inquisitive little boy wonders what really makes a church. When he compares various churches he discovers that it's the people who make the church. Ages 4-7.

(L81) Hunnicutt, C. W., Jean D. Grambs, *et al., Singer Social Studies Series.* New York: The L. W. Singer Company, Inc. (a division of Random House), 1966 revisions. Grades 3-6.

(L82) Hunt, Mabel Leigh, *Ladycake Farm.* Philadelphia: J. B. Lippincott Co., 1952. Moving to the country, a Negro family learns to farm and to face realistically problems of race.

(L83) Huus, Helen, *Children's Books to Enrich the Social Studies.* Bulletin No. 32. Washington, D.C.: National Council for the Social Studies, National Education Association, 1961.

(L84) Jay, Edith Sherman, *A Book About Me.* Chicago: Science Research Associates, Inc., 1952. Teacher's manual available. Picture book to develop reading readiness for primary-grade children.

(L85) Johnson, Christine A., *Muhammad's Children.* Chicago: University of Islam, 1963. A first-grade reader illustrated with photographs, written by and for the Black Muslims.

(L86) Johnson, E. Harper, *Kenny.* New York: Holt, Rinehart & Winston, Inc., 1957. The story of an American Negro boy's experiences in Africa, where his father is working for an oil company. Grades 6-9.

(L87) Johnston, Johanna, *That's Right, Edie.* New York: G. P. Putnam's Sons, 1966. A story to read aloud to the pre-school child. Edie happily scribbles in the conviction that she is really writing. When she starts school, she is too impatient to follow the teacher's instructions at first, but she finally learns to write.

(L88) Justus, May, *New Boy in School.* New York: Hastings House, 1963. A story of a Tennessee boy's experience going to a newly integrated school.

(L89) ———, *A New Home for Billy*. New York: Hastings House, 1966. Billy moves from a dreary apartment to a house in a white area, and Billy's father impresses the neighbors by fixing the place up.

(L90) Keats, Ezra Jack, *God Is in the Mountain*. New York: Holt, Rinehart & Winston, Inc., 1966. A collection of "voices and intimations" from different religions and philosophies all over the world in witness to the universality of religions.

(L91) ———, *John Henry*. New York: Pantheon Books, Inc., 1965. The illustrations bring to life the story of the Negro folk hero who "died with a hammer in his hand."

(L92) ———, *The Snowy Day*. New York: The Viking Press, Inc., 1962. (A Caldecott Award.) A very colorful depiction of a Negro boy's fun in the snow.

(L93) ———, *Whistle for Willie*. New York: The Viking Press, Inc., 1964. A little Negro boy named Peter wants to learn to whistle. Simple words and beautiful illustrations.

(L94) ——— and Pat Cherr, *My Dog Is Lost*. New York: Thomas Y. Crowell Company, 1960. A Puerto Rican boy loses his Spanish-speaking dog and finds many friends in his search for Pepito.

(L95) Kidwell, Carl, *The Angry Earth*. New York: The Viking Press, Inc., 1964. Story of slavery in the Indian economy.

(L96) King, Edmund, *Other Sandals*. New York: Holt, Rinehart & Winston, Inc., 1966. An energetic girl from a kibbutz and her introverted cousin from Haifa switch sandals, and lives, for a summer. Daily life in today's Israel, and the insights the girls gain about themselves and each other, provide meaningful reading. For older elementary children.

(L97) Konkel, Janet, *Schoolroom Bunny*. Chicago: Children's Press, 1965.

(L98) Korshak, Jack, *The Strange Story of Oliver Jones*. Chicago: Mid-American Publishing Co., 1966.

(L99) Kurflink, Anne E., *Somebody's Brother*. New York: The American Jewish Committee. 3rd printing, 1964. 8 pp. A very short open-ended story that asks, "Why did they call me nigger?"

(L100) LaFarge, Oliver, *The Mother Ditch*. Boston: Houghton Mifflin Company, 1954. Description of the irrigation ditch that supplies the town of Cerito, New Mexico, with the water necessary for farming in that semi-arid area.

(L101) Lenski, Lois, *Cotton in My Sack*. New York: Dell Publishing Co.,

1949. Joanda picks cotton to fill her long sack, knowing both the fun of spending the money she's earned and the anguish of being without it. A revealing account of life among the sharecroppers, tenants, and owners of the Cotton Belt.

(L102) ———, *High-Rise Secret*. Philadelphia: J. B. Lippincott Co., 1966. The anatomy of a housing project, with all the tensions of a heterogeneous community.

(L103) ———, *Judy's Journey*. Philadelphia: J. B. Lippincott Co., 1947. (Dell paperback reprint, 1966.) Migratory farm girl, aged 11-12.

(L104) ———, *Mama Hattie's Girl*. Philadelphia: J. B. Lippincott Co., 1953.

(L105) Levy, Mimi Cooper, *Corrie and the Yankee*. New York: The Viking Press, Inc., 1959. In an exciting reversal of plot, a Negro girl helps a runaway Yankee soldier escape to the Union lines. Enlightening, perceptive.

(L106) Lewis, Richard, *Miracles*. New York: Simon and Schuster, Inc., 1967. A collection of children's poems from around the world.

(L107) ———, *A Summer Adventure*. New York: Harper & Row, Publishers, 1962. Ross, who happens to be a Negro, grows up when he regretfully frees his beloved tamed animals after he experiences the loss of some of his freedom during a hospital stay. Wonderful nature book.

(L108) Lewiton, Mina, *Candita's Choice*. New York: Harper & Row, Publishers, 1966. A sympathetic picture of the adjustment problems of Puerto Ricans in New York.

(L109) Lexan, Joan M., *I Should Have Stayed in Bed!* New York: Harper & Row, Publishers, 1965. The friendship of a Negro and a white boy in an integrated school. Grades 1-2.

(L110) ———, *José's Christmas Secret*. New York: The Dial Press, Inc., 1963.

(L111) Lipkind, Will, *Four-leaf Clover*. New York: Harcourt, Brace & World, Inc., 1959. Several boys, one of whom is Negro, romp and play through summer days.

(L112) *Little Plays for Little People*. New York: Parents' Magazine Press, 1965. Selected from *Humpty Dumpty's Magazine*. Illustrates some simple ways to provide dramatic sketches for children. Some should help in furthering understanding of motives and feelings.

(L113) McCellan, Jack, *et al.*, *Citizens All*. Boston: Houghton Mifflin Company, 1967.

(L114) McGovern, Ann, and R. M. Powers, *Runaway Slave, The Story of Harriet Tubman*. New York: Scholastic Book Services, 1965. Lower elementary grades.

(L115) McLemore, Dale, and M. Vere DeVault, *Sociology*. Austin, Texas: Steck Publishing Co., 1962. A brief, simplified presentation of the basic concepts in sociology. Could be used at fourth-grade level and above.

(L116) Mann, Peggy, *The Street of the Flower Boxes*. New York: Coward-McCann, Inc., 1966. Dramatizes poverty and cultural differences in an overcrowded and run-down block in New York.

(L117) Manrique, Manuel, *Island in Harlem*. New York: The John Day Company, Inc., 1966. A young Negro Puerto Rican boy, Antonio, is transported from the poverty of a small cane-cutting village in Puerto Rico to the steaming jungle of New York's Spanish Harlem.

(L118) Marshall, Catherine, *Julie's Heritage*. New York: Longmans, Green & Co., Inc., 1957. An interracial friendship cools temporarily as the girls adjust to new friends at the start of junior high school.

(L119) Martin, Patricia Miles, *The Little Brown Hen*. New York: Thomas Y. Crowell Company, 1960. This realistically drawn picture book will appeal to intermediate-grade children. In an appealing rural setting, two problems are solved: a birthday present for Willie's mother and the disappearance of Willie's pet hen.

(L120) ———, *Trina's Boxcar*. Nashville: Abingdon Press, 1967. Set in a Wyoming town early in the twentieth century, the story presents a little Mexican girl's dilemma in learning the English language. A glossary of Spanish words and phrases is included. Ages 8-10.

(L121) "MATCH Boxes," *American Education*, III, No. 1 (December, 1966–January, 1967), 9. Describes a unique program to bring reality into the elementary classroom, developed by the Boston Children's Museum.

(L122) Mawhinney, Paul E., "The Shoes," *NEA Journal*, Vol. 55 (October, 1966), 12-14. An excellent example of the kind of story that, if cut at the appropriate climax, can be used for stimulating creative endings. The theme is poverty.

(L123) Means, Florence Crannell, *Carver's George*. Boston: Houghton

Mifflin Company, 1952. A sensitive, well-written biography of the famous Negro scientist.

(L124) ———, *It Takes All Kinds.* Boston: Houghton Mifflin Company, 1964. How poverty affects different people differently, a lesson learned when a family moves to a new town.

(L125) ———, *Knock at the Door, Emmy.* Boston: Houghton Mifflin Company, 1956. Pa had little use for folks or schooling, but Emmy's deep desire was for an education. Grades 7-9.

(L126) ———, *The Moved-Outers.* Boston: Houghton Mifflin Company, 1945. Story of a California family of Japanese origin, in the months following Pearl Harbor. Grades 7-9.

(L127) ———, *Shuttered Windows.* Boston: Houghton Mifflin Company, 1938. A Negro girl moves South. The description of college life may seem dated to more sophisticated students today. Grades 7-9.

(L128) ———, *Us Maltbys.* Boston: Houghton Mifflin Company, 1966. A prejudiced town learns to accept six foster children. Grades 7-12.

(L129) Miller, Dorothy Shirley, *Showboat 'Round the Bend.* New York: Dodd, Mead & Co., 1957. Girls' story of an interracial friendship in Iowa at the turn of the century.

(L130) Miller, Floyd, *Ahdoolo!: The Biography of Matthew A. Henson.* New York: E. P. Dutton & Co., Inc., 1963. The story of the Negro who went to the North Pole.

(L131) *Negro Americans.* Washington, D.C.: National Education Association, 1964. (*Time* magazine reprint.) Picture story of accomplishments of Negro Americans.

(L132) *Negro Folk Tales.* Washington, D.C.: Associated Publishers, 1966. Supplementary reader for primary grades.

(L133) Ness, Evaline, *Exactly Alike.* New York: Charles Scribner's Sons, 1964. Because her four freckle-faced brothers look exactly alike, Elizabeth has an extraordinary problem. A "wise friend" gives her advice and she solves the mystery with an exciting discovery.

(L134) ———, *Josefina February.* New York: Charles Scribner's Sons, 1963. A little Haitian girl faces a difficult choice when she finds a black baby burro. How Josefina finds out what was most important to her makes a warm and appealing story.

(L135) Newell, Hope, *A Cap for Mary Ellis.* New York: Harper & Row,

Publishers, 1963. How it feels to be one of the first Negroes admitted to a school for nurses.

(L136) Ormsby, Virginia H., *What's Wrong with Julio?* Philadelphia: J. B. Lippincott Co., 1965. A Spanish-speaking first grader won't talk until the other children talk to him in Spanish.

(L137) Palmer, Candida, *Snow Storm Before Christmas.* Philadelphia: J. B. Lippincott Co., 1965. Two Negro boys doing their last-minute shopping are caught in a snowstorm in downtown Philadelphia.

(L138) Panetta, George, *Sea Beach Express.* New York: Harper & Row, Publishers, 1966. Slum life here is treated for its exotic and comic value, as the Italian father is persuaded to take his family and a Puerto Rican child to Coney Island.

(L139) Raftery, Gerald, *Twenty-Dollar Horse.* New York: Julian Messner, Inc., 1955. With some melodramatic coincidences, a Negro and a white boy solve the problems of how to stop housing discrimination in a small town and take care of their commonly owned flea-bitten horse.

(L140) Randall, Blossom E., *Fun for Chris.* Chicago: Albert Whitman and Co., 1956. Jimmy decides he can have more fun playing with Chris and a new friend who is Negro than he can have by taunting them.

(L141) Riley, Louise, *A Spell at Scoggin's Crossing.* New York: Abelard-Schuman Limited, 1960. Gus, a Negro magician, takes the children on unbelievable adventures in Canada, *Train for Tiger Lily* (next reference) is its sequel.

(L142) ———, *Train for Tiger Lily.* New York: The Viking Press, Inc., 1954.

(L143) Robinson, Jackie, and Alfred Duckett, *Breakthrough to the Big League, The Story of Jackie Robinson.* New York: Harper & Row, Publishers, 1965.

(L144) Rockwell, Anne, *Gypsy Girl's Best Shoes.* New York: Parents' Magazine Press, 1966. A gypsy girl finds a place to dance in the city. Integrated pictures.

(L145) Rodman, Bella, *Lions in the Way.* New York: Follett Publishing Company, 1966. A realistic treatment of the problems faced by the eight Negro youngsters chosen to integrate the local high school.

(L146) *Round About the City.* New York: Child Study Association of America, 1966. Stories about city children of various backgrounds. Also published by Thomas Y. Crowell Company.

(L147) Rydberg, Ernie, *The Dark of the Cave*. New York: David McKay Co., Inc., 1965. The friendship of two nine-year-old boys, one of whom is blind; the other, Negro.

(L148) Sayres, William, *Do Good*. New York: Holt, Rinehart & Winston, Inc., 1966. Into a sleepy, contented South American village comes Peter, American to his toenails, on a mission to help. The villagers barely look up. Peter's transformation into a friend of the villagers makes a crisp comedy. For older elementary children.

(L149) Schechter, Betty, *The Peaceable Revolution*. Boston: Houghton Mifflin Company, 1963. The story of nonviolent resistance from Thoreau to Gandhi to today's freedom riders. Ages 12 up.

(L150) Scott, Ann Herbert, *Big Cowboy Western*. New York: Lothrop, Lee & Shepard Co., 1965. The story of a small Negro boy who gets a cowboy suit and guns for his birthday and shoots at everything.

(L151) Selsam, Millicent E., *Tony's Birds*. New York: Harper & Row, Publishers, 1961. (A Science I Can Read Book.) Tony discovers the joy of bird-watching under his father's encouraging guidance. Only the illustrations reveal that Tony and his father are Negroes.

(L152) Shotwell, Louisa, *Roosevelt Grady*. New York: Grosset & Dunlap, Inc., 1964. Very effective with middle-grade children, this book tells the story of a Negro migrant family and provides a real feeling of the poverty and struggle of the migrant worker.

(L153) Showers, Paul, *Your Skin and Mine*. New York: Thomas Y. Crowell Company, 1965. Explains skin color differences in simple scientific terms.

(L154) Simpson, Dorothy, *A Matter of Pride*. Philadelphia: J. B. Lippincott Co., 1959. Social-class differences; how it feels to be too poor to have shoes. Grades 5-6.

(L155) *Skyline Series*. New York: McGraw-Hill Book Company, 1967–68.

(L156) Smucker, Barbara C., *Wigwam in the City*. New York: E. P. Dutton & Co., Inc., 1967. Woodcuts by Bil Miret. Describes the prejudices encountered by an Indian family when it moves to Chicago from the reservation.

(L157) Sproel, Dorothy T., ed., *Tensions Our Children Live With*. Boston: Beacon Press, 1959. Very short stories to be read aloud and discussed with children.

(L158) Steele, William O., *Wayah of the Real People*. New York: Holt,

Rinehart & Winston, Inc., 1964. A young Cherokee Indian boy's indoctrination into the white man's ways. Wayah's story can help students in their own personal development.

(L159) Sterling, Dorothy, *Robert Smalls, Captain of the Planter*. Garden City, N.Y.: Doubleday & Company, Inc., 1958. A story of the true adventure of a Negro who captured a ship under Confederate guns and guided it to safe waters.

(L160) Sterne, Emma G., *I Have a Dream*. New York: Alfred A. Knopf, Inc., 1965. For upper elementary children. The story of ten Negro leaders who have helped toward the realization of full citizenship for the Negro. Excellent bibliography of related books.

(L161) Stolz, Mary, *The Bully of Barkham Street*. New York: Harper & Row, Publishers, 1963. The adjustment problems of a boy who is too fat. Grades 4-6.

(L162) *Stories You Can Finish*, by the Editors of *Read Magazine*. Columbus, Ohio: American Educational Publications, 1966. Intriguing and entertaining story beginnings which suggest a pattern not only for the inventive teacher, but for the inventive student.

(L163) Swift, Hildegard H., *The Railroad to Freedom*. New York: Harcourt, Brace & World, Inc., 1960 (reprinted). A novel written about the life of Harriet Tubman.

(L164) Talbot, Charlene Joy, *Tomás Takes Charge*. New York: Lothrop, Lee & Shepard Co., 1967. Alone in New York, Tomás and his smaller sister hide in an abandoned warehouse in order to escape the welfare authorities, whose supervision they fear.

(L165) Thompson, E. B., *Africa, Past and Present*. Boston: Houghton Mifflin Company, 1966. A historical as well as contemporary survey of Africa, for grades 5 and 6.

(L166) Udry, Janice May, *What Mary Jo Shared*. Chicago: Albert Whitman and Co., 1966. A Negro child overcoming shyness in school.

(L167) *Urban Social Studies Series*. New York: Holt, Rinehart & Winston, Inc., 1966. *William, Andy, and Ramon* and other titles.

(L168) Vogel, Ilse-Margaret, *Hello Henry*. New York: Parents' Magazine Press, 1965. Two Henrys, one white and one black, plus a friendly bear, put a supermarket in an uproar. Younger elementary age.

(L169) Weik, Mary Hays, *The Jazz Man*. New York: Atheneum Publishers,

Inc., 1967. A small, crippled Negro boy, sensitive about his handicap, stays away from school and lives an isolated life, his unhappiness intensified by his parents' neglect.

(L170) Weir, Ester, *Easy Does It*. New York: Vanguard Press, Inc., 1963. When a Negro family moves into a white neighborhood, a friendship blossoms in spite of the pressures on both families involved.

(L171) Weiss, Edna, *Truly Elizabeth*. Boston: Houghton Mifflin Company, 1957. A girl from Vermont who moves to New York City longs for her former home until some new city friends help her enjoy the diversity of big city life.

(L172) Weiss, Harvey, *Horse in No Hurry*. New York: G. P. Putnam's Sons, 1961. The assorted comic adventures of two boys (one Negro), a girl, a dog, and a lazy horse.

(L173) ———, *Paul's Horse Herman*. New York: G. P. Putnam's Sons, 1958. More low-keyed adventures of Paul, John Thomas, and Jessica.

(L174) Wells, Helen, *Escape by Night*. New York: Holt, Rinehart & Winston, Inc., 1953. This story of the Underground Railroad, like most such stories, is told from the point of view of a white family acting as conductors; but another conductor is a Negro. Further, a runaway slave, a young boy, returns to the South and later frees his little sister.

(L175) Williamson, Stan, *The No-Bark Dog*. Chicago: Follett Publishing Company, 1962. A simple picture book with a nonracial plot. A group of children of several races share Tim's concern over a nonbarking dog.

(L176) Woody, Regina, *Almena's Dogs*. New York: Ariel Books, 1954. Some may not approve of the fact that Almena's mother is a maid and her father a stablehand, but the book is primarily concerned with a girl's love for a dog and her struggle to keep it in a house with a no-animals lease.

(L177) Yates, Elizabeth, *Amos Fortune, Free Man*. New York: E. P. Dutton & Co., Inc., 1950. The story of an African chief, sold as a youth, who eventually buys his freedom and that of others in early New Hampshire. Grades 7-9.

(L178) Yoshika, Uchida, *The Promised Year*. New York: Harcourt, Brace & World, Inc., 1966. A Japanese girl comes to live with her grandparents in America. Excellent for showing cultural differences as young people feel them.

(L179) Ziner, Feenie, and Paul Galdone, *Counting Carnival.* New York: Coward-McCann, Inc., 1962. A counting book for the youngest readers, showing a blend of city children from many backgrounds.

M. SECONDARY EDUCATION: BACKGROUND

(M1) Association for Supervision and Curriculum Development, *The Junior High School We Saw.* Washington, D.C.: ASCD, 1964. A report of observations of eighth graders in schools across the country.

(M2) Coles, Robert, "Serpents and Doves: Non-Violent Youth in the South," in *Youth: Change and Challenge,* ed. Erik H. Erikson. New York: Basic Books, Inc., Publishers, 1963.

(M3) Davis, James A., *Great Aspirations.* Chicago: Aldine Publishing Co., 1966. An analysis of the career choices and postgraduate plans of 33,982 college seniors in 135 colleges and universities.

(M4) Douvan, Elizabeth, and Joseph Adelson, *The Adolescent Experience.* New York: John Wiley & Sons, Inc., 1966. Superior analysis and summary of current research on the adolescent today.

(M5) Fader, David N., and M. H. Shawitz, *Hooked on Books* (paperback). New York: Berkeley Medallion Books, 1966. Shows how reluctant readers can be "hooked." Provides an example of a three-week study guide for "West Side Story."

(M6) Faust, Irvin, "Operation Buena Vista," *Paris Review,* XXXV (1966), p. 87. A short story whose focus is the "other" side of such programs as Higher Horizons and others that shift the achievement goals of Negro children. Language probably too strong for public school students, but useful for teachers.

(M7) Friedenberg, Edgar, *Coming of Age in America: Growth and Acquiescence.* New York: Random House, Inc., 1965. Describes youth and school culture, with a particularly interesting research report on prejudice.

(M8) Ginzberg, Eli, *et al., The Optimistic Tradition and American Youth.* New York: Columbia University Press, 1962. The effects of an idealized "open" society on those who can or cannot get "out."

(M9) Golburgh, Stephen, ed., *The Experience of Adolescence.* Cambridge, Mass.: Schenkman Publishing Co., 1965. Verbatim autobiographies of young college students illustrating the impact of early experience and education on their development.

(M10) Hechinger, Grace, and Fred M. Hechinger, *Teen-Age Tyranny* (paperback). Greenwich, Conn.: Fawcett Publications, 1964. A portrait of today's adolescent society, including some of the upper socio-economic group.

(M11) Heller, Celia Stopnicka, *Mexican-American Youth: Forgotten Youth at the Crossroads*. New York: Random House, Inc., 1966. Concerns our third largest minority.

(M12) Horvath, John J., *Motivating Underprivileged Negro Students in Northton: A Study in Frustration*. Case Series in Educational Administration, No. 30. Columbus, Ohio: University Council for Educational Administration, Ohio State University, n.d. A brief "case" describing efforts of a teacher to provide assistance to Negro students while being thwarted by community barriers.

(M13) John, Charles S., *Growing Up in the Black Belt*. Washington, D.C.: American Council on Education, 1941. A classic report on how it feels for an adolescent to be "between" two cultures —North and South.

(M14) Kaufman, Bel, *Up the Down Staircase*. Englewood Cliffs, N.J.: Prentice-Hall, Inc., 1965. Secondary school life in a slum school. Witty, and accurate in many ways.

(M15) Kerlin, Robert T., *Negro Poets and Their Poems*. Washington, D.C.: Associated Publishers, 1936. Especially designed for use by English teachers.

(M16) Lacey, Paul, "Teaching Billy Budd," *Idea Exchange,* I, No. 5 (October, 1966), 12-17. Published by Educational Projects Inc., 1125-15th St., N.W., Washington, D.C.

(M17) McAllister, Jane Ellen, "Mississippi: Outpourings Over a Decade," *Journal of Secondary Education,* XL, No. 5 (May, 1965), 219-26. Comments on the racial issue by Negro high school children in Mississippi.

(M18) MacIver, R. M., ed., *Dilemmas of Youth Today*. New York: Harper & Row, Publishers, 1961. Thoughtful essays by leading social scientists.

(M19) Mayerson, Charlotte L., ed., *Two Blocks Apart* (paperback). New York: Holt, Rinehart & Winston, Inc., 1965. Compares the lives of Juan Gonzales and Peter Quinn in New York City. Shows how life styles are affected by environment.

(M20) Myers, R. E., and E. Paul Torrance, *Invitations to Speaking and Writing Creatively*. Boston: Ginn and Company, 1967. Workbook and teachers' guide, grades 6-9. Full of ideas which will help both the able and the less able students to be intrigued into writing.

(M21) Patterson, Franklin K., *Man and Politics.* The Social Studies Curriculum Program, Occasional Paper No. 4. Cambridge, Mass.: Educational Services Incorporated, 1965. Outlines a possible new approach to social studies in the junior high school.

(M22) Pelto, Pertti J., *The Study of Anthropology* (paperback). Columbus, Ohio: Charles E. Merrill Books, Inc., 1965. Especially valuable are the teaching suggestions by Raymond Muessig and Vincent Rogers, which comprise the last third of the volume.

(M23) *Posters of the Past.* Harriman, Tenn.: Dept. LAT. American history illustrated by old, rare pictures, playbills, ads, handbills, political posters, woodcuts, etc., in exact reproduction.

(M24) Prince, Richard, "Values, Grades, Achievement, and Career Choice of High-School Students," *The Elementary School Journal,* LX, No. 7 (April, 1960). 376-84. Published by University of Chicago Press.

(M25) Raths, Louis E., *et al., Values and Teaching.* Columbus, Ohio: Charles E. Merrill Books, Inc., 1966. Puts theory into practice. If values are important, here is a guide for developing teaching situations.

(M26) Schwitzgebel, Ralph, *Streetcorner Research: An Experimental Approach to the Juvenile Delinquent.* Cambridge, Mass.: Harvard University Press, 1965. A brief, intriguing account of an exploratory effort to reduce a proclivity to commit crime by paying thirty delinquents to provide their own therapy: they recorded their lives and problems in front of a sympathetic listener who was a social worker, a student in education, a psychologist, or a Jesuit priest.

(M27) Shaw, Otto L., *Youth in Crisis.* New York: Hart Publishing Co., 1966. A current report on what youth faces today.

(M28) Sherif, Muzafer, and Carolyn Muzafer, eds., *Problems of Youth: Transition to Adulthood in a Changing World.* Chicago: Aldine Publishing Co., 1965. Chapters by outstanding observers of youth in today's world.

(M29) Smith, Ernest A., *American Youth Culture.* New York: The Free Press, 1962. A view of the subcultures of American youth and the groups they form.

(M30) Smith, K. U., "The Testing Hoax," *New South,* XXI, No. 3 (Summer, 1966). Published by Southern Regional Council, Inc., Atlanta, Georgia. How tests discriminate against lower-class and Negro children.

(M31) Stewart, Charles W., *Adolescent Religion: A Developmental Study of the Religion of Youth.* Nashville: Abingdon Press, 1967. The beliefs, behavior, and adjustment to the world around them of young people.

(M32) Terkel, Studs, *Division Street: America.* New York: Pantheon Books, Inc., 1967. First-person life stories of some seventy people who constitute a cross-section of the nation. Through the voices of Appalachian migrants, policemen, taxi drivers, the poor and rich, we can see what has happened to our country during our lifetime.

(M33) Thomas, Nida, *Intergroup Relations, A Resource Handbook for 12th Grade Social Studies.* Albany: University of the State of New York, The State Department of Education, 1965.

(M34) Thomas, Piri, *Down These Mean Streets.* New York: Alfred A. Knopf, Inc., 1967. A Puerto Rican youth describes his growing up in New York Spanish Harlem; rough and sad, providing an inside view of the causes of urban unrest.

(M34a) Trout, Lawana, "Teaching the Protest Movement," *Holt's Dialog,* Fall, 1967, pp. 5-13. Published three times a year by Holt, Rinehart and Winston, Inc., New York.

(M35) Watson, Goodwin, *No Room at the Bottom.* Washington, D.C.: National Education Association, 1963. The effect of automation on the less skilled and less educated youth.

(M36) Weeks, Christopher, *The Job Corps: Dollars and Dropouts.* Boston: Little, Brown & Company, 1967.

(M37) Welsch, Erwin K., *The Negro in the United States: A Research Guide.* Bloomington: Indiana University Press, 1965. A good running commentary on some current material for studying the Negro.

N. BOOKS FOR YOUTH: FICTION AND NONFICTION

(N1) Allee, Marjorie H., *The Great Tradition.* Boston: Houghton Mifflin Company, 1937. A Negro girl at the University of Chicago; for grades 8-9.

(N2) Alpenfels, Ethel J., *Sense and Nonsense About Race.* New York: Friendship Press, 1965. The author answers questions asked about race by young people in high schools, colleges, churches, and clubs. The questions are answered from an anthropologist's point of view.

(N3) American Foundation for Political Education, *The Case of the Lively Ghost.* Chicago: American Foundation for Political Education, 1957. An open-ended presentation of a Southern school board and desegregation.

(N4) Angell, Pauline K., *To the Top of the World,* pp. 13-15. Skokie, Ill.: Rand McNally & Co., 1964. An account of Peary and a Negro companion, Matthew Henson, analyzing their different backgrounds which led to their common feat of being first men to the North Pole.

(N5) Archer, Elsie, *Let's Face It:* A guide to good grooming for Negro girls. Philadelphia: J. B. Lippincott Co., 1959.

(N6) *At Work in Industry Today.* Schenectady, N.Y.: Equal Opportunities Progress, No. ERC-41, Relations Publications Bldg. 2, General Electric Co., 1 River Road, 1965. Five case reports of Negroes at work, their hopes and plans for future progress.

(N7) Baldwin, James, *Blues for Mister Charlie.* New York: Dell Publishing Co., Inc., 1964. Explosive and painful play by one of America's most outspoken and articulate Negro writers. Requires a sturdy ego to read and absorb.

(N8) ———, *The Fire Next Time.* New York: The Dial Press, Inc., 1963. (Also available in Dell paperback.) Essays by outstanding contemporary Negro writers.

(N9) ———, *Going to Meet the Man.* New York: The Dial Press, Inc., 1965. First collection of Baldwin's stories.

(N10) ———, *Nobody Knows My Name.* New York: The Dial Press, Inc., 1961. (Also available in Dell paperback.)

(N11) ———, *Notes of a Native Son.* New York: The Dial Press, Inc., 1961. See especially the chapter on "The Harlem Ghetto" regarding Negroes' use of Jews as scapegoats.

(N12) Ball, John, *In the Heat of the Night.* New York: Harper & Row, Publishers, 1965. This novel tells of a Negro police officer from Pasadena, California, who is arrested in a Southern town for a murder he did not commit. He proves his innocence and takes charge of the police investigation.

(N13) Barrett, William, *Lilies of the Field.* Garden City, N.Y.: Doubleday & Company, Inc., 1962.

(N14) Belfrage, Sally, *Freedom Summer.* New York: The Viking Press,

Inc., 1965. Report of a summer spent working with Negroes in the freedom schools of Louisiana.

(N15) Bennett, Lerone, Jr., *What Manner of Man*. New York: Simon and Schuster, Inc., Essandess Special Edition, #10078.

(N16) Black, Algernon, *First Book of Ethics*. New York: Franklin Watts, Inc., 1966. A simply stated presentation of the major ethical problems facing mankind. The ideas are deep and complex, but the presentation can be understood by an average junior or senior high student. Recommended for in-depth class discussion. Beautifully printed; short.

(N17) Blanton, Catherine, *Hold Fast to Your Dreams*. New York: Julian Messner, 1955.

(N18) Bonham, Frank, *Durango Street*. New York: E. P. Dutton & Co., Inc., 1965. A novel for teenagers about the real problems of growing up in a black ghetto.

(N19) Bontemps, Arna, *Lonesome Boy*. Boston: Houghton Mifflin Company, 1955.

(N20) Bowen, David, *The Struggle Within,* pp. 13-15. New York: W. W. Norton & Company, Inc., 1965. An analysis of the Negro's problems in America, in all its dimensions, from early days to the demonstrations in Selma, Alabama.

(N21) Boyd, Andrew, and Van Rensburg, *An Atlas of African Affairs*. New York: Frederick A. Praeger, Inc., 1963.

(N22) Bragdon, Elsbeth, *There Is a Tide*. New York: The Viking Press, Inc., 1964. A boy, expelled from all the schools he has attended, is helped by being with his father.

(N23) Braithwaite, E. R., *To Sir, With Love*. Englewood Cliffs, N.J.: Prentice-Hall, Inc., 1960. A poignant autobiographical reprint of a British West Indies Negro trying to teach in the slum schools of London. (See movie of the same title.)

(N24) Brick, John, *Yankees on the Run*. New York: Duell, Sloan and Pearce, 1961.

(N25) Browin, Frances William, *Looking for Orlando*. New York: Criterion Books, Inc., 1961.

(N26) Brown, Jimmy, and Myron Cope, *Off My Chest*. Garden City, N.Y.: Doubleday & Company, Inc., 1964. A Negro athlete tells his story.

(N27) Brown, Sterling A., Arthur P. David, and Ulysses Lees, eds., *The Negro Caravan: Writings by American Negroes*. New York: Citadel Press, 1945. Out of print.

(N28) Burke, Carl F., *God Is for Real, Man.* New York: Association Press, 1966. Paraphrases of religious concepts and stories, by young people from the inner city; provides an interesting insight into the imaginative language of the "nonverbal."

(N29) Butcher, Margaret Just, *The Negro in American Culture.* New York: Alfred A. Knopf, Inc., 1956. A good review of the contributions of Negroes to American culture.

(N30) Buttero, Dorothy Gilman, *Heartbreak Street.* Philadelphia: Macrae Smith Co., 1958.

(N31) ———, *Masquerade.* Philadelphia: Macrae Smith Co., 1961.

(N32) Cain, Alfred E., *The Negro Heritage Reader for Young People.* New York: Educational Heritage, Inc., 733 Yonkers Ave., N.Y. 10704.

(N33) Carson, John F., *The Coach Nobody Liked.* New York: Dell Publishing Co., Inc. Ace basketball player Sid Hawkes is torn between his admiration for the new coach, who wants the team to play clean basketball, and his allegiance to his father, who wants the team to win at any price.

(N34) ———, *Floorburns.* New York: Dell Publishing Co., Inc. More than a good basketball story, this novel shows how varsity star Les Beach, a belligerent young athlete from the "wrong" side of the tracks, overcomes his short temper and rejoins the team.

(N35) Case, Elinor, *Mission 313.* Philadelphia: Westminster Press, 1963.

(N36) Chapman, Elwood N., *Your Attitude Is Changing.* Chicago: Science Research Associates, 1966. (Teachers' Guide available.) Oriented toward young adults facing first job responsibilities; numerous case studies and simplified approach useful for a wide audience.

(N37) ———, *Your Attitude Is Showing.* Chicago: Science Research Associates, 1964. (Teachers' Guide available.) Human relations materials written for the young adult; useful adaptation of standard psychological insights into human motivation.

(N38) Charyn, Jerome, *The Man Who Grew Younger and Other Stories.* New York: Harper & Row, Publishers, 1967. Short stories about growing up in primarily Jewish lower- and lower-middle-class areas of New York City twenty or more years ago.

(N39) Clarke, John Henrik, *American Negro Short Stories.* New York: Hill and Wang, 1966.

(N40) Coleman, Pauline, *The Different One.* New York: Dodd, Mead & Co., 1955.

(N41) Cousy, Robert, *Last Loud Roar.* Englewood Cliffs, N.J.: Prentice-Hall, Inc., 1964.

(N42) Cox, Alva I., *The Delinquent, The Hipster, The Square and the Sandpile Series.* St. Louis, Mo.: The Bethany Press, 1962. Three plays and the scripts for three TV plays on problems confronting youth today from a religious point of view.

(N43) Cuban, Larry, *The Negro in America.* Chicago: Scott, Foresman & Co., 1964. Written particularly for high school youth by a master teacher.

(N44) Daly, Maureen, *Seventeenth Summer.* New York: Dodd, Mead & Co., 1948.

(N45) David, Basil, *The African Past.* Boston: Atlantic Monthly Press Book, Little, Brown And Company, 1964. All the books listed here by this author are good historical background.

(N46) ———, *A Guide to African History.* Garden City, N.Y.: Doubleday & Company, Inc., 1965.

(N47) ———, *The Lost Cities of Africa.* Boston: Atlantic Monthly Press Book, Little, Brown And Company, 1959.

(N48) ———, *The Years of the African Slave Trade.* Boston: Little, Brown And Company, 1961.

(N49) Davis, John P., *The American Negro Reference Book.* Englewood Cliffs, N.J.: Prentice-Hall, Inc., 1966. Basic source material.

(N50) Davis, Ossie, *Purlie Victorious.* New York: Samuel French, Inc., 1961. A parody in comic strip terms of white notions of Negro life. Also made into a film, *Gone Are the Days.*

(N51) David, Russell F., *Anything for a Friend.* New York: Crown Publishers, Inc., 1963.

(N52) DeCarva, Roy, and Langston Hughes, *The Sweet Flypaper of Life.* New York: Simon and Schuster, Inc., 1955. Sardonic and delightful reflections on Negro life in the slums, with poignant photographs.

(N53) De Leeuw, Adele, *The Barred Road.* New York: The Macmillan Company, 1954.

(N54) Dobler, Lavinia, and E. A. Toppin, *Pioneers and Patriots.* New York: Doubleday & Company, Inc., 1965.

(N55) Douglas, Gilbert, *Hard to Tackle.* New York: Dell Publishing Co., Inc., 1967. Clint faces a crisis of conscience when Jeff Washington, a Negro teammate, is subjected to the violent prejudice of their conservative community.

(N56) Duberman, Martin B., *In White America*. Boston: Houghton Mifflin Company, 1964. A documentary play given off-Broadway with great success. Also available as a recording. Based on authentic sources with related music. Excellent for creating mood and empathy as well as reporting some often-evaded facts.

(N57) DuBois, W. E. B., *The Souls of Black Folk*. New York: Fawcett, Crest-Premier R354. A passionate unfolding of the Negro's bitter struggle for his human rights.

(N58) Ellison, Ralph, *Invisible Man*. New York: Signet Books, 1953. National Book Award winning novel of the inner feeling of the Negro who is not "seen."

(N59) Eyerly, Jeannette, *Dropout*. Philadelphia: J. B. Lippincott Co., 1963.

(N60) Fair, Ronald L., *Hog Butcher*. New York: Harcourt, Brace & World, Inc., 1967. A tale of contemporary Chicago and its Negro ghetto. Much of the story revolves around ten-year-old Wilford Robinson and his best friend, Earl.

(N61) Forbes, Kathryn, *Mamma's Bank Account*. New York: Harcourt, Brace & World, Inc., 1949. Adjustment of an immigrant family to big city poverty.

(N62) Freedman, Benedict, and Nancy Freedman, *Mrs. Mike*. New York: Coward-McCann, Inc., 1947.

(N63) Frick, Constance H., *Tourney Team*. New York: Harcourt, Brace & World, Inc., 1954.

(N64) Gault, William C., *Backfield Challenge*. New York: E. P. Dutton & Co., Inc., 1967. Racial problems intrude on the football championship. Both youth and adult attitudes are explored in realistic fashion.

(N65) Gilbreth, Frank, Jr., and Ernestine G. Carey, *Cheaper by the Dozen*. New York: Thomas Y. Crowell Company, 1963. Life in a large family.

(N66) Golden, Harry, *Harry Golden on . . . .* New York: Anti-Defamation League of B'nai B'rith, 1966.

(N67) ———, *Mr. Kennedy and the Negroes*. New York: Fawcett, 1964.

(N68) Goldschmidt, Walter, *The Ways of Mankind*. Boston: Beacon Press, 1953. Both the scripts and the recordings are exceptionally valuable introductions to anthropology. The teacher would also want to read *Exploring the Ways of Mankind,* edited by the same author, which provides the content background for the series.

(N69) Goss, Jocelyn Pretlow, *The Thomases Live Here*. New York: Holt, Rinehart & Winston, Inc., 1964. For adult literacy program, fourth-grade reading level. Story of life in the country, featuring Negro characters.

(N70) Green, Ely, *Ely, An Autobiography*. New York: Seabury Press, 1967. The poignant story of a despised and bewildered mulatto's efforts to live by the Golden Rule in turn-of-the-century Tennessee.

(N71) Green, Paul, *Five Plays of the South* (paperback). New York: Hill & Wang, 1963. Five powerful dramas which show the heart of the South in an earlier period.

(N72) Gregory, Dick, *From the Back of the Bus*. New York: E. P. Dutton & Co., Inc., A wry picture and joke book by the Negro comedian in which, by using humor, he shows some of the inner hurt and pain of the Negro situation today. Also, *What's Happening?* (1965).

(N73) ———, *Nigger*. New York: E. P. Dutton & Co., Inc., 1964. The autobiography of a well-known Negro comedian and activist in the civil rights movement. His story highlights the problems faced by today's Negro and provides insight into the person who engages in civil rights action.

(N74) Griffin, John H., *Black Like Me*. Boston: Houghton Mifflin Company, 1961. A white man disguises himself as a Negro and reports what it feels like and what things happen to him when he travels through the South in this role.

(N75) Grubb, Davis, *Shadow of My Brother*. New York: Holt, Rinehart & Winston, Inc., 1966. This novel, through flashbacks, traces the evolution of a Louisiana lynching.

(N76) Guy, Rosa, *Bird at My Window*. Philadelphia: J. B. Lippincott Co., 1965. Story of a Harlemite, Wade Williams, who has been exposed to the harshest aspects of ghetto life and then learns, quite by accident, that he is a brilliant child. Chance offers him a way out of the ghetto.

(N77) Haas, Ben, *The Troubled Summer*. Indianapolis: The Bobbs-Merrill Company, Inc., 1967. A Negro boy gains insight into race relations through activities in the civil rights movement in a small Southern town.

(N78) Handlin, Oscar, ed., *Children of the Uprooted*. New York: George

Braziller, Inc., 1966. Excerpts from comments by youth of immigrant parents.

(N79) ———, *Immigration as a Factor in American History*. Englewood Cliffs, N.J.: Prentice-Hall, Inc., 1959.

(N80) ———, *The Uprooted*. New York: Grosset & Dunlap, Inc., 1951. A perceptive historian reports on the emotional impact of immigration.

(N81) Hansberry, Lorraine, *A Raisin in the Sun*. New York: New American Library, 1958. The prize-winning play upon which the movie was based. Would be of great interest to the adolescent. Very well written and authentic. Very popular with teenagers.

(N82) Haugaard, Erik Christian, *A Slave's Tale*. Boston: Houghton Mifflin Company, 1965. A realistic tale of Norse life filled with war, death, love, adventure. Provides an understanding of what slavery and freedom mean to the human spirit.

(N83) Hentoff, Nat, *Call the Keeper*. New York: The Viking Press, Inc., 1966. A highly accurate report, disguised as a short novel, on the relations between eight New York Negroes and whites, among them a white jazz guitarist, an evil Negro detective, a dangerous Negro writer, and an icy white intellectual.

(N84) ———, *Jazz Country*. New York: Harper & Row, Publishers, 1966. A vivid picture of the driving quest for expression in a sixteen-year-old jazz trumpeter who tries to win acceptance by Negro musicians.

(N85) Heuman, William, *Backcourt Man*. New York: Dodd, Mead & Co., 1960. Sports novel.

(N86) Hill, Herbert, ed., *Soon, One Morning*. New York: Alfred A. Knopf, Inc., 1965.

(N87) Hirshberg, Al, *Bill Russell of the Boston Celtics*. New York: Julian Messner, 1963.

(N88) Hoffman, Edwin D., *Pathways to Freedom*. Boston: Houghton Mifflin Company, 1964. How ordinary people achieved freedom. Grades 7-12.

(N89) Holt, Len, *An Act of Conscience*. Boston: Beacon Press, 1965. Civil rights motivation explained.

(N90) Horne, Lena, and Richard Schickel, *Lena*. Garden City, N.Y.: Doubleday & Company, Inc., 1965. The autobiography of a successful Negro entertainer.

(N91) Hughes, Langston, ed., *The Best Short Stories by Negro Writers*. Boston: Little, Brown And Company, 1967. A collection of interest, not only because the authors are Negro, but because of the wide range of topics, from 1899 to the present.

(N92) ———, ed., *The Book of Negro Humor*. New York: Dodd, Mead & Co., 1966.

(N93) ———, ed., *New Negro Poets, U.S.A.* Bloomington: Indiana University Press, 1964.

(N94) ———, *Selected Poems*. New York: Alfred A. Knopf, Inc., 1959.

(N95) ———, *Simple's Uncle Sam*. New York: Hill and Wang, 1965. The "Simple" stories of Langston Hughes have been published widely since the mid-1940's, primarily for a Negro audience. With wit, irony, and flashing insight, these anecdotes reveal more about the Negro view of American society than many weighty tomes. See also *Simple Speaks His Mind*.

(N96) ——— and Arna Bontemps, eds., *The Book of Negro Folklore*. New York: Dodd, Mead & Co., 1959.

(N97) ———, *The Poetry of the Negro*. Garden City, N.Y.: Doubleday & Company, Inc., 1949.

(N98) Huie, William Bradford, *Three Lives for Mississippi*. New York: Trident Press, 1965. A report on the three young men, two white and one Negro, who were killed while working for civil rights.

(N99) Jacobs, Emma Atkins, *A Chance to Belong*. New York: Dell Publishing Co., Inc. Member of an immigrant family from Czechoslovakia, Jan wants to shape a new life in America but finds he must abide by his father's old-country attitudes and forsake important school activities and a "chance to belong," because of heavy family responsibilities.

(N100) Johnson, J. W., *The Autobiography of an Ex-Colored Man*. New York: Hill and Wang, 1960. A fictional account of racial insight, rejection, and re-identification.

(N101) ———, ed., *The Book of American Negro Poetry*. New York: Harcourt, Brace & World, Inc., 1931.

(N102) Jones, LeRoi, *The System of Dante's Hell*. New York: Grove Press, Inc., 1965. Childhood and youth remembered are given a new form in this novel structured according to the themes of Dante's *Inferno*. This is an account of childhood and adolescence in the Negro slums of Newark, the experiences of a Northern Negro in a small Southern town where the Air Force has sent him, and glimpses of life in New York.

(N103) ———, *Blues People*. New York: William Morrow & Co., Inc., 1963.

(N104) Kaufman, Bel, *Up the Down Staircase*. Englewood Cliffs, N.J.: Prentice-Hall, Inc., 1964. Ironic, funny, and biting "diary" of a teacher's life in a slum secondary school. High school students will find this easy and enjoyable reading, especially if they then try to see how their school and teachers are similar to or different from those described. (Also see movie by the same name.)

(N105) Kelley, William M., *A Different Drummer*. Garden City, N.Y.: Doubleday & Company, Inc., 1962. A strange and moving novel of the South when a mysterious migration of Negroes occurs.

(N106) Killens, John Oliver, *'Sippi*. New York: Trident Press, Simon and Schuster, Inc., 1967. When the Supreme Court issued its 1954 school desegregation decisions, many Negroes felt Jim Crow had been buried. Yet today there is more bitterness among Negroes, and more ill-feeling toward Negroes, than ever before. There has been a radical change in both the strategy and the attitudes of the Negro. This novel explores the background that has motivated these changes.

(N107) King, Martin Luther, *A Martin Luther King Treasury*. New York: Educational Heritage, Inc., 1964. Selected writings.

(N108) Kingsnoth, G. W., *Africa South of the Sahara*. New York: Cambridge University Press, 1963.

(N109) Kraft, Ivor, *When Teenagers Take Care of Children*. Philadelphia: Macrae Smith Co., 1965. A popular guide for the baby-sitter (and prospective mother).

(N110) Kuntsler, William M., *Deep in My Heart*. New York: William Morrow & Co., Inc., 1966. A New York lawyer tells what motivated him to engage in civil rights activities and describes his experiences since then.

(N111) Leavitt, Hart Day, and David A. Sohn, *Stop, Look and Write!* New York: Bantam Books, 1964. A method of teaching effective writing developed over ten years of experiment with high school students. Through the use of more than 100 remarkable photographs, students learn creative observation and are taught how to transfer ideas to paper. A great variety of examples and practical exercises are offered and the book covers many kinds of writing, from descriptive phrases to paragraphs to complete stories.

(N112) Lee, Harper, *To Kill a Mockingbird.* Philadelphia: J. B. Lippincott Co., 1960. Perceptive novel about small-town Southern life and prejudice in the 1930's. Also an excellent feature film.

(N113) Lewiton, Mina, *A Cup of Courage.* New York: Dell Publishing Co., Inc. Against the background of a crisis in her family's newspaper business, seventeen-year-old Brook Falter must face the stern reality of her journalist father's alcoholism and her own confusion over her affection for Philip Cantrell.

(N114) Loomis, Amy Goodhue, ed., *The Brass Ring.* St. Louis, Mo.: The Bethany Press, 1965. Four plays on themes of significance to youths of today. "Look Ma, I'm Different," a short open-ended playlet, is one of those included.

(N115) Lynd, Staughton, *Nonviolence in America: A Documentary History.* Indianapolis: The Bobbs-Merrill Company, Inc., 1966. An interesting and illuminating source book, from the Quakers to Martin Luther King.

(N116) McCard, William, *Mississippi: The Long Hot Summer.* New York: W. W. Norton & Company, Inc., 1965. A report of efforts of college students and others to reach Mississippi Negroes and of the tragedies that accompanied these efforts.

(N117) McCarthy, Agnes, and Lawrence Reddick, *Worth Fighting For.* Garden City, N.Y.: Doubleday & Company, Inc., 1965. For the slower reader, a review of the struggle for Negro rights.

(N118) McKone, Jim, *Lone Star Fullback.* New York: Vanguard Press, Inc., 1966. High school football interwoven with story of racial hurts.

(N119) Madison, Arnold, *Danger Beats The Drum.* New York: Holt, Rinehart & Winston, Inc., 1966. A mystery story focusing on interracial friendships and the evils of narcotics.

(N120) Malcolm X, with the assistance of Alex Haley, *The Autobiography of Malcolm X.* New York: Grove Press, Inc., 1965. Writes the late author in this first and last book: "When I am dead—I say it because from the things I know, I do not expect to live long enough to read this book in its finished form—I want you to just watch and see if I'm not right in what I say: that the white man, in his press, is going to identify me with 'hate.' "

(N121) Marshall, Catherine, *Julie's Heritage.* New York: David McKay Co., Inc., 1957. A girl finds out the difficulties of being judged as a person first, though people see her first as a Negro. Grades 7-9.

(N122) Mayerson, Charlotte L., *Two Blocks Apart.* New York: Holt, Rinehart & Winston, Inc., 1965. (Also in paperback.) Compares the lives of Juan Gonzales and Peter Quinn in New York City. Authentic and dramatic contrasts.

(N123) Means, Florence Crannell, *Reach for a Star.* Boston: Houghton Mifflin Company, 1957.

(N124) ———, *Tolliver.* Boston: Houghton Mifflin Company, 1963.

(N125) Merrill, Robert, and Sandford Body, *Once More from the Beginning.* New York: The Macmillan Company, 1966. Autobiography of a Jewish boy.

(N126) Miles, Richard, *Angel Loves Nobody.* Englewood Cliffs, N.J.: Prentice-Hall, Inc., 1967. A novel set in the inner-city slum. For adults and older adolescents.

(N127) Miller, Arthur, *The Crucible.* New York: The Viking Press, Inc., 1953. (Paperback, Compass, 1964.) Set during the grim days of the Salem witch trials, this Pulitzer Prize winning play brings into focus an issue that still weighs heavily on the progress of American civilization—the problem of guilt by association.

(N128) Miller, Warren, *The Cool World.* New York: Fawcett, 1959. Popular with young people, describes the slum world that a Harlem teenager sees. The story of a Negro boy's relentless quest for identity and his final rejection of violence as a means of escape from the ghetto.

(N129) Morris, Phyllis Davis, *Life with the Lucketts.* New York: Holt, Rinehart & Winston, Inc., 1965. For adult literacy programs; fourth-grade reading level. Story about problems of urban life, featuring Negro characters.

(N130) *Negro Thought in America, 1880–1915.* Ann Arbor: University of Michigan Press, 1966. Detailed study of Negro thought and culture from Reconstruction to World War I, the period when the seeds of the civil rights movement were sown.

(N131) Neville, Emily C., *Berries Goodman.* New York: Harper & Row, Publishers, 1966. In a typical New York suburb, real estate covenants and racial prejudices effectively stop a growing friendship between Bertrand Goodman and Sidney Fine.

(N132) Newell, Hope, *A Cap for Mary Ellis.* New York: Harper & Row, Publishers, 1953.

(N133) O'Dell, Scott, *The King's Fifth.* Boston: Houghton Mifflin Company, 1966. Esteban (a Negro) hunts for the Golden cities in Southwestern United States in the sixteenth century as a member of the Spanish exploring party. Grades 7-12.

(N134) Oliver, Paul, *Conversation with the Blues.* New York: Horizon Press, 1965. The author journeyed through the South and North to the Great Lakes with a tape recorder and camera. This book reveals inner meaning of the blues as private thought and feeling as well as music.

(N135) Olson, Gene, *The Tall One.* New York: Dodd, Mead & Co., 1956.

(N136) Page, J. D., *An Introduction to the History of West Africa.* New York: Cambridge University Press, 1962.

(N136a) Parks, Gordon, *The Learning Tree.* New York: Harper & Row, Publishers, Inc., 1963.

(N137) Person, Thomas, *New Dreams for Old.* New York: Longmans, Green & Co., Inc., 1957.

(N138) Philips, Jane, *Mojo Hand.* New York: Trident Press, Simon and Schuster, Inc., 1966. This is a brutal but tender and often amusing first novel about a young Negro girl who renounces her hitherto meaningless life and leaves her upper-middle-class protective home. She travels across the country in pursuit of an old blues singer and a man essentially of her own heritage and people. Though the novel ends on a tragic note, the young heroine does come to feel that she is part of her ethnic background and a true member of her group.

(N139) *Plays for Living.* New York: New York Mental Health Materials Center, various dates. A series of short plays, using few or no props, which focus on typical human relations problems. Suitable for high school classes and groups. Guaranteed to provoke student interest and discussion. See authors Nora Stirling and Rose Leivan Schiller.

(N140) Powdermaker, Hortense, *Stranger and Friend: The Way of an Anthropologist.* New York: W. W. Norton & Company, Inc., 1966. (Also in paperback.) The "Way"—to walk with men nor lose the common touch and the honest insight; to be measured humanist and compassionate scientist; to balance unavoidable dislike and ready admiration—here, in utterly simple talk, is a wise and fine anthropologist among Melanesians, white and colored Mississippians, Hollywood cinema-makers, Northern Rhodesians.

(N141) Riessman, Frank, and John Dawkins, *Play It Cool.* Chicago: Follett Publishing Co., 1967.

(N142) Rodman, Bella, *Lions in the Way.* Chicago: Follett Publishing Co., 1966. Novel for young people about desegregation.

(N143) Rogers, Joel A., *Africa's Gift to America.* 1961. Distributed by Sportshelf & Soccer, Box 634, New Rochelle, New York. 10802.

(N144) Rollins, Bryant, *Danger Song.* Garden City, N.Y.: Doubleday & Company, Inc., 1967. A young Negro attempts to reach beyond Boston's Negro ghetto. His efforts bring him briefly, poignantly, in touch with the gentler-seeming white world and danger. He discovers he can only be what he is—an American Negro.

(N145) Russell, William, *Go Up for Glory.* New York: Coward-McCann, Inc., 1966. Autobiography of a Negro professional basketball player.

(N146) Schechter, Betty, *The Dreyfus Affair: A National Scandal.* Boston: Houghton Mifflin Company, 1966. A detailed, provocative presentation of the historic Dreyfus case, the years of trials and retrials following the conviction of an innocent Jewish army officer in France in 1894.

(N147) ———, *The Peaceable Revolution.* Boston: Houghton Mifflin Company, 1965. The history of nonviolence from Gandhi to Dr. King.

(N148) Schiller, Rose Leivan, *Fences.* New York: New York Mental Health Materials Center, 1966. A play about how prejudice feels. For adolescent or adult groups.

(N149) *Scope.* Englewood Cliffs, N.J.: Scholastic Book Service. A publication designed especially for the nonmotivated, slow-reading high school student in urban areas. Highly recommended.

(N150) Sherburne, Zoa, *Too Bad About the Haines Girl.* New York: William Morrow & Co., Inc., 1967. A sensitively and authentically written novel about a girl and her family when she becomes pregnant.

(N151) Sklar, George, *And People All Around.* New York: Random House, Inc., 1967. Dramatized account of the recent murder of the three civil rights workers in Mississippi. A dramatic and disturbing enactment.

(N152) Smiley, Marjorie B., Richard Corbin, and John J. Marcatante, *Stories in Song and Verse.* New York: The Macmillan Company, 1966. (Gateway English, A Literature and Language Arts Program.)

(N153) Smiley, Marjorie B., Florence B. Freedman, Jacqueline Tilles, and John J. Marcatante, *Coping.* New York: The Macmillan Company, 1966. (Gateway English, A Literature and Language Arts Program.)

(N154) Smiley, Marjorie B., Florence B. Freedman, and John J. Marcatante, *A Family Is a Way of Feeling*. New York: The Macmillan Company, 1966. (Gateway English, A Literature and Language Arts Program.)

(N155) Smiley, Marjorie B., Domenica Paterno, and Betsy Kaufman, *Who Am I?* New York: The Macmillan Company, 1966. (Gateway English, A Literature and Language Arts Program.)

(N156) Speare, Elizabeth George, *The Witch of Blackbird Pond*. Boston: Houghton Mifflin Company, 1958. Historical narrative of a girl whose rebellion against bigotry and her Puritan surroundings culminates in a witch hunt and trial. Winner of Newbery Medal.

(N157) Speevack, Yetta, *The Spider Plant*. New York: Atheneum Publishers, Inc., 1966. A quiet, simply told story of a young Puerto Rican girl in New York City; lonely and homesick, she made her love for growing things the key to new friendships and acceptance in a strange land.

(N158) Speicher, John, *Looking for Baby Paradise*. New York: Harcourt, Brace & World, Inc., 1967. A novel about the defeat of a well intentioned, well-educated social worker who tries to bring "good" into the lives of youngsters in Washington Heights, New York City. Funny and tragic.

(N159) Sprague, Gretchen, *A Question of Harmony*. New York: Dodd, Mead & Co., 1966. A high school story in which the playing of Jeanne, a cellist, Dave, a pianist, and Mel, an outstanding Negro athlete and violinist, leads to a "sit-in" hotel situation.

(N160) Sterling, Dorothy, *Mary Jane*. Garden City, N.Y.: Doubleday & Company, Inc., 1959. A novel for junior high students about how a Negro girl faces and survives school integration.

(N161) Sterling, Phillip, ed., *Laughing on the Outside, The Intelligent White Reader's Guide to Negro Tales and Humor*. New York: Grosset & Dunlap, Inc., 1965.

(N162) Sterne, Emma Gelders, *I Have a Dream*. New York: Alfred A. Knopf, Inc., 1965. The book brings into focus ten Negro leaders, ending with the March to Washington.

(N163) Stevenson, Janet, *Sisters and Brothers*. New York: Crown Publishers, Inc., 1966. A fictionalized account of an historical event —the confrontation in a family of the white and the Negro relatives in post-Civil War years.

(N164) Stirling, Nora, *The Case of the Missing Handshake*. New York:

Human Relations Aids, 1952. Published for the American Theatre Wing Community Plays. A play about inconsistent behavior in pre-teenagers.

(N165) ———, *The Daily Special.* New York: Human Relations Aids. Published for the American Theatre Wing Community Plays, 1958. A play about the rights of every member of the family.

(N166) ———, *Fences.* New York: Human Relations Aids, 1967. Published for the American Theatre Wing Community Plays. The impact of prejudice is conveyed through role-playing technique.

(N167) ———, *Random Target.* New York: Human Relations Aids, 1954. Published for the American Theatre Wing Community Plays. The author's theme centers around the situation: "If a child has strong feelings of anger, it is better for him to have a chance to express these against the person or situation that caused them, than to lash out blindly at some inappropriate or random target."

(N168) ———, *The Room Upstairs.* New York: Human Relations Aids, 1953. Published for the American Theatre Wing Community Plays. Theme of old people and young people living together.

(N169) ———, *Tomorrow Is a Day.* New York: Human Relations Aids, 1955. Published for the American Theatre Wing Community Plays. A play about building self-confidence in children.

(N170) ———, *What Did I Do?* New York: Human Relations Aids, 1953. Published for the American Theatre Wing Community Plays. A play about how parents feel about their influence on children.

(N171) Stolz, Mary (Slattery), *The Noonday Friends.* New York: Harper & Row, Publishers, 1966. A story of Franny, whose humiliations because of poverty are offset by her relationships with a small, beloved brother and a large Puerto Rican family. Set in New York City.

(N172) ———, *Who Wants Music on Monday?* New York: Harper & Row, Publishers, 1963.

(N173) *Stories You Can Finish,* by the Editors of *Read Magazine.* Columbus, Ohio: American Educational Publications, Inc., 1962. Some excellent unfinished stories to interest reluctant writers in junior and senior high school.

(N174) Strachan, Margaret Pitcairn, *Where Were You That Year?* New

York: Washburn, 1965. A novel about a college girl's experiences with voter registration in the South.

(N175) *The Struggle for Freedom and Rights: The Negro in American History*. Detroit: Detroit Public Schools, 1965. Supplemental text for grade 8.

(N176) Styron, William, *The Confessions of Nat Turner*. New York: Harper & Row, Publishers, 1967. A novelization. Reveals in agonizing human terms the essence of Negro slavery. (Also in *Harper's*, September, 1967.)

(N177) Sugarman, Tracy, *Stranger at the Gates: A Summer in Mississippi*. New York: Hill and Wang, 1966. In the summer of 1964, students and young people from all over the country met in Oxford, Ohio, to train for civil rights work in Mississippi, to assist Negroes in securing the vote and claiming rights that had so long been denied them. By summer's end three of them had been killed, scores injured and arrested.

(N178) Sullivan, George, *Wilt Chamberlain*. New York: Grosset & Dunlap, Inc., 1966. A biography of one of the greatest basketball players of all times; begins with high school days in Philadelphia, moves through the University of Kansas where he led the Jayhawks to the highest national ratings.

(N179) Sutherland, Elizabeth, *Letters from Mississippi*. New York: McGraw-Hill Book Company, 1965. Letters from 650 volunteers who went South in the summer of 1964.

(N180) Thompson, Elizabeth B., *Africa Past and Present*. Boston: Houghton Mifflin Company, 1966. Grades 5-12.

(N181) Thompson, Jean, *The House of Tomorrow*. New York: Harper & Row, Publishers, 1967. The diary of a young girl awaiting the birth of her child in a house for unwed mothers. Authentic, vivid, nonsentimental.

(N182) Toyer, Aurelia, *Get Your Money's Worth*. New York: Holt, Rinehart & Winston, Inc., 1964. Adult literacy program; Negro author.

(N183) Trahey, Jane, *The Trouble with Angels*. New York: Dell Publishing Co., Inc., 1966. A rebellious ringleader during her days at the Convent of St. Mark's, the author describes adolescent rebellion in the enclosure of a Catholic school.

(N184) Uggams, Leslie, *The Leslie Uggams Beauty Book*. Englewood Cliffs, N.J.: Prentice-Hall, Inc., 1966. One of America's brightest young singing stars, a Negro, shares her professional secrets, telling the reader everything she needs to know about teenage beauty—inside and out—from hair care, make-up, and diet to good grooming, charm, and manners.

(N185) Vogt, Evon A., and Ethel M. Albert, *People of Rimrock: A Study of Values in Five Cultures.* Cambridge, Mass.: Harvard University Press, 1967. The long series of publications under the Harvard "Values Study" approaches its end with this volume; the five cultures—Zunis, Navajos, Spanish-Americans, Mormons, and homesteading Texans—are now compared. This book, many-authored, is for everyone.

(N186) Wade, Richard C., ed., *The Negro in American Life.* Boston: Houghton Mifflin Company, 1965. A selection of original source material on Negro history.

(N187) Walker, Margaret, *Jubilee.* Boston: Houghton Mifflin Company, 1966. True-life story of the author's great-grandmother. It is a picture of life on a Georgia plantation during the Civil War era. For the first time the entire antebellum, Civil War, and Reconstruction story is told from the Negro point of view by a Negro. Superb drama; good contrast to *Gone With the Wind.*

(N188) Warren, Robert Penn, *Band of Angels.* New York: Random House, Inc., 1955.

(N189) ———, *Who Speaks for the Negro?* New York: Random House, Inc., 1965. A revealing interview with Negro leaders by a poet-novelist.

(N190) Watkin, Edward, *At the Edge of Harlem.* New York: William Morrow & Co., Inc., 1965.

(N191) Watson, Marjorie E., and Irving M. Brown, *Help Wanted.* New York: Human Relations Aids, 1960. A play about family reaction to the subject of working wives and mothers.

(N192) White, W. L., *Lost Boundaries.* New York: Harcourt, Brace & World, Inc., 1948. Story of a boy who discovers at age 16 that his parents are Negro.

(N193) Whitney, Phyllis A., *A Long Time Coming.* New York: David McKay Co., Inc., 1954. Incident after incident shows Christie Allard that good intentions alone will never change her town's prejudice against migrant Mexican-American workers in the local canning factory.

(N194) ———, *Step to the Music.* New York: Thomas Y. Crowell Company, 1953. A novel about a girl who sympathizes with both sides during the Civil War.

(N195) Woodward, C. Vann, *The Strange Career of Jim Crow.* New York: Oxford University Press, Inc., 1957. A competent history of the legalization of segregation.

(N196) Wright, Charles S., *The Messenger.* New York: Farrar, Straus & Giroux, Inc., 1963. Novel of a young Negro in New York.

(N197) ———, *The Wig.* New York: Farrar, Straus & Giroux, Inc., 1966. Comedie noire.

(N198) Wright, Richard, *Native Son.* New York: New American Library (paper), 1962. A classic novel of the impact of poverty and racial discrimination.

(N199) Yefremov, Ivan, *Land of Foam.* New York: New American Library (paper), 1959. Portrays various ancient civilizations through the harrowing experiences of a sensitive young Greek in his fight for freedom.

(N200) Young, A. S., "Doc," *Negro First in Sports.* Chicago: Johnson Publishing Co., Inc., 1966. An authoritative reference book giving the history of the Negro's participation in various sports, and the celebrated "firsts" in their fields. A. S. "Doc" Young, a veteran Negro sportswriter, supplements his statistics with many lively anecdotes.

(N201) Young, Jefferson, *A Good Man.* Indianapolis: The Bobbs-Merrill Company, Inc., 1952.

O. BIOGRAPHIES AND AUTOBIOGRAPHIES FOR HIGH SCHOOL AND ADULT READERS

(O1) Bontemps, Arna, *We Have Tomorrow.* Boston: Houghton Mifflin Company, 1945. Biographies of twelve distinguished Negroes. Grades 7-9.

(O2) Broderick, Francis L., *W. E. B. DuBois, Negro Leader in a Time of Crisis.* Stanford, Calif.: Stanford University Press, 1966. A scholarly biography.

(O3) Brown, Claude, *Manchild in the Promised Land.* New York: The Macmillan Company, 1965. Tough, bitter, realistic autobiography of a boy in Harlem.

(O4) *Call Them Heroes.* Morristown, N.J.: Silver Burdett Company, 1966. A series of booklets developed by the Board of Education of the City of New York to interest junior and senior high school youth through real-life stories of persons who succeeded despite the handicap of belonging to some minority group.

(O5) Davis, Sammy, Jr., and Jane and Burt Boyar, *Yes I Can* (paperback). New York: Farrar, Straus & Giroux, Inc., 1965.

(O6) Dexter, Dave, Jr., *The Jazz Story: From the '90's to the '60's.* Englewood Cliffs, N.J.: Prentice-Hall, Inc., 1965. Includes the author's personal recollections of Charlie Parker, Mildred Bailey, Stan Kenton, Dizzy Gillespie, Woody Herman, and many others.

(O7) Einstein, Charles, *Willie Mays: Coast to Coast Giant.* New York: G. P. Putnam's Sons, 1963. Biography of a Negro star baseball player and athlete.

(O8) Frank, Anne, *Anne Frank: Diary of a Young Girl.* Garden City, N.Y.: Doubleday & Company, Inc., 1952. Paperback by Washington Square Modern Library, Pocket Books. A universal favorite of adolescent youth; tragic and poignant.

(O9) Gibson, Althea, *I Always Wanted to Be Somebody.* New York: Harper & Row, Publishers, 1958. The personal story of a Negro girl who became a championship tennis player.

(O10) Gregory, Dick, with Robert Lipsyte, *Nigger: An Autobiography.* New York: E. P. Dutton & Co., Inc., 1964. (Also in paperback, Pocket Books.) The openness of this autobiography has great appeal for adolescents.

(O11) Griffith, Beatrice, *American Me.* Boston: Houghton Mifflin Company, 1947. Exceptionally authentic report of how Mexican-American youth feel, with supporting research data. Although published twenty years ago, the material is still accurate.

(O12) Handlin, Oscar, *Children of the Uprooted.* New York: George Braziller, Inc., 1966. Primarily first-person accounts of what it meant to be an immigrant's child in nineteenth-century America. Joel Chandler Harris, Louis D. Brandeis, Fiorello La-Guardia, Reinhold Niebuhr, Walter Reuther, and others.

(O13) Horne, Lena, and Richard Schickel, *Lena.* Garden City, N.Y.: Doubleday & Company, Inc., 1965. Story of a Negro singer who found herself between the Negro and white worlds, before she was able to find herself as an artist.

(O14) Kazin, Alfred, *A Walker in the City.* New York: Harcourt, Brace & World, Inc., 1951. Particularly sensitive report of an immigrant Jewish child in the slum schools of New York earlier in the century.

(O15) McGill, Ralph, "W. E. B. DuBois," *The Atlantic* (November, 1965), 78-81. A talk with a man who was a spokesman for

Negro rights for many decades but who became embittered, turned Communist, left the United States for Africa, and died abroad, shortly after this interview was held.

(O16) Malcolm X, *The Autobiography of Malcolm X.* New York: Grove Press, Inc., 1965. Once a leader in the Black Muslim movement, the author was assassinated just prior to the publication of this book. Provides vivid insight into the life experiences that go into the Negro extremist protest.

(O17) Mays, Willie, "Willie Mays: My Story," *Look* (March 22, 1965), 117-22. Adapted from the autobiography.

(O18) Meredith, James, *Three Years in Mississippi.* Bloomington: Indiana University Press, 1966. Meredith's own story of his experiences as the first Negro to enter the University of Mississippi.

(O19) Miers, Earl Schenck, *The Trouble Bush.* Skokie, Ill.: Rand McNally & Co., 1966. In an autobiography characterized by humility, skill, and vitality, Mr. Miers, whose life has been a triumph over cerebral palsy, speaks passionately for an understanding of the physically handicapped. Mr. Miers is author or co-author of over forty books on American history.

(O20) Peare, Catherine O., *Mary McLeod Bethune.* New York: Vanguard Press, Inc., 1951. The story of a great Negro educator who founded a leading college in the South.

(O21) Redding, J. Saunders, *On Being Negro in America* (paperback). Indianapolis: The Bobbs-Merrill Company, Inc., 1951. A personal history of a sensitive Negro educator, which evokes for the reader a feeling of the individual Negro intellectual as he faces American society.

(O22) Robinson, John R., and Alfred Duckett, *Breakthrough to the Big League; the Story of Jackie Robinson.* New York: Harper & Row, Publishers, 1966. The plain-speaking autobiography of the first Negro to play baseball in the major leagues.

(O23) Russell, William, *Go Up for Glory.* New York: Coward-McCann, Inc., 1966. Autobiography of a Negro professional basketball player.

(O24) Sterling, Dorothy, and Benjamin Quarles, *Lift Every Voice.* Garden City, N.Y.: Doubleday & Company, Inc., 1966. The lives of Booker T. Washington, W. E. B. DuBois, Mary Church Terrell, and James Weldon Johnson, who strove to open doors for their people through education, writing, organization, and participation in politics.

(O25) Trilling, Calvin, *An Education in Georgia: The Integration of Charlayne Hunter and Hamilton Holmes.* New York: The Viking Press, Inc., 1964. The story of the first two Negro students to enter the University of Georgia. Originally published in the *New Yorker* magazine.

(O26) Walker, Margaret, *Jubilee.* Boston: Houghton Mifflin Company, 1966. A slave's view of the collapse of plantation life, told by one of her descendants.

(O27) Waters, Ethel, *His Eye Is on the Sparrow.* Garden City, N.Y.: Doubleday & Company, Inc., 1951. Unvarnished autobiography of the painful experiences of growing up Negro in the harshest slum environment.

(O28) Wright, Richard, *Black Boy.* New York: New American Library, 1945. Autobiography of the angry Negro author; his early years in the South during the Depression.

P. TEXTBOOK STUDIES

(P1) Abraham, Herbert, "How Biased Are Our Textbooks?" *The UNESCO Courier,* May, 1956.

(P2) Alexander, Albert, "The Gray Flannel Cover on the American History Textbooks," *Social Education,* January, 1960.

(P3) Alilunas, Leo, "Ethnocentrism in Public and Parochial School American History Textbooks," *Religious Education,* March–April, 1965.

(P4) Bach, Harry, "Censorship of Library Books and Textbooks in American Schools," *Journal of Secondary Education,* January, 1965.

(P5) Baldwin, James, "A Talk to Teachers," *Saturday Review,* December 21, 1963.

(P6) Bennett, Lerone, Jr., "Reading, 'Riting and Racism: The Negro in Textbooks," *Ebony,* March, 1967, pp. 130-38. Reviews related study of textbooks prior to recent efforts, and reports on current inclusion of Negroes and Negro history in school texts.

(P7) "Big Drive for Balanced Multiracial Textbooks," *Time,* August 19, 1966.

(P8) "Bigotry Through Textbooks," *America,* October 7, 1961.

(P9) Billington, R. A., "Bias in History Textbooks," *Saturday Review,* January 15, 1966.

(P10) Bron, Ralph, and Marion Bron, "How to Select a Social Studies Textbook," *Social Education,* December, 1961.

(P11) Burress, Lee, "Censorship Pressures on Wisconsin Public Schools," *Education Digest,* January, 1964.

(P12) Davis, L., "Current Controversy: Minorities in American History Textbooks," *Journal of Secondary Education,* November, 1966.

(P13) Eckert, George, "History Instruction and International Understanding: The Problem of International Textbook Improvement," *Approaches to an Understanding of World Affairs,* National Council for the Social Studies 25th Yearbook, 1954.

(P14) Elkin, Sol M., "Minorities in Textbooks: The Last Chapter," *Teachers College Record,* March, 1965.

(P15) Gast, David K., "Minority Americans in Children's Literature," *Elementary English,* January, 1967, pp. 12-23. Careful analysis shows variation of stereotypes of various groups as portrayed in current books for children.

(P16) Grambs, Jean D., " 'Dick and Jane Go Slumming': Instructional Materials for Culturally Disadvantaged Elementary Children," in *Developing Programs for the Educationally Disadvantaged,* A. Harry Passow, ed. New York: Teachers College Press, Columbia University, 1968.

(P17) "Guidelines for Textbook Selection," *Report of the Joint Committee of the National Education Association and the American Textbook Publishers Institute,* National Education Association, 1963.

(P18) Harris, Judah H., *The Treatment of Religion in Elementary School Social Studies Textbooks* (paperback). New York: Anti-Defamation League of B'nai B'rith, 1963. A critical look at school texts.

(P19) Klineberg, Otto, "Life Is Fun in a Smiling, Fair-Skinned World," *Saturday Review,* February 16, 1963.

(P20) Krug, Mark M., "Safe Textbooks and Citizenship Education," *School Review,* Winter, 1960.

(P21) LaFollette, Robert, "History Textbooks and International Understanding," *Social Education,* May, 1953.

(P22) Larrick, Nancy, "The All-White World of Children's Books," *Saturday Review,* September 11, 1965.

(P23) Marcus, Lloyd, *The Treatment of Minorities in Secondary School Textbooks.* New York: Anti-Defamation League of B'nai B'rith, 1961.

(P24) Margolis, Richard J., "The Well-Tempered Textbook," *The Education Digest,* December, 1965.

(P25) Mayer, Martin, "The Trouble with Textbooks," *Harper's,* July, 1962.

(P26) Millender, D. M., "Selecting Our Children's Books: Time for Some Changes," *Changing Education* (Journal of the American Federation of Teachers), I (Fall, 1966), 8-13.

(P27) Olson, Bernard E., "Inter-Group Relations in Protestant Teaching Materials," *Religious Education,* March–April, 1960.

(P28) Peter, Sister Mary, "New Textbook: More Relevant to Urban Needs," *Catholic School Journal,* February, 1966.

(P29) Polos, Nicholas C., "Textbooks—What's Wrong with Them?" *Clearing House,* April, 1964.

(P30) Price, R., "Textbook Dilemma in the Social Studies," *Social Studies,* January, 1966.

(P31) Ram, Marie L., "An Analysis of the Lois Lenski Literature from a Sociological Point of View (Parts 1 and 2)." Unpublished Dissertation, University of Buffalo, 1958. Dissertation Abstracts 19, June, 1959, 3307.

(P32) Roselle, Danie, "In the Defense of Good Textbooks," *Peabody Journal of Education,* September, 1966.

(P33) Shaver, J. P., "Reflective Thinking, Values, and Social Studies Textbooks," reply with rejoinder, B. R. Joyce, *School Review,* Autumn, 1966.

(P34) Sloan, Irving, "Balance and Imbalance: 'New' History Texts of the Negro," *Changing Education* (Journal of the American Federation of Teachers), I (Fall, 1966), 14-19.

(P35) Slotkin, Aaron N., "The Treatment of Minorities in Textbooks: The Issues and the Outlook," *Strengthening Democracy.* Board of Education of the City of New York, 1964. (Pamphlet.)

(P36) Stampp, Kenneth M., *The Negro in American History Textbooks.* Sacramento: California State Department of Education, June, 1964. A report of a study of the treatment of Negroes in American History textbooks used in Grades 5 and 8 in the California public schools.

(P37) Sutherland, J. W., "Teaching About the Negro in American History," *California Teachers Association Journal,* October, 1966.

(P38) "These Racially Integrated Materials Are Available," *Nation's Schools,* LXXIX (June, 1967), 40-52. A listing of published materials to date, with list of sources for further information.

(P39) Weinryb, Bernard D., "Inter-Group Content in Jewish Religious Textbooks," *Religious Education,* March–April, 1960.

Q. PICTURES AND THEIR UTILIZATION

(Q1) Association for Childhood Education International, *Feelings and Learning*. Washington, D.C.: The Association, 1965.

(Q2) Bermont, Hubert, and Shelley Langston, *The Child.* New York: Pocket Books, Inc., 1965. Wholly pictures—of children, their faces, their moods.

(Q3) Carson, Rachel, *The Sense of Wonder*. New York: Harper & Row, Publishers, 1965. Evocative pictures of the world around us.

(Q4) *Chandler Language-Experience Readers.* San Francisco: Chandler Publishing Co., 1965. This series emphasizes photographs for reading readiness in the form of large pictures that are loose in a slipjacket. The children pictured are multi-ethnic in urban settings.

(Q5) *Children at School and Play*. Chicago: Johnson Publishing Co., Inc., n.d. Ten photographs, 8 × 10, showing Negro children (elementary age).

(Q6) *The Deprived.* New York: Seabury Press, 1963. An exhibit of thirty-two pictures, black and white, 18 × 18, taken by social worker-photographer Daniel J. Ransohoff. Sponsored by the Executive Council of the Episcopal Church, 815 Second Ave., New York, New York. Particularly useful for major focus on white poverty.

(Q7) *Famous Contemporary Negroes.* Chicago: Johnson Publishing Co., Inc., n.d. A set of fourteen 8 × 10 black and white portraits with biographical captions.

(Q8) *Famous Negroes of the Past.* Chicago: Johnson Publishing Co., Inc., n.d. A set of twelve 8 × 10 black and white portraits with captions.

(Q9) *Focus on Problems Facing Youth.* A Picture Packet. New York: National Conference of Christians and Jews, 1955. Selected drawings present problems typical of those youth face. Designed for small group discussions in class or youth groups.

(Q10) Heyman, Ken, and Michael Mason, *Willie*. New York: The Ridge Press, Inc., 1963. The world of a four-year-old living in the slums of a great city, wondrously caught by the camera.

(Q11) Levitt, Helen, and James Agee, *A Way of Seeing*. New York: The

Viking Press, Inc., 1965. Superb photographs of children in the slums, with a terse commentary.

(Q12) Mead, Margaret, and Ken Heyman, *Family*. New York: The Macmillan Company, 1965. A global view of the family through the eyes of a sensitive camera and with the voice of an anthropologist who can write for everyman.

(Q13) Miller, Wayne, *The World Is Young*. New York: The Ridge Press, Inc. (distributed by Simon and Schuster, Inc.), 1958. A sensitive photographer shows the world of growing children in school and out. Particularly useful for exploration of feelings. Not integrated, but probably will have universal appeal.

(Q14) Osborn, Merton B., and Bruce Miller, *Sources of Free Pictures*. Riverside, Calif.: Bruce Miller Publications, 1964.

(Q15) ———, *So You Want to Start a Picture File: An Aid to Better Teaching*. Riverside, Calif.: Bruce Miller Publications, 1964.

(Q16) *Pictures of Distinguished Negroes*. Washington, D.C.: Associated Publishers, Inc., n.d.

(Q17) Pioneer History Society, Harriman, Tennessee. Source of facsimile historical posters. Brings the reality of history to the classroom. Example: poster advertising a slave auction.

(Q18) Potter, David, J. Joel Moss, and Herbert F. A. Smith, *Photosituations: A Technique for Teaching*. Minneapolis: Burgess Publishing Co., 1963. Particularly useful in teacher education.

(Q19) Purcell, Carl, *Teach Me!* Washington, D.C.: National Education Association, 1967. A photographic essay on the joys and challenges of teaching and learning. A lively collection of pictures of schools, classrooms, teachers, and students. Useful for provoking discussion and writing.

(Q20) Reese, Thelma Kier, *Discussion Pictures*. New York: Harper & Row, Publishers, 1958. Guidebook for teachers available. Large pictures that present family problem situations as well as "good" situations. Not integrated.

(Q21) Reich, Hanns, ed., *Children and Their Fathers*. New York: Hill and Wang, Inc., 1962. Pictures from around the world.

(Q22) ———, *Children and Their Mothers*. New York: Hill and Wang, Inc., 1964. Pictures from around the world of children with their mothers. Useful for comparative study showing the universal aspects of maternal feelings.

(Q23) *Rumor Clinic*. New York: Anti-Defamation League of B'nai B'rith. A "game" guaranteed to involve everyone in a lively discussion and self-teaching demonstration—we all have concepts of stereotypes of other groups that distort what we see and hear and may cause harmful rumors. Developed by the noted Harvard psychologist, Gordon Allport.

(Q24) Shaftel, Fannie, and George Shaftel, *Words and Action.* New York: Holt, Rinehart & Winston, Inc., 1966. Excellent large pictures designed to provoke classroom discussion. Very helpful teachers' guide with focus on use of pictures for role-playing. The best set now available.

(Q25) Smith, Lillian, *Our Faces, Our Words.* New York: W. W. Norton & Company, Inc., 1964. With excellent photographs, Lillian Smith tells the story of her awakening to the Negro situation in the South as she was growing up and the situation as she saw it before her death in 1966.

(Q25a) Steichen, Edward, *The Family of Man.* New York: Maco Magazine Corp. (for the Museum of Modern Art), 1955. Superb collection of pictures from around the world showing all the stages of man's life; how people differ and yet are the same no matter where in the world they may be found.

(Q26) Stern, Phillip M., *The Shame of a Nation.* New York: Ivan Obolensky, Inc., 1965. Pictorial presentation of poverty.

(Q27) *Table of Important Events and Dates in Negro History.* Washington, D.C.: Associated Publishers, Inc., 1936. Poster 19 x 24—convenient as teacher's guide.

(Q28) *To Be Alive!* New York: The Macmillan Company, 1965. Pictures from film produced for New York World's Fair, 1965–1966.

(Q29) *Urban Education Studies.* New York: The John Day Company, Inc., 1965. Series of very large photographs on heavy stock, to illustrate basic themes of life. Also, particular cities are pictured in separate folios.

(Q30) UNESCO. *Schools Around the World, Children Around the World, UNESCO Around the World.* Picture sets obtainable through UNESCO Publications Center, 317 East 34th Street, New York, New York 10016.

(Q31) Williams, Catherine M., *Learning from Pictures.* Washington, D.C. Department of Audiovisual Instruction, National Education Association, 1963. Discusses many ways to use and display pictures; rather pedestrian in approach, though many suggestions are useful.

(Q32) *Youth Profile at School.* Chicago: Johnson Publishing Co., Inc., n.d. Twelve 8 x 10 photographs of Negro youth in school and school-related activities.

R. FILMS, FILM SOURCES, FILM USE

(R1) *Africa.* Series of 4, 8mm color loop films, about 3 min. each. Gateway Educational Films Ltd., London, England, 1967. An excellent series with a fine commentary. Could be used in a basic geography class on the secondary level, but most effective use will be in upper elementary and junior high levels. Technical level of films is very high and photography excellent.

(R2) *Africa: The Hidden Frontiers.* 16mm, 60 min., B & W. NET Film Service, Indiana U. Audio-Visual Center, Bloomington. The independent African nation of Kenya is examined in terms of its attempts to unify its numerous African tribes, Europeans, and Asians into an organized nation, and in terms of the social progress that has been made in spite of this mixture of peoples.

(R3) *All the Way Home.* 29½ min., B & W. Anti-Defamation League. A house in an all-white neighborhood is for sale. When a Negro family stops to inquire about it, neighborhood fear and anxiety mount to a dangerous point while responsible community leadership asserts itself. An open-ended film.

(R4) *Anatomy of an Accident.* 28 min., color. American Telephone and Telegraph, 1961. A story of a careful driver who suffers tragic consequences because he permits himself to be irritated while driving. Acted by David Wayne and Phyllis Avery, this dramatization stresses the need for defensive driving, concentration, control, and common courtesy.

(R5) *Marian Anderson.* 26 min., B & W. Irving Lesser, 1952. Scenes from the famous singer's early childhood in the slums of Philadelphia up to her Town Hall recital in New York City. Depicts the hardships she overcame to become one of the world's greatest singers.

(R6) *Anti-Defamation League of B'nai B'rith.* 1966–1967 Catalog of Audio-Visual Materials. Inquire at local ADL offices for material available. Excellent source listing with annotations. Published annually.

(R7) *Ask Me, Don't Tell Me.* 22 min., B & W. Contemporary, 1961. Unemployed and restless teenagers are helped to help themselves. An American Friends project offers boys the opportunity of working on constructive projects in their own environment with the right to argue and vote on any enterprise.

(R8) *Audiovisual Instruction* (Journal). Washington, D.C.: Department of Audiovisual Instruction, National Education Association.

(R9) Beck, Lester F., "Television for the Preschool Child," *Audiovisual Instruction* (Department of Audiovisual Instruction, NEA), January, 1965.

(R9a) The Bill of Rights: A series of films dealing with the Bill of Rights: *Justice, Liberty and Law; Search and Privacy; Speech and Protest; Interrogation and Counsel.* Approx. 22 min. each, color. Churchill Films. For senior high school and college. The first film introduces the main concepts of the Bill of Rights. The others include interviews with persons involved in the particular issues: private citizens, police, judges, etc. Enacted episodes have provision for stopping the projector for discussion between sequences. Each episode is in the form of a "cliffhanger" leaving the class with a challenging question to consider. For the teacher who is prepared to encourage inductive learning. (Correlated with: *The Bill of Rights: Handbook* and *The Bill of Rights: Sourcebook.*) New York: Benziger Brothers, Inc., 1967.

(R10) *Brazil: The Vanishing Negro.* 16mm, 30 min., B & W. NET Film Service, Indiana U. Audio-Visual Center, Bloomington. Brazil, reputed to be a "racial paradise," is observed in terms of its past and present, the influence of Afro-Brazilian religious ceremonies, amalgamation and "racial democracy."

(R11) *Burden of Truth.* United Steelworkers of America, Pittsburgh, 1959. Superb hour-long film about the problems facing the educated and working-class Negro; fictional. May appear dated to some, but story remains authentic.

(R12) *The Captive.* 28 min. Appalachia and the story of a man's struggle to escape from the crushing bonds of poverty. Should shock the complacent into recognizing the responsibility that faces them for bringing new hope and freedom to the captive poor.

(R13) *Case History of a Rumor.* 52 min. United States Armed Forces and anti-Communist maneuvers are distorted into their exact opposite by extreme Rightist elements. Rumors spread false alarms among thousands and undermine the faith of the American people in their institutions and government.

(R14) *Cast the First Stone.* 42 min. Anti-Defamation League. This documentary features interviews on location with Americans whose lives have been affected by prejudice and discrimination. Negroes in Los Angeles and Chicago; Jews in Detroit; Puerto

Ricans in New York; Mexicans, Japanese, and Chinese in the Midwest.

(R15) *Children Without.* 30 min., B & W. National Education Association, Washington, D.C. Too many children in American cities are without parental love and care, without the basic requisites of daily living, without the many experiences that help them develop their potentialities. The film takes the viewer into a Detroit public school where teachers and counselors establish the warm relationships such children need and provide positive learning experiences for them. Focus is on white poverty.

(R16) *The Cities and the Poor: Part I.* 16mm, 60 min. NET Film Service, Indiana U. Audio-Visual Center, Bloomington. In this study of the frustrations, aspirations, and fears of America's poor, sections of Chicago and Los Angeles are examined in an attempt to understand the nature of social welfare work, the lack of motivation among the poor, and the growing impatience prevalent in some poverty-stricken areas.

(R17) *The Cities and the Poor: Part II.* 16mm, 60 min. NET Film Service, Indiana U. Audio-Visual Center, Bloomington. In this second National Educational Television film on poverty in urban areas, emphasis is centered on the continuing unrest in the nation's slums and the effects of this discontent on poverty programs now in existence.

(R18) *The Civil Rights Movement:* Film Series.

1. *The Civil Rights Movement: A Personal Review*
2. *The Civil Rights Movement: Historic Roots*
3. *The Civil Rights Movement: The South*
4. *The Civil Rights Movement: The North*
5. *The Civil Rights Movement: The Mississippi Project*

Encyclopedia Britannica Educational Corporation, Chicago, 1966.

(R19) *Color of Man.* 10 min. AFL-CIO. Discusses latest scientific findings and theories as to why man's skin color differs from one group to another.

(R20) *Common Fallacies About Group Differences.* 15 min. Group differences in behavior are the result of the culture people grow up in, not heredity. Behavior of an individual should not be generalized to represent the behavior of a group.

(R21) *Confronted.* 16mm, 60 min., B & W. NET Film Service, Indiana U. Audio-Visual Center, Bloomington. The confrontation of several Northern communities with the issue of Negro integration in schools, jobs, and housing has evoked varied reactions in both Negroes and whites.

(R22) *The Cool World.* The world of Harlem and its youth. See *Saturday Review,* January 21, 1967, for review.

(R23) Culkin, John M., S.J., "I Was a Teen-age Movie Teacher," *Saturday Review,* July 16, 1966.

(R24) ———, "The Motion Picture as an Art Form: Film Study in the High School," *Bulletin* (of the National Catholic Education Association), 1966. Valuable for bibliography of feature films and ways they are useful.

(R25) de Heusch, Luc, *The Cinema and Social Sciences.* New York: UNESCO Publications Center, 1962. Survey of ethnographic and sociological films. Excellent source for finding documentary films of value.

(R26) *The Dispersed.* 16mm, 60 min., B & W. NET Film Service, Indiana U. Audio-Visual Center, Bloomington. A study of Jewish people throughout the world today to gather their views on the extent of anti-Semitism, the assimilation of the Jews with the Gentiles, the retainment of Jewish customs and religious training, the loss of Jewish identity, and their hopes in terms of the new homeland of Israel.

(R27) Dolan, Harry E., *Losers Weepers. NBC-TV,* 1967. New "experimental" series by a 36-year-old new playwright who was a member of Budd Schulberg's writing workshop in the Watts area of Los Angeles. The production was filmed on location in the Watts area.

(R28) *Due Process of Law Denied.* 29 min., B & W. Teaching Film Custodians, 1943. An excerpt from the feature film "Oxbow Incident." Dramatizes some of the unlawful trials and mob violence which took place in the early days of the West. Illustrates the necessity to recognize the rights of an accused person as provided under the Constitution. Schools only. Superb introduction to discussion of civil rights today.

(R29) Educational Film Library Association, *Films for Children with 1965 Supplement.* New York: The Association, 1965. An annotated list of films mostly just for fun; a few listed are outstanding documentary stories.

(R30) *The Exiles.* Kent Mackenzie, Contemporary Films. Social problems of urbanized American Indians.

(R31) *Exploding the Myths of Prejudice.* A film produced with the assistance of Ethel Alpenfels, anthropologist.

(R31a) *The Eye of the Beholder.* Fascinating film demonstrating how one's perceptions may change "reality." Also available in French and Spanish editions.

(R32) *5½: Reflections of an Age.* Office for Audio-Visuals of the Stewardship Council, United Church of Christ, 1501 Race Street, Philadelphia. Superb film showing the feelings and self-concepts of a 5½-year-old middle-class Negro boy.

(R33) *Four Lessons in Human Values.* United World Films, 221 Park Avenue South, New York.

(R34) *Free at Last.* 16mm, 30 min., B & W. NET Film Service, Indiana U. Audio-Visual Center, Bloomington. Tracing the history of the American Negro from emancipation to the end of World War II, this film examines the Depression, the end of the so-called Negro renaissance of the twenties, and past Negro leaders.

(R35) *Freedom to Read.* 14 min., B & W. Available from Anti-Defamation League. One of four films in The Challenge series, Mr. Jones, representing a community group, wants certain books removed from the public library in the interest of national security.

(R36) *The Future and the Negro.* 16mm, 75 min., B & W. NET Film Service, Indiana U. Audio-Visual Center, Bloomington. A panel discussion, moderated by Ossie Davis, examines such questions as the worldwide future of the Negro, racism, amalgamation, the economic position of the Negro, and the relationship of American Negroes to Africa.

(R37) *The Game.* National Film Board of Canada, 1967. Available through McGraw-Hill Book Company. A casual relationship that ceases to be casual, confronting a teenage boy with an agonizing moral dilemma.

(R38) *The Great Rights.* 14 min., color. Brandon, 1964. A humorous animated film, which dramatizes the way life in this country might be without the Bill of Rights. Without flagwaving, the film subtly conveys our privileges as individuals as well as our need to protect them by protest and responsibility.

(R39) *Hand in Hand.* British Production. Focuses on religious differences. The friendship of a Catholic and a Jewish child precipitates adult awareness of prejudice.

(R40) *Hangman.* 12 min., color. Lack of "involvement" among humans is attacked eloquently. Boldly stark drawings illustrate Maurice Ogden's allegorical poem. A penetrating statement of the necessity for individual responsibility to speak out against injustice or be doomed. Students won't easily forget this powerful prod toward involvement in "freedom with responsibility."

(R41) *The Hard Way*. 16mm, 60 min., B & W. NET Film Service, Indiana U. Audio-Visual Center, Bloomington. The problem of poverty in America, the richest country in the world, is discussed emphasizing the ways in which the poor of today are different from those of past generations.

(R42) *Heritage of the Negro*. 16mm, 30 min., B & W. NET Film Service, Indiana U. Audio-Visual Center, Bloomington. Series host Ossie Davis examines the civilization of ancient Africa and explores the "old culture" through art, sculpture, and present-day pageantry.

(R43) *The High Wall*. 30 min. Anti-Defamation League. This prize-winning film shows how the hostility of a teenager toward those of other national, religious, and racial groups is a product of the prejudices and frustrations of his parents, along with their emphasis on discipline instead of love. Shows some of the basic origins and meanings of prejudice.

(R44) Hoban, Charles F., *Focus on Learning*. Washington, D.C.: American Council on Education, 1942. The what and why of children's learning from films; a classic.

(R45) ———, "The Usable Residue of Educational Film Research," *New Teaching Aids for the American Classroom*. Washington, D.C.: U.S. Office of Education, 1960.

(R46) *Home of the Brave*. 85 min., B & W. Association Films, 1949. The feature film produced by Stanley Kramer. Concerns four white and one Negro soldier in the South Pacific during World War II. Negro emerges from a cloud of inferiority and shame into full and equal standing with his fellow men.

(R47) *House on Cedar Hill*. 17 min., B & W. *Contemporary Films*, 1953. A biographical study of Frederick Douglass, the Negro slave who became a leader of the anti-slavery movement before the Civil War and a leader in the fight for Negro rights after it. His life and struggles are pictured through his personal belongings, drawings, and photographs.

(R48) *Incident on Wilson Street, Parts I and II*. 51 min., B & W. McGraw-Hill Book Company, 1966. Newspapers in many cities have recently reported frequent attacks on teachers by pupils. This film shows individual and group reaction to an in-school "incident" when a young student suddenly strikes out at her teacher.

(R49) International Film Bureau, 332 Michigan Ave., Chicago. Distributors of four open-ended short films suitable for senior high school and adult groups. The film, *Teaching—a Question of Method,* focuses on the problem of religious conviction and the role of public education.

(R50) *The Interview.* 5 min., color. Brandon, 1960. A "square" announcer and a "hip" French horn player manage to confuse each other utterly by their jargon and ignorance of each other's terminology. A spoof at jazz, the middle class, and communications.

(R51) *Just Like Me.* Karl B. Lohmann, Jr. Thorne Films. Human relations; elementary grades.

(R52) *Liberty in a Featherbed.* 30 min., B & W. Committee on Jewish Education, United Synagogue, 1953. Dramatizes the efforts of Thomas Kennedy to remove civil and political inequalities in the state legislature of Maryland in 1818.

(R53) *Lonely Boy.* 28 min., B & W. National Film Board of Canada, 1962. The story of Paul Anka, the young Canadian singer and songwriter. A candid look at his rise to fame and stardom in the multi-million dollar entertainment business. Shows the pressure, emotion, and illusions of a teenage idol. Astonishing insight but no patronizing narration.

(R54) *Louisiana Diary.* 16mm, 59 min., B & W. NET Film Service, Indiana U. Audio-Visual Center, Bloomington. A documentary film on the special efforts by a CORE group to assist Negroes in the Sixth Congressional District in Louisiana during a registration campaign in the summer of 1963.

(R55) Maccoby, E. E., and W. C. Wilson, "Identification and Observational Learnings from Films," *Journal of Abnormal and Social Psychology,* LV, July, 1957. Useful as a guide in using audio-visual materials.

(R56) *Major Religions of the World.* 20 min., Encyclopedia Britannica Films. Beliefs and important rituals of Hinduism, Buddhism, Judaism, Christianity, and Islam. Animated diagrams illustrate rise of newer religions from older ones.

(R57) *Marked for Failure.* 16mm, 60 min., B & W. NET Film Service, Indiana U. Audio-Visual Center, Bloomington. This film report focuses on the problems facing both educators and children in America's slum schools and illuminates the reasons why these children, mostly Negro, are kept out of the cultural and, ultimately, the economic mainstream of society.

(R58) *Meeting Place.* 14 min., B & W. Methodist Publishing House, 1959. A Negro and a white doctor wait together in vain for the arrival of committee members, all of whom fail to appear because of a recent racial crisis. Considers questions of how men can work to overcome tension caused by racial feelings.

(R59) *Men for Others.* 16mm, 60 min., B & W. NET Film Service, Indiana U. Audio-Visual Center, Bloomington. Shows members of the Woodlawn Organization in Chicago and Peace Corps workers in Africa. This film observes people interested in the welfare of their fellow men and the various ways they are serving others through spiritual, social, and economic channels.

(R60) *The Merry Go Round.* National Film Board of Canada, 1967. Available through McGraw-Hill Book Company. Three divergent opinions on premarital sex, set off against the story of a boy and girl who are verging on a physical relationship.

(R61) *The Messenger from Violet Drive.* 16mm, 30 min., B & W. NET Film Service, Indiana U. Audio-Visual Center, Bloomington. Elijah Muhammad, leader of the controversial Black Muslim movement, discusses Black Muslim philosophies, including their desire for total separation of Negroes from whites in America.

(R62) *Minorities Have Made America Great.* A film produced with the assistance of Ethel Alpenfels, anthropologist.

(R63) *A Morning for Jimmy.* 28 min., B & W. National Urban League, 1960. A young Negro boy, seeking a part-time job, encounters discrimination for the first time head on and is discouraged until his teacher takes him to visit Negroes successfully employed in many fields. Presents a strong case to finish school and to take a stand for your rights.

(R64) *The Neglected.* A Mental Health Film Board Production, sponsored by the Office of Children and Youth, Pennsylvania Department of Welfare, and the U.S. Children's Bureau. Inquire: International Film Bureau, 332 S. Michigan Avenue, Chicago, Ill. Film shows how child protective services help to stabilize families whose children have come under the protection of community authorities because of abuse or neglect. Reveals the wide range of problems of the disadvantaged and makes clear that they need more than merely an increased income.

(R65) *The Negro and the American Promise.* 16mm, 60 min., B & W. NET Film Service, Indiana U. Audio-Visual Center, Bloomington. Dr. Martin Luther King, Malcolm X, Dr. Kenneth Clark, and James Baldwin discuss their motivations, doctrines, methods, goals, and place in the American Negro's movement for social and racial equality.

(R66) *The Negro and the South.* 16mm, 30 min., B & W. NET Film Service, Indiana U. Audio-Visual Center, Bloomington. A study of the thoughts, fears, hopes, frustrations, and rationalizations of both Southern Negroes and whites living the enigmatic "Southern way of life."

(R67) *Neighbors.* 9 min., color. International Film Bureau, 1952. A startling presentation of the way in which violent disputes may arise from the most trivial incidents. A modern parable of the latent hostility in local issues, as we see two men fighting over a flower. This film has been particularly good with emotionally disturbed youngsters and potential dropouts.

(R68) *New Mood.* 16mm, 30 min., B & W. NET Film Service, Indiana U. Audio-Visual Center, Bloomington. The "New Mood" reviews historical moments in the civil rights struggle of the last decade and traces the impact of the new Negro militancy on both Negro and white Americans.

(R69) *Nigeria: A School for Jacob.* 16mm, 30 min., B & W. NET Film Service, Indiana U. Audio-Visual Center, Bloomington. Jacob Ajibola is an eleven-year-old Nigerian boy typical of the young African today who has ambition yet lacks the education necessary to find his own place in the world. Contrasting Jacob with a boy in Appalachia with similar aspirations, this film raises the question: Can U.S. taxpayers afford to educate both Americans and those abroad who are in need?

(R70) *Nine from Little Rock.* United States Information Agency film, not available as yet for showing in the U.S. Survey of what has become of the nine Negro youths who entered Little Rock High School in the fall of 1957.

(R71) *No Hiding Place.* 51 min. One of the most powerful and dramatic programs to be presented on the *East Side/West Side* television series. It is a daring drama about a Negro family who has moved into an all-white Northern suburban community. Ironically, it is a Southern white housewife and not her Northern husband who displays courage and understanding when some of their neighbors are panicked into selling their homes.

(R72) *Nothing But a Man.* What a Negro male feels confronted by today's conflicting demands. Reviewed in *Saturday Review,* January 21, 1967.

(R73) *Occurrence at Owl Creek Bridge.* 27 min., B & W. Contemporary. A gripping re-creation of an incident during the Civil War. Told with sparse dialogue and careful detail, the story is almost totally visual and portrays a day in the life of a man condemned to be hanged on a bridge—his escape, his memories and fantasies. This film has unlimited discussion possibilities.

(R74) *Omowale: The Child Returns Home.* 16mm, 30 min., B & W. NET Film Service, Indiana U. Audio-Visual Center, Bloomington. Focusing on Mississippi-born novelist John William and his odyssey to Africa to explore his ancestral roots, this film studies the relationship of the American Negro to Africa and Africans.

(R75) *One Potato, Two Potato.* A feature film focusing on interracial feelings. See review in *Saturday Review,* January 21, 1967.

(R76) *Our Country, Too.* 16mm, 30 min., B & W. NET Film Service, Indiana U. Audio-Visual Center, Bloomington. The inner world of the American Negro—his values, attitudes, and impressions of life—is examined through observing aspects of life in the American Negro community.

(R77) *A Patch of Blue.* A film about a blind girl and a Negro protector.

(R78) *Phoebe.* National Film Board of Canada, 1967. Available through McGraw-Hill Book Company. A day of emotional anguish in the life of an unmarried pregnant teenage girl.

(R79) *A Place in the Sun.* Encyclopedia Britannica Films. A very short cartoon-type film which uses analogy to show that each person must have his place in the sun for any to survive.

(R80) *Police Power.* 16mm, 60 min., B & W. NET Film Service, Indiana U. Audio-Visual Center, Bloomington. A debate on the role of police power in a modern democratic society and on related issues, including conflicts between civil liberties and police methods, attitudes of the police and the public toward one another, and the effect of Supreme Court decisions on police authority.

(R81) *Politics: The High Cost of Conviction.* Horizon Film Productions,

International Film Bureau. Individual endorsement of political candidates, an open-ended film.

(R82) *Portrait of a Disadvantaged Child: Tommy Knight.* 16 min., B & W. McGraw-Hill Book Company, 1966. This film brings the viewer face to face with the reality of a day in the life of a slum child.

(R83) *Portrait of the Inner City.* 15 min., B & W. McGraw-Hill Book Company, 1966. This film looks at the community as a passer-by might see it, and also from the viewpoint of young people who are growing up in this environment.

(R84) *Portrait of the Inner City School: A Place to Learn.* McGraw-Hill Book Company, 1966. This film illustrates how, even unconsciously, a teacher can discriminate against pupils from disadvantaged homes and neighborhoods.

(R85) *Poverty in Rural America.* 16mm, 28½ min., B & W. Sound. Motion Picture Service, Office of Information, Department of Agriculture, Washington, D.C. Defines the problems of rural poverty and then explores several situations where local people are working to remove the causes of such poverty.

(R86) *Profiles in Courage.* Available from I.Q. Films, Inc., 689 Fifth Ave., New York. Based on biographies by John F. Kennedy. A series of 26 films originally produced for TV.

(R87) *The Rafer Johnson Story.* 52 min., B & W. Sterling, 1965. The determination and triumph of one of the most honored athletes of our time, from Johnson's early childhood days of hardship and struggle to world decathlon champion and first member of the Peace Corps, finally being honored by the President of the United States.

(R88) *Remember Us.* 60 min. Anti-Defamation League. A documentary on the atrocities committed by the Nazis. Concentration-camp survivors, now living in the United States, give a first-hand account of their experience under the Hitler regime.

(R89) *Rental (Free) Library of Audio-Tapes.* New York City Commission on Human Rights.

Order No.	*Title*	*Duration*
5050-1	*Adventures in Negro History*	20 min.
5050-2	*Birmingham—A Testament of Non-Violence*	20 min.
5050-4	*Housing and the Minority Buyer*	20 min.
5050-5	*Lessons from the Harlem Riots*	20 min.
5050-8	*The Puerto Rican in New York City*	20 min.

Order No.	Title	Duration
5050-9	*Portrait of a Ghetto-Bedford Stuyvesant Story*	20 min.
5050-10	*Segregation and the Puerto Rican*	20 min.
5050-15	*The Negro and the American Theatre*	20 min.
5050-16	*The Neighborhood*	20 min.
5050-22	*Let's Talk Sense About School Integration*	10 min.
5050-24	*The Negro Woman*	10 min.
5050-28	*The White Liberal*	10 min.
5050-30	*School Integration*	10 min.
5050-35	*Harlem, The Ghetto and the Riots*	20 min.
5050-37	*Integration in Education*	13½ min.
5050-38	*School Integration—After Boycott of February 3, 1964*	10 min.
5050-43	*Poverty*	60 min.
5050-45	*New Horizons of the Negro Woman*	30 min.
5050-48	*Equality in Our Time*	60 min.

Free of charge, any or all of the above tapes are available for loan to schools or organizations. Order by title and order number. Department of Public Relations, Curriculum Center for Human Relations, 80 Lafayette St., New York City, New York.

(R90) *Right or Wrong?* (Making moral decisions.) 11 min. Coronet Films, 1952. Open-ended. Gang of high school boys breaks a warehouse window; one is caught. Shall he tell the names of his buddies who really did the deed?

(R91) *Rumor Clinic.* Anti-Defamation League of B'nai B'rith, New York. Includes Rumor Clinic film strip and also instructions in how to conduct a rumor clinic. Local ADL offices will help in providing trained personnel to put on a rumor clinic. Very helpful.

(R92) *The Run from Race.* 16mm, 30 min., B & W. NET Film Service, Indiana U. Audio-Visual Center, Bloomington. Filmed in Philadelphia, Negroes, a minister, a university professor, a real estate salesman, and a housewife tell of life and problems in a Negro community and speculate on why some people run from racial problems, particularly problems in housing.

(R93) *Runner.* 11 min., B & W. National Film Board of Canada, 1962. A close-up, flowing study of Bruce Kidd, a young long-distance runner, showing what it takes to be a track star. You see the runner caught up in the race, concentrating on timing and stamina. Enhanced by an excellent jazz score and commentary by William Auden.

(R94) *Scrap of Paper and a Piece of String.* John Korty for NBC. Contemporary Films. Human relations; for grades K-9.

(R95) *Selected Quality Feature Films in Programs for the Culturally Disadvantaged.* Films, Inc. (a subsidiary of Encyclopedia Britannica Films). Lists full-length films available for education use in terms of human relations topics.

(R96) Sheridan, Marion C., *et al., The Motion Picture and the Teaching of English.* New York: Appleton-Century-Crofts, 1965.

(R97) *Slavery.* 16mm, 30 min., B & W. NET Film Service, Indiana U. Audio-Visual Center, Bloomington. Based on the testimony and vivid memory of former Southern slaves, this dramatic and choral work portrays life under slavery and examines the tragic and sometimes humorous experiences of life in the old South.

(R98) *South Africa Essay Part I: Fruit of Fear.* 16mm, 60 min., B & W. NET Film Service, Indiana U. Audio-Visual Center, Bloomington. The South African dual standards of living separate the affluent world of the whites, where lavish living is accepted as a right and not a privilege, from the world of the ghettos, where the black majority lives a segregated life.

(R99) *Speech Chain.* Teaching package. Bell Telephone Company. Physics and biology of spoken language; grades 7-12.

(R100) *The Story of Sammy Lee.* 30 min. Anti-Defamation League. The documentary illustrating that many unprejudiced children grow up to experience discrimination or to discriminate, even against Olympic champions, while others share in happy experiences of living and working together.

(R101) *The Streets of Greenwood.* 20 min. Photographed in Mississippi in the summer of 1964. In this documentary the Negro drive for freedom is pitted against the determination of the white community to keep Greenwood as it is. A white political rally in an open field with a racist speech by a candidate for office is contrasted with a Negro freedom festival in another field with folk singer Pete Seeger.

(R102) *Study in Color.* A trilogy of films consisting of "Boy," "The Job," and "Study in Color." A group of three plays which represent a strong indictment of racial prejudice. With modern dramatic techniques and symbolism, they appeal to moral considerations and impel audiences to analyze their own inner feeling about color and race. Although created as a trilogy, each film is an entity and can be used either for a single program or as one of a series of three.

"Boy." 12 min., B & W. Cleared for TV. An experience in the search for identity. Through imaginative role-playing, a Negro boy indulges in a fantasy which reveals his deep sensitivity to name-calling and stereotyped attitudes toward racial minorities. The hard-hitting dialogue exposes the degradation to which a prejudiced person subjects his fellow human beings.

"The Job." 29 min., B & W. Cleared for TV. A sophisticated approach to the problem of racial prejudice, this sometimes humorous, but biting satire attacks the hypocrisy of using the race angle as a promotion gimmick for "selling" movies, plays, or books. A Negro celebrity who is hired to promote a new movie on "The American Negro" is the central character of this play, which is both entertaining and thought-provoking.

"A Study in Color." 28 min., B & W. Cleared for TV. Two players discuss "color" in separate soliloquies—one is a white man who wears a Negro mask, the other a Negro wearing a white mask. Through the use of these theatrical devices, the members of the audience are given an opportunity to place themselves in the role of the Negro and to try to empathize their deepest feelings.

(R103) *Superfluous People.* 56 min. Approaches the problem of the thousands of unwanted, displaced, and poverty-stricken individuals in American society today. Pictures infants in institutions and hospitals awaiting placement in foster homes and shows interviews with young adults walking the streets without jobs. Explains the plight of many elderly people who have been moved from their old homes by urban renewal.

(R103a) *Susan B. Anthony Is Tried for Voting.* 27 min., B & W. McGraw-Hill Book Company. From CBS *You Are There* series. Shows the second day of legal proceedings.

(R104) *Take an Option on Tomorrow.* Louis de Rougemont Associates for International Business Machines and New York State Division for Youth. Youth rehabilitation.

(R105) *Tanzania—The Quiet Revolution.* 16mm, 60 min., B & W. NET Film Service, Indiana U. Audio-Visual Center, Bloomington. A study of the peoples of Tanzania and their struggle with the problems of extreme poverty, illiteracy, and racism; also President Julius K. Nyerere's policy of nonalignment, which he presents as the only practical method of obtaining the money and manpower necessary to solve his country's problems.

(R106) *Teaching: A Question of Method.* Horizon Film Productions;

International Film Bureau distributors. Teacher's responsibility for challenging religious beliefs. An open-ended film.

(R107) *That's Me.* 15 min., B & W. Contemporary, 1965. A social worker tries to help a young Puerto Rican who finds it very difficult to adjust to life in New York City. This serio-comic dramatic sketch conveys the true situation with economy and wit.

(R108) *A Time for Burning.* Lutheran Film Associates, 1966. Probes problems of integration in one community. Story of youthful pastor, William Youngdahl, and his odyssey. An authentic story of a dedicated person.

(R109) *A Time Out of War.* 22 min., B & W. Contemporary, 1954. Across a river tired soldiers of the North and South during the Civil War call a brief truce. From this slight theme based on Robert Chamber's short story, "Pickets," emerges a powerful documentary film without patronizing narration.

(R110) *To Hear Your Banjo Play.* 19 min., B & W. Brandon. Pete Seeger plays his banjo and narrates a story which traces the history of American folk music from the first banjo made by a Negro slave. The story and dialogue by Alan Lomax is interspersed with examples of popular folk songs and square dances.

(R111) *To Sir, With Love.* 1967. Feature-length film. Stars Negro actor Sidney Poitier. Based on the book of the same name by Braithwaite. A Negro teacher in a London slum school.

(R112) *Tragedy in a Temporary Town.* 47½ min. Anti-Defamation League. Kinescope of the NBC program by Reginald Rose, starring Lloyd Bridges. What occurs at a temporary construction workers' camp when a rumor causes an innocent victim to be accused of a crime he did not commit. Hysteria ensues as blind prejudice against a minority group erupts.

(R113) *The Troubled Cities.* 16mm, 60 min., B & W. NET Film Service, Indiana U. Audio-Visual Center, Bloomington. An inquiry into the crises of American cities and a report on the attempts of four metropolitan areas (New York, Detroit, Boston, and Newark) to solve their growing social and financial problems, including inadequate housing, low standards of living, racial tension, and crime.

(R113a) *Twelve Angry Men.* Feature-length film, demonstrating how people can influence a group; also the role of prejudice and prejudgment in forming opinions and distorting reality. A powerful drama for high school students and adults.

(R114) *Up the Down Staircase.* 1967. Feature-length film based on the novel of the same name by Bel Kaufman. Realistic and effective presentation of teaching problems in a slum high school.

(R115) *Vandalism: Crime or Prank?* Horizon Film Production; International Film Bureau. An open-ended film: shall vandalism be reported?

(R116) *Walk in My Shoes.* 42 min., B & W. A documentary in the "Close-Up" series, exploring the innermost feelings of the Negro as he reacts to prejudice and discrimination in America. Originally presented by ABC-TV, the film endeavors to project what it is like to "walk in the shoes" of the Negro—whether as a professional in Chicago or a laborer in New York. An effective presentation of the contemporary Negro protest.

(R117) *Wanted—A Place to Live.* 15 min., B & W. Anti-Defamation League, 1953. Uses stop-projector technique. A Negro is rejected when he answers an ad to share a room with three other university students. In the second ending, a Jew is rejected as the room-seeker.

(R118) *Weston Woods.* Weston, Conn. A production firm which specializes in preparing audiovisual materials to accompany books children read or teachers read to them.

(R119) *What Is a Story?* Film Associates of California. Elementary through high school.

(R120) *What "Liberty and Justice" Means.* 10 min., color, B & W. Churchill Films. Grades 1-6. Relates concepts to children's own lives.

(R121) *What to Do About Upset Feelings.* Coronet Films. Primary grades.

(R122) *What Will You Tear Down Next?* 16mm, 30 min., B & W. NET Film Service, Indiana U. Audio-Visual Center, Bloomington. The conflicts in reshaping a metropolitan complex in upper New York State are examined showing the physical problems encountered, the reactions of the people, and the rationale behind this change and others that threaten tradition.

(R123) *Who Do You Kill?* 51 min., B & W. Carousel Films, 1964. A young Negro couple in Harlem faced with anti-Negro prejudices, frustrations, and bitterness. Their child, bitten by a rat, dies and the effect of this event reveals social conditions of Negroes, reaction to second-class citizenship, living in substandard housing, and discrimination in employment by unions and employers. A very moving film.

(R124) *Willie Catches On.* 25 min. Incidents in the life of a Canadian boy show how careless words and thoughtlessness on the part of adults perpetuate stereotypes and discriminatory attitudes even in a relatively unprejudiced environment.

(R125) *With Liberty and Justice For All.* 60 min., B & W. McGraw-Hill Book Company, 1956. A dramatization of the growth of social justice as illustrated by famous decisions of the Supreme Court, especially in relation to the Bill of Rights and amendments to the Constitution. Joseph Welch provides narration and commentary to unify the case histories. Part I is focused mainly on the 13th and 14th Amendments of the Constitution.

(R126) *You Can't Run Away.* 32 min., B & W. Teaching Films Custodians, 1952. An excerpt from the feature film "Intruder in the Dust," which presents the near lynching of a Negro.

(R127) *The Young Americans.* 16mm, 60 min., B & W. NET Film Service, Indiana U. Audio-Visual Center, Bloomington. A study of the youth of America—who they are, what they want, where they fit in, how they affect society, what they believe in, and why.

S. RECORDINGS

(S1) *Adventures in Negro History.* A Pepsi-Cola Production. Re-creation of the pageant of Negroes in history: a pilot on Columbus' ship (Nino), a soldier in Washington's army (Prince Whipple), a scientist and teacher (George Washington Carver), an outstanding statesman (Dr. Ralph Bunche).

(S2) Baldwin, James, *Black Man in America.* Distributed by Credo, 102 Mt. Auburn Street, Cambridge, Mass. Interview of Baldwin as a man, as an artist, and as a Negro of this violent but hopeful age of emancipation.

(S3) Chad Mitchell Trio, *Typical American Boys.* Mercury, Stereo, SR 60992. Includes such titles as "Which Hat Shall I Wear to the PTA?"

(S4) *Decision.* 33⅓ RPM long-playing microgroove transcriptions. Available from Anti-Defamation League. Allows for open-ended discussion. Some of the problems dramatized are: Where does hate begin? How can a newspaper preserve democracy? What rumors do you spread? Is the tooth and claw the first law of nature? Some of the stars are Walter Abel, Sir Cedric Hardwicke, Stefan Schnabel, Bill Stern, and Conrad Nagel. Secondary school and adult levels.

(S5) Fisher, Miles Mark, *Negro Slave Songs in the United States.* The Citadel Press, New York, 1963.

(S6) *Folk Music.* Washington, D.C.: Music Division, Recording Laboratory, Reference Department, Library of Congress, 1965. A catalog of folk songs, ballads, dances, instrumental pieces, and folk tales of the United States and Latin America on records. Records available from the Library of Congress loan library.

(S7) *Folkways Records, Inc.,* 117 West 46th Street, New York.

(S8) *The Frederick Douglass Years, 1817–1895.* A Pepsi-Cola Production. Story of Frederick Douglass, a slave who became an orator, journalist, and advisor to President Lincoln. The spirit of this fiery American comes alive in your own living room.

(S9) *The Nashville Sit-In Story.* Folkways Records, FH 5590, 12" L.P. A semidocumentary recording re-enacted to tell the story of the Nashville sit-in. Songs of movement are included. Accompanying text by Rev. Kelly Miller Smith.

(S10) *The Negro Woman.* Folkways Records. Edited by Jean M. Brannon and read by Dorothy Washington. Selections from the lives and works of Phillis Wheatley, Sojourner Truth, Harriet Tubman, Frances Ellen Watkins Harper, Ida B. Wells Barnett, Mary Church Terrell, and Mary McLeod Bethune. Hi-fi L.P. record is available, together with a documentary illustrated text booklet.

(S11) *Sit-In Songs: Songs of the Freedom Riders.* Dauntless DM 4301, 12" L.P. Includes twelve songs.

(S12) *The Sit-In Story.* Folkways Records, FH 5502, 12" L.P. A report of the lunchroom sit-ins in 1960. Edwin Randall narrates; other voices include Dr. Martin Luther King, Ralph McGill, Rev. Ralph Abernathy, and a student who participated in the sit-ins. Accompanying text.

T. BIBLIOGRAPHIES

(T1) American Jewish Committee, *The Police and Race Relations: A Selected Bibliography.* New York: The Committee, 1966.

(T2) ———, *Negro-Jewish Relations: A Selected Bibliography.* New York: The Committee, 1966.

(T3) Armstrong, Helen T., and Ruth Ann Robinson, "Books on Africa for Children," *Top of the News,* June, 1965. American Library Association. A brief bibliography of what is available on Africa in fiction and nonfiction published since 1960. Earlier books are in bibliography by Augusta Baker in *Top of the News,* March, 1961.

(T4) Baker, Augusta, *Books About Negro Life for Children* (rev.). New York: The New York Public Library, 1963. An annotated listing. Also includes books on Africa.

(T5) *A Bibliography of Books for Children.* Bulletin No. 37. Washington, D.C.: Association for Childhood Education International, 1962.

(T6) Board of Education of the City of New York, *Materials for the Literature Program, Grades 1-6.* New York: Board of Education of the City of New York, 1958.

(T7) Brown, Richard C., *They Were There: A Guide to Firsthand Literature for Use in Teaching American History.* Washington, D.C.: The Service Center for Teachers of History, American Historical Association, 1962. An invaluable bibliography for the history and English teacher to use in finding authentic source material about the "feel" of American history.

(T8) Committee of the International Reading Association, *Children, Books and Reading (Perspectives in Reading No. 3).* Newark, Del.: International Reading Association, 1964.

(T9) Crosby, Muriel, ed., *Reading Ladders for Human Relations* (rev. ed.). Washington, D.C.: American Council on Education, 1963.

(T10) *A Graded List of Books for School Libraries.* New York: Harcourt, Brace & World, Inc., 1964. Special listings: sight-saving books, books for slow readers, books by curriculum topics.

(T11) Hall, Elvajean, *Personal Problems of Children.* Boston: Campbell & Hall, 1964. A list of books organized around children's problems.

(T12) Hartman, John J., *Annotated Bibliography on Simulation in the Social Sciences.* Ames, Iowa: Iowa Agriculture and Home Economics Experimental Station, 1966.

(T13) Harvard Clearinghouse on Educational Differences. Cambridge, Mass.: Graduate School of Education, Harvard. A source of selected bibliographies; reprint service.

(T14) Huus, Helen, *Children's Books to Enrich the Social Studies.* Bulletin No. 32. Washington, D.C.: National Council for the Social Studies, National Education Association, 1961.

(T15) *Index to Periodical Articles By and About Negroes.* Boston: G. K. Hall and Co., Decennial cumulation, 1950–1959, Annuals, 1960–.

(T16) *Insight.* Harrisburg, Pa.: Department of Public Instruction. Published monthly since October, 1965. A review or bibliographical newsletter which focuses on intergroup relations.

(T16a) Keating, Charlotte M., *Building Bridges of Understanding.* Tucson, Ariz.: Palo Verde Publishing Co., Inc., 1967. An exceptionally valuable bibliography, annotated with skill, insight, and compassion by a mother who tried out many of the books on her own children. Should be on every library shelf as guide to selection of books about children representing all ethnic, religious, and socio-economic groups.

(T17) Kircher, Clara, *Behavior Patterns in Children's Books: A Bibliography.* Washington, D.C.: The Catholic University of America Press, 1966. This bibliography lists books in which good character traits are embodied, for the purpose of the books' being used therapeutically to develop such traits in children. Especially valuable for a bibliography of articles and books on the use of bibliotherapy.

(T18) Koblitz, Minnie W., *The Negro in Schoolroom Literature.* New York: Center for Urban Education, 1967. Annotated bibliography of books, K-6, which portray integrated situations.

(T19) Lewis, Gertrude, and Esther Murow, *Educating Disadvantaged Children in the Elementary Schools.* Washington, D.C.: U.S. Department of Health, Education and Welfare, Government Printing Office, 1966. An annotated bibliography. Disadvantaged Children Series #5.

(T20) Millender, Dharathula H., *Books About Negro Life and History.* Chicago: American Federation of Teachers, AFL-CIO, 1967. A personal appraisal of a variety of reading materials for children and adults.

(T21) Miller, Elizabeth W., *The Negro in America: A Bibliography.* Cambridge, Mass.: Harvard University Press, 1966. Annotated bibliography listing over 3,500 books, articles, and pamphlets written mostly since the 1954 Supreme Court school decision. Does not cover many problems very completely.

(T22) *The Negro Movement: Past and Present.* Detroit, Mich.: Wayne County Intermediate School District, Desegregation Advisory Project, 1967. An annotated bibliography. A selected listing of over 800 titles collected by the Wayne County staff. Useful for desegregation and for coverage of the Negro in America.

(T23) Office of Economic Opportunity, *Catalog of Federal Programs for*

Individual and Community Improvement. Washington, D.C.: Information Center, Office of Economic Opportunity, December, 1965, 413 pp. Sixty-five pages provide a list of current programs; balance of volume describes each in greater detail. For more current information, consult specific agency and program.

(T24) Penn, Joseph E., *et al., The Negro American in Paperback*. Washington, D.C.: National Education Association, Professional Rights and Relations Committee on Civil and Human Rights of Educators, 1967. A selected list of paperbound books compiled and annotated for secondary school students. A good list, though many worthwhile items are omitted or overlooked.

(T25) *Readings and References in Intergroup Relations*. Washington, D.C.: National Association of Intergroup Relations Officials, 2027 Massachusetts Ave., N.W., 1966. A brief bibliography, listing basic periodicals as well as standard references.

(T26) "Report of Reading List Sub-committee, Young Adult Service Division, Library Service to Disadvantaged Youth." Chicago: American Library Association, 50 E. Huron St., Chicago, Illinois 60611, 1967. (Mimeographed.)

(T27) Salk, Erwin A., ed., *A Layman's Guide to Negro History*. Chicago: Quadrangle Books, 1966. An extremely valuable reference source for teachers and librarians. Includes basic information about the Negro, plus extensive bibliographies of material for all ages.

(T28) United States Commission on Civil Rights, *Catalog of Publications, 1964*. Washington, D.C.: The Commission.

(T29) Welsch, Erwin K., *The Negro in the United States: A Research Guide*. Bloomington: Indiana University Press, 1966. (Also available in paperback.) Annotated citations of books, periodicals, and articles are skillfully woven into a narrative of Negro life and history.

(T30) *We Read*. Washington, D.C.: The Children's Services Division of the American Library Association, Office of Economic Opportunity, 1966. Selected lists of children's books and recordings.

(T31) Wolfe, Ann G., *About 110 Books* (5th rev. ed.). New York: American Jewish Committee, Institute of Human Relations, 165 E. 56th Street, New York, New York, 1966. Contains titles of children's books that deal with interracial and interreligious relationships, poverty, war and peace, and international understanding.

U. JOURNALS

(U1) *The American Child.* (As of 1967, titled *New Generation.*) National Committee on Employment of Youth, National Child Labor Committee, 145 East 32nd Street, New York, N.Y. 10016.

(U2) *American Education.* Office of Education, U.S. Department of Health, Education and Welfare, Washington, D.C. Published ten times a year.

(U3) *Atlas.* The Magazine of the World Press, 31 West 57th Street, New York, N.Y.

(U4) *Audio-Visual Instruction.* Department of Audio-Visual Instruction, National Education Association, Washington, D.C.

(U5) *Bulletin* of the Council on Interracial Books for Children. 9 East 40th Street, New York, N.Y.

(U6) *Crisis.* National Association for the Advancement of Colored People, 1790 Broadway, New York, N.Y. 10019. Monthly. General articles and pictures.

(U7) *The Disadvantaged Child.* Seattle, 71 Columbia Street, Seattle, Wash. Vol. I published March, 1967. To appear as an annual review of the literature.

(U8) *Ebony.* Johnson Publishing Co., Inc., 1820 South Michigan Avenue, Chicago, Ill. 60616. All schools should subscribe to this monthly, which provides a *Life* style presentation of Negroes today in America, plus other feature articles.

(U9) *Freedomways.* 799 Broadway, Suite 542, New York, N.Y. 10003. A quarterly review of the Negro Freedom Movement.

(U10) *Golden Legacy.* Fitzgerald Publishing Co., Hollis, New York. A monthly publication devoted to bettering intergroup relations through providing readable material of historical interest for young people. Early issues devoted to leading Negro heroes and heroines from the past.

(U11) *Hi Neighbor.* Hastings House, New York, N.Y., 1960–1965. A series of publications, of which eight are now available, showing the work of UNICEF. Four countries are described in each issue. Designed to provide elementary school children with a sense of the cultures of different countries.

(U12) *Human Relations.* Tavistock Publications, Tavistock Institute of

Human Relations, London. A scholarly journal published four times a year.

(U13) *Integrated Education.* Integrated Education Associates, 343 South Dearborn Street, Chicago, Ill. Published bi-monthly.

(U14) *IRCD Bulletin.* Project Beacon, Ferkauf Graduate School of Education, Yeshiva University, New York, N.Y. 10003. A bi-monthly publication from the Information Retrieval Center on the Disadvantaged. Each issue contains a relevant article and a comprehensive bibliography.

(U15) *The Journal of Applied Behavioral Science.* National Training Laboratories, National Education Association, Washington, D.C. Research and theory articles related to problems of changing human behavior.

(U16) *The Journal of Intergroup Relations.* National Association of Intergroup Relations Officials, 2027 Massachusetts Avenue, N.W., Washington, D.C. Published quarterly.

(U17) *The Journal of Negro Education.* Howard University Press, Washington, D.C. Published for The Bureau of Educational Research.

(U18) *The Journal of Negro History.* Howard University, Washington, D.C.

(U19) Negro Book Club, Inc., 160 West 85th Street, New York, N.Y. 10024. Specializing in books by and about Negroes.

(U20) *Newsletter on Intellectual Freedom.* The Intellectual Freedom Committee of the American Library Association, 50 East Huron Street, Chicago, Ill. 60611.

(U21) *New South.* Southern Regional Council, 5 Forsyth Street, N.W., Atlanta, Ga. A quarterly review of Southern affairs.

(U22) *Quarterly Review of Higher Education Among Negroes.* Johnson C. Smith University, Charlotte, N.C. 28208. Published since 1933. Index.

(U22a) *Race.* Institute of Race Relations, 36 Jermyn Street, London, S.W.1. Oxford University Press, Press Road, Neasden Lane, London, N.W.10. Published quarterly.

(U23) *Race Relations Law Reporter.* Vanderbilt University, School of Law, Nashville, Tenn.

(U23a) *Research Annual on Intergroup Relations.* (Melvin M. Tumin, ed.) Anti-Defamation League of B'nai B'rith, 315 Lexington Avenue, New York, N.Y. 10016.

(U24) *Scope.* Published by Scholastic Magazines, Inc., Dayton, Ohio.

(U25) School Paperback Institute, Inc., 124 East 40th Street, New York, N.Y. 10016. Provides articles and reference materials on paperbacks and other nontext materials.

(U26) *Sociology of Education*. American Sociological Association, 1001 Connecticut Avenue, N.W., Washington, D.C.

(U27) *Sociometry*. American Sociological Association, 1001 Connecticut Avenue, N.W., Washington, D.C.

(U28) *Southern School Report*. Nashville, Tenn.

(U29) *Trans-Action: Social Science and Modern Society*. Washington University Press, St. Louis, Mo. Contains excellent articles on contemporary social problems. Published bi-monthly.

(U30) *Trends in Housing*. National Committee Against Discrimination in Housing, New York, N.Y. Newspaper published bi-monthly.

(U31) *The UNESCO Courier*. UNESCO Publication Center, 317 East 34th Street, New York, N.Y.

(U32) *The Urban Review*. The Center for Urban Education, 33 West 42nd Street, New York, N.Y. A bi-monthly publication. Vol. I published in 1966.

(U33) *The World and the School*. The Atlantic Information Centre for Teachers, Benjamin Franklin House, 36 Craven Street, London, W.C.2. A review for teachers of current international affairs, published three times a year.

V. ORGANIZATIONS

(V1) American Civil Liberties Union, New York and local chapters. Publishes an annual report of civil rights activities, plus other material on a national and local level.

(V2) American Jewish Committee, 165 East 56th Street, New York, N.Y. 10022.

(V3) Anti-Defamation League of B'nai B'rith, 315 Lexington Avenue, New York, N.Y., or see listing in local area. Offices maintained in most large cities.

(V4) Catholic Interracial Council. National Catholic Conference for Interracial Justice, 1307 South Wabash Avenue, Chicago, Ill. 60605. Sixty local Catholic Interracial Councils operate under the direction of the Conference.

(V5) The Council on Human Relations, 281 The Arcade, Cleveland, Ohio 44114.

(V6) Ferkauf Graduate School of Education, Yeshiva University, 55 Fifth

Avenue, New York, N.Y. 10003. Publishes *IRCD* (Information Retrieval Center on the Disadvantaged) *Bulletin.*

(V7) League of United Latin American Citizens, 2218 South Birch Street, Santa Ana, Calif. Publishes monthly magazine, *LULAC.* Annual convention. Founded by civic-minded persons in 1929 for the advancement of Latin Americans.

(V8) National Association for the Advancement of Colored People, 20 West 40th Street, New York, N.Y. 10018; also regional offices.

(V9) National Association of Intergroup Relations Officials, 2027 Massachusetts Avenue, N.W., Washington, D.C. 20036. Publishes a journal and holds an annual conference. Also has local chapters.

(V10) National Conference of Christians and Jews, 43 West 57th Street, New York, N.Y. 10019, or see local offices. Provides material, consultation, and speakers on intergroup matters.

(V11) Negro Book Club, 160 West 85th Street, New York, N.Y. 10024.

(V12) Southern Regional Council, 5 Forsyth Street, Atlanta, Ga. Publishes quarterly journal, *New South.*

(V13) Urban League, 55 East 52nd Street, New York, N.Y. 10022; also regional offices.